Reading Plato through Jung

"This is a gem of a book! Once again, Paul Bishop demonstrates why he's a master of insight and a leading light in Jungian scholarship. Bishop guides us expertly through the twists and turns of Jung's interpretation of Plato's cosmology and treats us to a feast of weighty ideas and philosophical traditions along the way. Crafted with Bishop's usual assiduity and delightful style, this book provides much needed clarification of Jung's complex relation to Plato, and Jung's cryptic accounts of the 'third' and the 'fourth'."
—Lucy Huskinson, *Professor of Philosophy, Bangor University, UK*

"No serious reader of Jung can avoid encountering and, frankly, being perplexed by Jung's numerous excited references to the third becoming the fourth. What does this idea mean? And why was it so important to Jung? With his characteristic erudition, insight, and open-mindedness, as well as a good deal of sheer sleuthing, Paul Bishop brilliantly explicates Jung's major statements on this theme, especially as they relate to works of Plato, Goethe, and Dorn. What might initially have seemed an esoteric curiosity turns out, after Bishop's masterful analysis, to be a key to understanding the real-world significance and ethical challenge of Jung's entire clinical and cultural thought. This is a stunningly illuminating piece of scholarship."
—Roderick Main, Professor, *Department of Psychosocial and Psychoanalytic Studies, University of Essex, UK*

"Paul Bishop applies a unique lens to Jung's philosophical framework and evinces fascinating insights into how the influence of Plato resonates through the archetypal underpinnings to analytical psychology. In doing so, the spirit of Plato's enduring presence in the annals of western thought is marvelously illuminated via Bishop's accessible and erudite writing style. This is a book brimming with original ideas and new connections and will be of keen interest to Jungian thinkers and practitioners, as well as to academics and students of philosophy. I highly recommend this to anyone interested in the living legacy of Platonic thought and its influence on depth psychology."
—Phil Goss, Associate Professor, *Centre for Lifelong Learning, University of Warwick, UK, and Jungian Analyst*

Paul Bishop

Reading Plato through Jung

Why must the Third become the Fourth?

Paul Bishop
School of Modern Languages and Cultures
University of Glasgow
Glasgow, UK

ISBN 978-3-031-16811-6 ISBN 978-3-031-16812-3 (eBook)
https://doi.org/10.1007/978-3-031-16812-3

© The Author(s), under exclusive licence to Springer Nature Switzerland AG 2022

This work is subject to copyright. All rights are solely and exclusively licensed by the Publisher, whether the whole or part of the material is concerned, specifically the rights of translation, reprinting, reuse of illustrations, recitation, broadcasting, reproduction on microfilms or in any other physical way, and transmission or information storage and retrieval, electronic adaptation, computer software, or by similar or dissimilar methodology now known or hereafter developed.

The use of general descriptive names, registered names, trademarks, service marks, etc. in this publication does not imply, even in the absence of a specific statement, that such names are exempt from the relevant protective laws and regulations and therefore free for general use.

The publisher, the authors, and the editors are safe to assume that the advice and information in this book are believed to be true and accurate at the date of publication. Neither the publisher nor the authors or the editors give a warranty, expressed or implied, with respect to the material contained herein or for any errors or omissions that may have been made. The publisher remains neutral with regard to jurisdictional claims in published maps and institutional affiliations.

Cover pattern © Melisa Hasan

This Palgrave Macmillan imprint is published by the registered company Springer Nature Switzerland AG.
The registered company address is: Gewerbestrasse 11, 6330 Cham, Switzerland

Yes, Plato, you are right! All truths are within us: they are US, and when we think we have discovered them, we are merely looking within ourselves and saying YES!
(de Maistre, Les Soirées de Saint-Pétersbourg, Septième entretien)

Acknowledgements

First and foremost I am grateful to Marcus West and Nora Swan-Foster, as well as to an anonymous reader, for their comments and encouragement on the first draft of this study, originally intended to be an article for *The Journal of Analytical Psychology*. Their advice and input at this early stage turned out to be crucial, and I am greatly indebted to them for their help and advice on a manuscript already exploding the lengths of a conventional article. Next, I should also like to thank the three reviewers who generously gave their time to report on a proposal for an extended version of this manuscript for the Palgrave Pivot series; their suggestions were all ones which I have been glad to incorporate.

Many years ago, Alan Cardew drew my attention to the complex relation between Plato and Jung, and I owe him a large debt of thanks for our conversations about this and much else ever since. For his assistance locating a passage in the fourth edition of Adolf von Harnack's *Lehrbuch der Dogmengeschichte*, an email exchange on the topic of the Third and the Fourth in Jung, and general encouragement in difficult times, I should like to express my profound gratitude to Peter Kingsley. And for his helpful guidance in relation to synchronicity and to Gerhard Dorn and the stage of the *coniunctio*, I am greatly indebted to Roderick Main.

I am extremely grateful to Dr Barbara J. Becker, formerly of the History Department, University of California, Irvine, for permission to reproduce two diagrams and for taking the time to explain how Plato's "X" can be interpreted in terms of the intersection of the celestial equator and the ecliptic. And I owe to Terence Dawson the comforting thought that, however clean the final version of a text might seem to be, like a good carpet maker one should always leave a niggle or two, just to remind oneself that no one is perfect. Last but not least, my final thanks go to Beth Farrow at Palgrave Macmillan for progressing the proposal so swiftly and for her support throughout this project, and to Esther Rani, Production Editor for Springer Nature.

CONTENTS

1 Introduction: Psychoanalysis and the Problem of the Third and the Fourth 1

2 Jung's Reading of Plato and the *Timaeus* 17

3 Jung on the Doctrine of the Trinity 51

4 The *Timaeus* and Cosmology; The Third and the Fourth in Alchemy and Synchronicity 91

5 Conclusion 127

Bibliography 135

Index 151

List of Figures

Fig. 2.1	How the Demiurge arranges the fabric of the universe. (Diagram reproduced with the kind agreement of Dr Barbara J. Becker, Department of History, University of California, Irvine. https://faculty.humanities.uci.edu/bjbecker/ExploringtheCosmos/week1c.html)	29
Fig. 2.2	How the Demiurge structures the universe. (Diagram reproduced with the kind agreement of Dr Barbara J. Becker, Department of History, University of California, Irvine. https://faculty.humanities.uci.edu/bjbecker/ExploringtheCosmos/week1c.html)	29
Fig. 3.1	Schematic representation of the Trinity. (A compact version of a basic minimal (equilateral triangular) version of the "Shield of the Trinity" or "Scutum Fidei" diagram of traditional Christian symbolism, with original Latin captions. In the public realm and available at https://en.wikipedia.org/wiki/Shield_of_the_Trinity#/media/File:Shield-Trinity-Scutum-Fidei-compact.svg)	53
Fig. 3.2	Plato's elements arranged as a quaternity	66
Fig. 3.3	Plato's elements arranged as a quincunx	67
Fig. 3.4	Cornford's "full scheme" of the composition of the soul	69
Fig. 4.1	The "chi"	96

CHAPTER 1

Introduction: Psychoanalysis and the Problem of the Third and the Fourth

Abstract This introductory chapter examines the notion of the Third and the Fourth in a range of psychoanalytic thinkers as practitioners identified by Ann Belford Ulanov in 2007. Ulanov traced the notion of the Third as a source of healing back to Paul Tillich, who criticized Jung for his "anxiety" about metaphysics. In Jung's defence, Edward F. Edinger highlighted the revelatory function of the symbol in Jung's thought and examined the rôle of the Third in the dialectic of development Jung proposed. While Jung's early work emphasized the Third as the "transcendent function", he increasingly insisted on the importance of the Fourth as something that makes itself known in the human psyche yet lies outside it—the "recalcitrant" Fourth, as he called it, which he related to Plato's *Timaeus* and Goethe's *Faust II*. It is the thinking behind these relations that the present study undertakes to examine in more detail, in order to answer the question: why *must* the Third become the Fourth?

Keywords Jung • Ulanov • Tillich • Edinger • The Third • The Fourth

One of the major tropes of psychoanalytic discourse is the notion that "the Third" is an agent that can in some way or another bring about healing. This notion of "the Third" as a source of healing can be traced back, as the US psychoanalyst Ann Belford Ulanov explored in 2007 in an article in

The Journal of Analytical Psychology, to the theologian Paul Tillich: and, in fact, various analysts have understood "the Third" in different ways: as "the space in between" (in the case of Winnicott), as located in the mind of the mother or of the analyst (André Green), as speech (Lacan), as intersubjectivity (Thomas Ogden), or as process (Jessica Benjamin) (Ulanov 2007, 585–589). This demonstrates an extremely wide range of how this term is understood; let us consider each one briefly.

In *Playing and Reality* (1971), the English psychoanalyst and object relations theorist Donald Winnicott (1896–1971) argued that play, especially in its use of a transitional object, enables individuals not just to develop in early childhood but to engage with "the abstractions of politics and economics and philosophy and culture seen as the culmination of natural growing processes", thereby opening up a "third area"—the area of "cultural experience which is a derivative of play", that is, play as a third area which "expands into creative living and into the whole cultural life of [humankind]" (Winnicott 2005, 187 and 138). Then again, in his lecture "On thirdness" (1991), the French psychoanalyst André Green (1927–2012) argued that "the real problem with the developmental perspective is not the journey from two to three—from the dyad to the triad—but the transition from the stage of potential thirdness (when the father is only in the mother's mind) to effective thirdness when he is perceived as a distinct object by the child" (Green 2000, 46). Drawing on the work of the American philosopher and semiotician Charles Sanders Peirce (1839–1914), Green proposed another view of what he called "the crux of the matter: that one day this paradise has to come to an end, that two in one becomes two who are kept apart, and this is why a third is needed"— namely, that "firstness is being, secondness relating, and thirdness thinking" (ibid., 50 and 63). Thirdness is said to be "the highest capacity of the mind", because "thought is the manipulation of signs" and "this capacity of thought opens the way for an infinite system of interpretation" (ibid., 64 and 66).

Although he was affiliated to the SSP (Société psychanalytique de Paris), in the early 1960s Green began attending the seminar of Jacques Lacan (1901–1981). According to Lacan, the human psyche can be understood in terms of three "orders" or "registers", which he calls the Imaginary, the Symbolic, and the Real. On this account, speech itself is a kind of third, represented by the symbolic father who stands between the mother and the infant (or between the analysand and the unconscious) (Evans 1996, 131–132; Ulanov 2007, 587). On 1 November 1974, Lacan gave an address to the 7th Congress of the École freudienne de Paris in Rome entitled "La Troisième", that is, "The Third", where he declared: "It is not because the unconscious is structured like a language that lalangue does not have to play against its own enjoyment, since it is made out of this very enjoyment. The subject supposed to know, who is the analyst in the transference, is not supposed in error, if he knows what the unconscious consists of, in being a knowledge that is articulated from lalangue, the body that speaks only being knotted to it by the real that it enjoys" (Lacan 2019, 94–95; cf. Lacan 2011). (As it happens, this address opens with an allusion to (or a misquotation from? a playful calque on?) a piece of numerological esotericism by the French Romantic poet Gérard de Nerval (1808–1855), his poem "Artémis" (the sixth in a sequence of eight sonnets published under the title *Les Chimères* [*The Chimeras*] in 1854), which opens, "La Treizième revient ... C'est encor la première" [i.e. "The Thirteenth returns ... It's still the first"] [Nerval 1966, 702].)[1]

Along with his use of *reverie*, his focus on the use of language in psychoanalysis, and his approach to the relationship between psychoanalysis and literature, Thomas Ogden (b. 1946) introduced into psychoanalysis in 1992 the concept of the *analytic third*. In addition to the analyst and the analysand, he argued, there is a third subject of analysis—the "intersubjective analytic third" or simply the "analytic third", defined as standing "in dialectical tension with the analyst and analysand as separate individuals with their own subjectivities", inasmuch as each participates "in the unconscious intersubjective construction (the analytic third)", albeit asymmetrically (Ogden 1997, 109). On this account, the relationship of the rôles of analyst and analysand "structures the analytic interaction in a way that strongly privileges the exploration of the unconscious internal object world of the analysand", because the analytic relationship itself fundamentally "exists for the purpose of helping the analysand make psychological changes that will enable him to live his life in a more fully human way" (ibid., 109).

In the case of the New York-based psychoanalyst Jessica Benjamin (b. 1946), thirdness is bound up with the idea of intersubjectivity (Benjamin 2004). For Benjamin, this idea of passes into psychoanalysis thanks to Lacan, whose view of intersubjectivity "derived from Hegel's theory of recognition and its popularization by the French Hegelian writer Kojève" (ibid., 11; see Lacan 1991; Kojève 1980). Whereas, on her account, Lacan saw the Third as something which "keeps the relationship between two persons from collapsing" in various ways: in the form of merger (oneness), of the elimination of difference, or of the polarized opposition of the power struggle (ibid., 11–12), Benjamin conceives as thirdness "both as a mental function and as an intersubjective state" (Benjamin 2005, 197). As an intersubjective state, thirdness is "the position that turns the opposition of dichotomies into tensions, spaces, possibilities for creative dissonance and harmony"—hence an image of thirdness "based on a musical metaphor" of "two or more people following a score, not one they have already read but one that reveals itself only as they go along" (ibid., 197).

In their various ways, all these analysts are seen by Ulanov as having endorsed the view of the importance of the Third expressed by the German-US Christian existentialist philosopher and theologian, Paul Tillich (1886–1965).[2] On Tillich's account, there are three fundamental concepts in the Christian tradition: first, *esse qua esse bonum est*, that is, "being as being is good"; second, the universal fall, in the sense of "the transition from this essential goodness into existential estrangement from oneself", is something that happens "in every living being and in every time"; and third, there is the possibility of salvation, in the sense of *salvus* or *salus*, that is, "healing" or "wholeness" (Tillich 1959, 118–119). For Tillich, all "genuine theological thinking" contains these three principles: (1) "essential goodness"; (2) "existential estrangement"; and (3) "the possibility of something, a 'third,' beyond essence and existence, through which the cleavage is overcome and healed" (ibid., 119). (In so arguing, Tillich concluded, our "essential and existential nature" points to our "teleological nature" (in the sense of our *telos*, aim, or that for which and towards which our life drives) [ibid., 119].)

In his contribution to a public memorial meeting held in 1961 in honour of C.G. Jung after his death and sponsored jointly by the New York Association for Analytical Psychology and the Analytical Psychology Club of New York, Paul Tillich paid tribute to the way in which "many of Jung's ideas are of great help to theology and especially to Protestant theology" (see Bertine et al., 28–32). Yet he went on to criticize what he saw as Jung's scepticism about metaphysics, going so far as to speak of "Jung's anxiety about what he calls metaphysics":

> This, it seems to me, does not agree with his actual discoveries, which on many points reach deeply into the dimension of a doctrine of being, that is, an ontology. This fear of metaphysics, which he shares with Freud and other nineteenth-century conquerors of the spirit, is a heritage of this century. [...] In taking the biological and, by necessary implication, the physical

1 INTRODUCTION: PSYCHOANALYSIS AND THE PROBLEM OF THE THIRD... 5

realm into the genesis of archetypes, he has actually reached the ontological dimension "imprinted upon the biological continuum." And this was unavoidable, given the revelatory power he attributes to the symbols in which the archetypes express themselves. For to be revelatory one must express what needs revelation, namely, the mystery of being. (Ibid., 31)

(Some of Jung's current critics in the academy might raise their eyebrows at the suggestion that Jung was not sufficiently metaphysical!) In Jung's defence, the American analyst Edward F. Edinger (1922–1998) later argued that Jung was not so much afraid of metaphysics as of metaphysicians, pointing to the parallel between Tillich's call for symbols that are "revelatory" inasmuch as they "express what needs revelation, namely, the mystery of being", and Jung's statement in *Aion* (1951) about the importance of the shadow, the syzygy, and the self:

> [It] is possible, through them, to relate so-called *metaphysical* concepts, which have lost their root connection with natural experience, to living, universal psychic processes, so that they can recover their true and original meaning. In this way the connection is re-established between the ego and projected contents now formulated as "metaphysical" ideas. Unfortunately, [...] the fact that metaphysical ideas exist and are believed in does nothing to prove the actual existence of their content or of the object they refer to, although the coincidence of idea and reality in the form of a special psychic state, a state of grace [*eines status gratiae*], should not be deemed impossible, even if the subject cannot bring it about by an act of will. Once metaphysical ideas have lost their capacity to recall and evoke the original experience they have not only become useless but prove to be actual impediments on the road to wider development. One clings to possessions that have once meant wealth; and the more ineffective, incomprehensible, and lifeless they become the more obstinately people cling to them. (Naturally it is only sterile ideas that they cling to; living ideas have content and riches enough, so there is no need to cling to them.) Thus in the course of time the meaningful turns into the meaningless. This is unfortunately the fate of metaphysical ideas. (Jung 1959, §65)

In fact, Edinger himself drew attention to the fact that one of Jung's "major discoveries" had been "the psychological significance of the number four as it relates to the symbolism of psychic wholeness and the four functions", arguing that the significance of the quaternity is "basic to his whole theory of the psyche, both as regards its structure and its developmental goal", that is, the individuation process (Edinger 1973, 179). At the same time, however, Edinger conceded that one encounters other numerical motifs in dreams as in myth and folklore, notably the theme of three, but that "because of the predominant value that Jung attached to the quaternity, he tended in most cases to interpret trinitarian images as incomplete or amputated quaternities" (ibid., 179). Such an approach, Edinger noted, could provoke objections, such as the one expressed by Victor White (1902–1960), the English Dominican priest with whom Jung famously conducted a lengthy correspondence about psychology and theology. As White wrote in *Soul and Psyche* (1960):

> [...] Are we *always* compelled to ask, when confronted with the number three, "Where is the fourth"? Are we to suppose that always and everywhere the number three us to be understood only a four minus one?—that every triangle is only a failed square? [...] Or could it possibly be that ternary symbols are, so to speak, archetypal images in their own right, which present a content distinct from that of the quaternity? (White 1960, 106)

In his chapter in *Ego and Archetype* (1972) entitled "The Trinity Archetype and the Dialectic of Development", Edinger picks up this challenge, proposing that "th[e] ternary symbol is a separate and valid entity in itself" and distinguishing between (a) the quaternity image as expressing "the totality of the psyche in its structural, static or eternal sense"; and (b) the trinity image as expressing "the totality of psychological experience in its dynamic, developmental, temporal aspect" (Edinger 1973, 182). For support for this position, Edinger turns to the English psychoanalyst H.G. Baynes (1882–1943), who wrote in *Mythology of the Soul* (1940) that "the triune archetype symbolizes the dynamic or vital aspect" and that "the number three is specifically associated with the creative process": "Every function of energy in nature has, indeed, the form of a pair of opposites, united by a third factor, their product. Thus the triangle is the symbol of a pair of opposites joined above or below by a third factor" (Baynes 1969, 565 and 405).

And Edinger can point to other threefold developmental models as well. According to William Inge (1860–1954), the mystical process of spiritual development is threefold (purgative, illuminative, and unitive) (Inge 1918, 9–10); the Italian theologian and apocalyptic thinker, Joachim of Fiore (c. 1135–1202), developed a theory of historical time, dividing history into three stages (the Age of the Father, corresponding to the Old

Testament; the Age of the Son, corresponding to the New Testament; and the Age of the Holy Spirit, corresponding to an imminent utopian age and a new dispensation of universal love); the Swiss physician and alchemist known as Paracelsus (c. 1493–1541) combined the mediaeval view of the human being as composed of body, soul, and spirit and the alchemical view of metals as composed of three primary principles of mercury, sulphur, and salt, when he identified mercury as the spirit, sulphur as the soul, and salt as the body (Paracelsus 1967, 125); G.W.F. Hegel (1770–1831) (or, rather, Hegelians) proposed an understanding of the process of history in terms of three stages of thesis, antithesis, and synthesis[3]; while Alfred North Whitehead (1861–1947) distinguished three stages in the natural learning process (the stages of romance, precision, and generalization) (Whitehead 1929). Closer to his psychoanalytic home, Edinger could point to Freud's three stages of psychosexual development (oral, anal, and genital)[4]; the distinction made by Gerhard Adler (1904–1988) between feminine and masculine triads (Adler 1961, 26–261); the three stages of psychological development identified by M. Esther Harding (1888–1971) (autos, ego, and Self) (Harding 1963, 22–23); and, indeed, Edinger's own scheme of psychological development, involving (1) the stage of the Self, in which the ego is identified with the Self; (2) the stage of the ego, in which the ego becomes alienated from the Self; and (3) the stage of the ego-Self axis, in which the ego becomes reunited with the Self—three phases of a repetitive cycle which recurs time and again throughout the individual's lifetime (Edinger 1973, 186).

Yet originally, however, Jung had been as keen as any post-Hegelian thinker might have been to think in terms of triads. In his early work, for instance, we find an emphasis on the Third as the so-called transcendent function. In an important essay with this title written in 1916 (in other words, during the time that he was working on the fifth and sixth of his *Black Books*), but not discovered in his files until 1953 and not published until 1957, Jung sought to answer the "universal question", viz.: "How does one come to terms in practice with the unconscious?" (*Wie setzt man sich praktisch mit dem Unbewußten auseinander?*) (Jung 1969b, 67). In this paper Jung distinguished two key stages in the analytic process: after (1) the unconscious content has been "given form" and "the meaning of this formulation is understood", the question arises as to (2) "how the ego will relate to this position" and "how the ego and the unconscious are to come to terms [with each other]" (*damit hebt die Auseinandersetzung zwischen dem Ich und dem Unbewußten an*) (Jung 1969b, §181). This second stage is, Jung believed, the more important one, because it involves "the bringing together of opposites for the production of a third: the transcendent function"—a stage in which "it is no longer the unconscious that takes the lead, but the ego" (ibid., §181).

Jung claimed that, despite its name, there was "nothing mysterious or metaphysical" about the term "transcendent function" (perish the thought!), and that as a psychological function it was comparable to the mathematical function of the same name, that is, a function of real and imaginary numbers (Jung 1969b, §131). (According to the *Encyclopedia Britannica*, a transcendental function is a function not expressible as a finite combination of the algebraic operations of addition, subtraction, multiplication, division, raising to a power, and extracting a root. It includes the functions log x, sin x, cos x, e^x (and any functions containing them), which are are expressible in algebraic terms only as infinite series. In short, the term transcendental means nonalgebraic.) Jung's choice of the term *transzendente Funktion* is nevertheless problematic, because it risks terminological confusion around the terms *transzendent* and *transzendental*, and their different implications in the discourses of mathematics and philosophy. In the philosophy of Immanuel Kant (1724–1804), "transcendental" is defined as "all cognition […] that is occupied not so much with objects but rather our *a priori* concepts of objects in general" (*Critique of Pure Reason*, A 11; Kant 1997, 133). So "transcendental" refers to what is prior to or makes experience possible, while "transcendent" refers to what goes beyond experience. (Does Jung himself always, if ever, stick to this distinction?)

Faced with the products of the unconscious, Jung argues, the ego must seize the initiative and, like Faust when faced with the sign of the Earth Spirit, should ask: "How am I affected by this sign?" (*Wie anders wirkt dies Zeichen auf mich ein?*) (Jung 1969b, §188; cf. *Faust*, Part One, l. 460). To answer this question requires more than "clever talk" (*gescheites Geschwätz*), it involves "the shuttling to and fro of arguments and affects [which] represents the transcendent function of opposites":

> The confrontation of the two positions generates a tension charged with energy and creates a third, living thing [*Lebendiges … ein Drittes*]—not a logical stillbirth in accordance with the principle *tertium non datur* [i.e., the law of the excluded third or *principium tertii exclusi*, viz.: "no third possibility is given"], but a movement out of the suspension between opposites, a living birth that leads to a new level of being, a new situation. (Ibid., §189)

Thus the transcendent function "manifests itself as a quality of conjoined opposites" and "so long as these are kept apart—naturally for the purpose of avoiding conflict—they do not function and remain inert [*toter Stillstand*]" (ibid., §189; see Miller 2004).

Nearly thirty years later, in a letter to Olga Fröbe-Kapteyn of 20 August 1945 Jung wrote that the *opus* consists of three parts (insight, endurance, and action), and he speaks here in powerful, dramatic terms about how "everyone goes through this mill, consciously or unconsciously, voluntarily or forcibly", of "a conflict that rages in itself and against itself [...] in the fire of suffering": we are, he told her, "crucified between the opposites and delivered up to the torture until the 'reconciling third' takes shape" (Jung 1973–1975, vol. 1, 375). ("A life without inner contradiction is either only half a life or else a life in the Beyond, which is destined only for angels", he concluded, adding: "But God loves human beings more than the angels" [ibid., 375].)

Ten years after this letter, in *Mysterium coniunctionis* (1955–1956) Jung reaffirms that "what the union of the opposites really 'means' transcends human imagination", and he repeats (yet again) the law of the excluded middle, *tertium non datur* (Jung 1970, §201).[5] This third thing is "an eternal image, an archetype, from which individuals can turn away their mind for a time but never permanently"—a point substantiated, Jung argued (here as elsewhere), by the promulgation in 1950 of the dogma of the Assumption of the Virgin Mary by Pope Pius XII in his apostolic constitution *Munificentissimus Deus*) (ibid., §201).[6] For Jung, this insight was of the greatest existential significance: "Whenever this image is obscured our life loses its proper meaning and consequently its balance", but "so long as we know that we are the carrier of life and that it is therefore important for us to live, then the mystery of our soul lives also—no matter whether we are conscious of it or not" (ibid., §201). But the converse is also true, and "if we no longer see the meaning of our life in its fulfilment, and no longer believe in humankind's eternal right to this fulfilment, then we have betrayed and lost our soul, substituting for it a madness which leads to destruction"—as was demonstrated, Jung believed, by his time (and, one might add, as it is by ours, too) (ibid., §201).

Over time, however, this emphasis on the Third as the "transcendent function" gave way in Jung's thinking to an increasing insistence on the importance of "the Fourth" as something that makes itself known in the human psyche, yet lies outside us; this mysterious Fourth is said to lead "straight to the Anthropos idea that stands for human wholeness, that is, the conception of a unitary being": as Jung put it in "Individual Dream Symbolism in Relation to Alchemy" (1936), "the one joins the three as the fourth and thus produces the synthesis of the four in a unity" (Jung 1968, §210).[7] In the alchemical terms of the Hermetic *Basilian Aphorisms*, the Fourth is like the "life force (*vis animans*)" or the "'glue of the world' (*glutinum mundi*)"—"the medium between mind and body and the union of both" (ibid., §209). Leaving to one side the reasons for Jung's strategic preference for alchemical literature, we should note that, in this paper, he also highlights the presence of the issue of the Third and the Fourth in two rather more traditionally canonical works, Plato's *Timaeus* and Johann Wolfgang Goethe's *Faust*.

For her own part, Ann Belford Ulanov (b. 1938) herself illustrates how, in the wake of Jung, many practitioners of analytical psychology have embraced this shift from the reconciling, uniting the Third to the Fourth— the "recalcitrant" Fourth, as Jung liked to call it (Jung 1969a, §191). In her paper, "The third in the shadow of the fourth", Ulanov advanced Jung's own work on the Fourth by "playing around", as Amy Lamborn has put it, with the notion that "the fourth does three things" (Lamborn 2011, 114). First, the Fourth reveals to us "the limits of our perceptions", inasmuch as it is "ever living and moving us, not captured in a fixed definition of time" (Ulanov 2007, 602). Second, without the Fourth, "the purposiveness gains no purpose, no channel into living, no stepping over into concrete life" (ibid., 602–603). And third, the Fourth shows itself as the One—not the original One of undifferentiation, but "the unity with multiplicity and the multiplicity within unity" (Lamborn 2011, 114; cf. Ulanov 2007, 603). Thus the functioning of the Fourth allows us to glimpse what the German-US psychoanalyst Hans Loewald (1906–1993) called *sublimation*: "In genuine sublimation, this alienating differentiation is being reversed in such a way that a fresh unity is created by an act of uniting. In this reversal—a restoration of unity—there comes into being a differentiated unity (a manifold) that captures separateness in the act of uniting, and unity in the act of separating" (Loewald 1988, 24), or what Winnicott termed "the separation that is not a separation but a form of union" (Winnicott 2005, 132).

Yet why *must* "the Third become the Fourth"? And what does the problem of the Third and the Fourth have to do with Plato—and with Goethe? In this short study I shall go on in the second chapter to offer a brief survey of some of the work that has been done on Jung's relation to Plato, before turning to consider the central ideas of the dialogue Jung most frequently cites, the *Timaeus*. Jung attached a particular significance to its account of the composition, division, and fashioning of the World Soul into two circles (which can be interpreted in different ways), commenting on this episode in *Transformations and Symbols of the Libido* (1911–1912) and drawing (via Arthur Drews) on the *Enneads* of Plotinus. In the third chapter we shall examine the essay "A Psychological Approach to the Dogma of the Trinity", first delivered as a lecture at Eranos in 1940. Here Jung suggests that the *Timaeus* (with its opening question, "One, two, three,—but where, my dear Timaeus, is the fourth of our guests [...]?" [17a])[8] invites an interpretation of the text in terms of Pythagoras's theory of number and the numerology of Gerhard Dorn. After pausing to explore Jung's reference to Plato's career as a political thinker, we return to the *Timaeus* and its opening question, which Jung links to the Cabiri scene in the second part of Goethe's *Faust*. Jung argues that the Three "yearns" to become a Four, although he curiously neglects to consider other examples of number symbolism in the *Timaeus*—even though they might have helped confirm his reading. Finally, in the fourth chapter, we consider Jung's account in the *Black Books* of "an unforgettable night in the desert" when he "saw the X for the first time" and "understood the Platonic myth"; examine Jung's further discussions of the motif of the Third and the Fourth (as well as the Seventh and the Eighth) in various alchemical texts, as well as in his paper on "Synchronicity" (1952); and investigate how the parallel interpretative approaches to the problem of the Third and the Fourth in the *Timaeus* and in the Cabiri scene in *Faust* recur (and in fact converge) in Jung's late, great work, *Mysterium coniunctionis*. By way of a conclusion, the fifth chapter argues that Jung's Platonism is paradoxical, characterized by an apparent rejection of metaphysics while nevertheless reformulating them in psychological terms. Even more paradoxically, in his embrace of the quest to experience the perfection of wholeness (symbolized by the circle), Jung thereby reveals himself to be a true student of Plato.

NOTES

1. Not surprisingly, Jung too was attracted to the mysterious figure of Nerval, famous for his pet lobster, Thibault, whom he took for walks on a silk ribbon lead, explaining to Théophile Gautier that lobsters know the secrets of

the sea and do not bark. In 1945, Jung delivered a lecture in Zurich on Nerval's visionary memoir, *Aurélia ou le rêve et la vie* (1855), recently edited by Craig Stephenson (Jung 2015), and Nerval's poem, "Artémis", represents a point of intersection between Nerval and the Mexican poet Octavio Paz (1914–1998), whose work has been explored from a Jungian perspective (Williamson 2007, 52–54).

2. For a recent reappraisal of Tillich and Jung, see Dourley (2008). A key link between Jung and Tillich was the significance both attached to Friedrich Nietzsche (1844–1900). In his seminar on Nietzsche's *Thus Spoke Zarathustra* given in Zurich between 1934 and 1939, for instance, Jung related in the session held on 21 November how his first serious engagement with Nietzsche's key text had been almost literally out-of-this-world. "I read *Zarathustra* for the first time with consciousness", he told his audience, "in the first year of the war, in November 1914, twenty years ago; then suddenly the spirit seized me and carried me to a desert country in which I read *Zarathustra*" (Jung 1989, vol. 1, 259). Although Jung claimed that this reading was more "conscious" than his previous one from the time when he was a university student had been, he nonetheless describes it in ecstatic terms, suggesting an emotional as well as an intellectual experience. At around the same time (in 1916), and also in his thirties, Tillich had his own "Zarathustra-Erlebnis" which is reported in his biography in very similar terms (Pauck and Pauck 1978, vol. 1, 63–64). But what exactly was this *Erlebnis*? According to his biographers Wilhelm and Marjon Pauck, "the traditional conception of God no longer had any validity for Tillich, and he discovered in Nietzsche something that conclusively liberated him from this conception": "In a wood in France he began, at the age of thirty, to read *Thus Spoke Zarathustra*, and the ecstatic affirmation of existence which he found in this work and which after the war was to prevail in reaction to the years of hunger and death, transported him into something approaching ecstasy. Like many other soldiers who read Nietzsche, Tillich felt himself drawn back to passion and life. He was particularly attracted to Nietzsche's rejection of bourgeois hypocrisy. When he went on holiday he devoted himself enthusiastically to the powerful pleasures of life" (ibid., vol. 1, 63–64). And in her autobiography, Hannah Tillich (1896–1988) mentions the importance of Nietzsche for her husband: on her account, reading Nietzsche "lured" the young Tillich "away from middle-class respectability", while his *Zarathustra* "broke with everything Paulus had learned from [his] father" (Tillich 1973, 101), serving (along with Huysmans's *Là-bas* and Baudelaire's *Les Fleurs du mal*) in effect as a kind of entry-level drug to pornography, to which Tillich later became virtually addicted (Jones 1994, 156). In 1944, Tillich participated in a symposium held in New York in celebration of the centenary of Nietzsche's birth under the auspices of the Conference on

Methods in Philosophy and the Sciences to which he contributed a comment, hailing Nietzsche's significance as a critic of bourgeois society (Tillich 1945, 307–309).
3. As Walter Kaufmann observed, "whoever looks for the stereotype of the allegedly Hegelian dialectic in Hegel's *Phenomenology* will not find it", and he rightly points to J.G. Fichte and to F.W.J. Schelling (in his *On the Ego as Principle of Philosophy* [1795]) as sources of this pattern (Kaufmann 1978, 153–162); cf. Mueller (1958); reprinted in Stewart (ed.) 1996, 301–305.
4. Strictly speaking, Freud identifies five stages (oral, anal, phallic, latent, and genital); see his *Three Essays on the Theory of Sexuality* (1905) (Freud 1977, pp. 31–169).
5. The classic statements of the law of the excluded third (also known as the law or the principle of excluded middle) can be found in Parmenides, fragment B 8: "[Being] must either altogether or not be" (Barnes 1987, 134); in Aristotle's discussion of the principle of non-contradiction in *De Interpretatione*, §9, where he says that of two contradictory propositions, one must be true and the other false (Aristotle 1984, vol. 1, 28–29), and his statements in his *Metaphysics*, book 3, that "everything must be either affirmed or denied" and "a thing cannot at the same time be and not be" (996b 26–30) and in book 4 that "there cannot be an intermediate between contradictories" (1011b 26–27) (ibid., vol. 2, 1575); and in Leibniz's statement in his *Nouveaux Essais sur l'entendement humain* (1704), book 4, chapter 2, that "a proposition is either true or false" (Leibnitz 1896, 405). For a technical discussion, see Alfred North Whitehead and Bertrand Russell, *Principia Mathematica*, 3 vols (1910–1913).
6. The text of this apostolic constitution can be found on the Vatican website; see Pius XII 1950. For discussion of the history of this dogma, see Shoemaker (2004).
7. For a meditation on why Four functions as an expression of wholeness, see Le Mouël (2011/2012).
8. In this study the *Timaeus* is cited (using the usual Stephanus numbers) from the translation in the Loeb edition by R.G. Bury (1869–1951), the Irish-born Anglican. clergyman, classicist, and philologist.

BIBLIOGRAPHY

Adler, Gerhard. 1961. *The Living Symbol: A Case Study in the Process of Individuation*. New York: Pantheon.
Aristotle. 1984. *The Complete Works of Aristotle*. Ed. by Jonathan Barnes, 2 vols. Princeton, NJ: Princeton University Press.
Barnes, Jonathan. 1987. *Early Greek Philosophy*. Harmondsworth: Penguin.
Baynes, H.G. 1969. *Mythology of the Soul; A Research into the Unconscious from Schizophrenic Dreams and Drawings*. London: Ryder.

Benjamin, Jessica. 2004. Beyond Doer and Done To: An Intersubjective View of Thirdness. *The Psychoanalytic Quarterly* 73 (1): 5–46.

———. 2005. From Many into One: Attention, Energy, and the Containing of Multitudes. *Psychoanalytic Dialogues* 15 (2): 185–201.

Dourley, John P. 2008. *Paul Tillich, Carl Jung and the Recovery of Religion*. London and New York: Routledge.

Edinger, Edward F. 1973. *Ego and Archetype: Individuation and the Religious Function of the Psyche*. Baltimore, ML: Penguin Books.

Evans, Dylan. 1996. *Dictionary of Lacanian Psychoanalysis*. London and New York: Routledge.

Freud, Sigmund. 1977. *On Sexuality* [*Pelican Freud Library*, Vol. 7]. Trans. under James Strachey, ed. by Angela Richards. Harmondsworth: Penguin.

Green, André. 2000. *André Green at the Squiggle Foundation*. Ed. Jan Abram. London: Karnac Books.

Harding, M. Esther. 1963. *Psychic Energy: Its Source and its Transformation*. Princeton, NJ: Princeton University Press.

Inge, William. 1918. *Christian Mysticism: Considered in Eight Lectures Delivered before the University of Oxford* [The Bampton Lectures, 1899], 4th ed. London: Methuen.

Jones, E. Michael. 1994. *Dionysos Rising: The Birth of Cultural Revolution Out of the Spirit of Music*. San Francisco: Ignatius Press.

Jung, C.G. 1959. *Aion: Researches into the Phenomenology of the Self*. Trans. by R.F.C. Hull. *Collected Works*, Vol. 9/ii. Princeton, NJ: Princeton University Press.

———. 1968. *Psychology and Alchemy*. Trans. by R.F.C. Hull = *Collected Works*, Vol. 12, 2nd ed. London: Routledge.

———. 1969a. *Psychology and Religion: West and East*. Trans. by R.F.C. Hull = Collected Works, Vol. 11, 2nd ed. London: Routledge & Kegan Paul.

———. 1969b. *The Structure and Dynamics of the Psyche*. Trans. by R.F.C. Hull. *Collected Works*, Vol. 8, 2nd ed. Princeton, NJ: Princeton University Press.

———. 1970. *Mysterium coniunctionis: An Inquiry into the Separation and Synthesis of Psychic Opposites in Alchemy*. Trans. by R.F.C. Hull = *Collected Works*, Vol. 14, 2nd ed.. Princeton, NJ: Princeton University Press.

———. 1973–1975. *Letters*. Ed. by Gerhard Adler and Aniela Jaffé, trans. by R.F.C. Hull, 2 vols. Princeton, NJ: Princeton University Press.

———. 1989. *Nietzsche's "Zarathustra": Notes of the Seminar Given in 1934–1939*. Ed. by James L. Jarrett, 2 vols. London: Routledge.

———. 2015. *On Psychological and Visionary Art: Notes from C.G. Jung's Lecture on Gérard de Nerval's "Aurélia"*. Ed. by Craig Stephenson. Princeton and Oxford: Princeton University Press.

Kant, Immanuel. 1997. *Critique of Pure Reason*. Ed. and trans. by Paul Guyer and Allen W. Wood. Cambridge: Cambridge University Press.

Kaufmann, Walter. 1978. *Hegel: A Reinterpretation*. Notre Dame, IN: University of Notre Dame Press.

Kojève, Alexandre. 1980. *Introduction to the Reading of Hegel* [²1947], Assembled by Raymond Queneau, ed. by Allan Bloom, trans. by James H. Nichols, Jr. Ithaca and London: Cornell University Press.
Lacan, Jacques. 1991. *The Seminar of Jacques Lacan, Book I: Freud's Papers on Technique, 1953–1964* [1975]. Ed. by Jacques-Alain Miller, trans. by John Forrester. New York and London: Norton.
———. 2011. La Troisième. Ed. by Jacques-Alain Miller, *La Cause freudienne*, no. 79: 11–33.
———. 2019. *The Third*. Trans. by Philip Dravers, *The Lacanian Review*, no. 7, Get Real. Spring, 83–109.
Lamborn, Amy Bentley. 2011. Revisiting Jung's 'A Psychological Approach to the Dogma of the Trinity': Some Implications for Psychoanalysis and Religion. *Journal of Religion and Health* 50: 108–119.
Le Mouël, Christophe. 2011/2012. Four: A Reflection on the Wholeness of Nature. Parts 1 and 2. *Psychological Perspectives* 54 (2) and (June and December): 54–79 and 175–196; Part 3. *Psychological Perspectives*, Vol. 55, Vol. 2 (June): 219–245.
Leibnitz, Gottfried Wilhelm. 1896. *New Essays Concerning Human Understanding*. Trans. by Alfred Gideon Langley. New York: Macmillan.
Loewald, Hans W. 1988. *Sublimation: Inquiries into Theoretical Psychoanalysis*. New Haven: Yale University Press.
Miller, Jeffrey C. 2004. *The Transcendent Function: Jung's Model of Psychological Growth through Dialogue with the Unconscious*. Albany, NY: State University of New York Press.
Mueller, Gustav E. 1958. The Hegel Legend of 'Thesis-Antithesis-Synthesis.' *Journal of the History of Ideas* 19 (3): 411–414; reprinted *The Hegel Myths and Legends*, ed. by Jon Stewart, pp. 301–305. Evanston, IL: Northwestern University Press, 1996.
Nerval, Gérard de. 1966. *Œuvres*. Ed. by Henri Lemaitre. Paris: Garnier.
Ogden, Thomas E. 1997. *Reverie and Interpretation: Sensing Something Human*. Northvale, NJ, and London: Jason Aronson.
Paracelsus. 1967. *The Hermetic and Alchemical Writings of Paracelsus*. Trans. by A.R. Waite, Vol. 1. New Hyde Park, NY: University Books.
Pauck, Wilhelm, and Marjon Pauck (1978). *Paul Tillich: Sein Leben und Denken*, 2 vols. Stuttgart; Frankfurt am Main: Evangelisches Verlagswerk; Lembeck.
Pius XII. 1950. *Apostolic Constitution of Pope Pius XII Munificentissimus Deus defining the dogma of the Assumption*. Available https://www.vatican.va/content/pius-xii/en/apost_constitutions/documents/hf_p-xii_apc_19501101_munificentissimus-deus-html.
Shoemaker, Stephen J. 2004. *The Ancient Traditions of the Virgin Mary's Dormition and Assumption*. New York: Oxford University Press.

Tillich, Paul. 1945. Nietzsche and the Bourgeois Spirit. *Journal of the History of Ideas* 6 (3): 307–309.
———. 1959. *Theology of Culture*. Ed. by Robert C. Kimball. New York: Oxford University Press.
Tillich, Hannah. 1973. *From Time to Time*. New York: Stein and Day.
Ulanov, Ann Belford. 2007. The Third in the Shadow of the Fourth. *Journal of Analytical Psychology* 52 (5): 585–605.
White, Victor. 1960. *Soul and Psyche: An Enquiry into the Relationship of Psychotherapy and Religion*. New York: Harper.
Whitehead, A.N. 1929. *The Aims of Education*. New York: Macmillan.
Williamson, Rodney. 2007. *The Writing in the Stars: A Jungian Reading of the Poetry of Octavio Paz*. Toronto, Buffalo, and London: University of Toronto Press.
Winnicott, Donald W. 2005. *Playing and Reality* [1971]. Abingdon: Routledge.

CHAPTER 2

Jung's Reading of Plato and the *Timaeus*

Abstract The question of the relationship between C.G. Jung and Plato can best be described as a vexed one. This chapter surveys the critical literature on Jung's relationship to Plato, before turning to consider the central ideas of the dialogue Jung most frequently cited, the *Timaeus*. Its account of the composition, division, and fashioning of the World Soul into two circles can be interpreted in different ways, and Jung attached a particular significance to this passage. In *Transformations and Symbols of the Libido* Jung commented on this episode and drew (via the account offered by Arthur Drews) on the *Enneads* of Plotinus.

Keywords Jung • Plato • Wolfgang Giegerich • Peter Kingsley • *Timaeus* • World Soul • Plotinus • Arthur Drews

The question of the relationship between C.G. Jung and Plato can best be described as a vexed one. In a lecture on "Archetypes of the Collective Unconscious" (1934; 1954), Jung defined the term "archetype" as an "explanatory paraphrase" of the Platonic concept of *eidos* (εἶδος), a term meaning "idea", "essence", or "type" found in Plato's theory of forms and Aristotle's theory of universals (Jung 1969a, §5). In addition, Jung defined "archetype" as a concept found in the *imago dei* of Philo of Alexandria, in the Church Father St Irenaeus's treatise *Against Heresies*

© The Author(s), under exclusive license to Springer Nature
Switzerland AG 2022
P. Bishop, *Reading Plato through Jung*,
https://doi.org/10.1007/978-3-031-16812-3_2

(II.7 §5), in the notion of "archetypal light" (τὸ ἀρχέτυπον φῶς) in the *Corpus Hermeticum*,[1] and in the writings (*The Celestial Hierarchy*, II.4; *The Divine Names*, I.6) of Pseudo-Dionysius the Areopagite.[2] In a later lecture on "Psychological Aspects of the Mother Archetype" (1938; 1954), Jung rehearsed again some of these sources, yet distanced himself from them by claiming to be "an empiricist, not a philosopher", while nevertheless adding that Kant's doctrine of the categories "destroys in embryo every attempt to revive metaphysics in the old sense of the world, but at the same time paves the way for a rebirth of the Platonic spirit" (Jung 1969a, §149–§150).

Yet Jung also had a "big picture" account of the Platonic tradition: in one session (given on 6 February 1935) in his series of seminars on Nietzsche's *Zarathustra* (1934–1939), Jung told his audience that "ancient philosophy really started from a different reality than ours" as well as from "a very different psychology" (Jung 1989, vol. 1, 366–367). The problem, Jung believed, was a linguistic one, since in ancient times speech was "very unwieldy". For this reason, Jung argued, Plato had recourse to "parables and all sorts of means in order to express his philosophical thought". Jung cited the famous allegory of the cave in the *Republic* as a case in point, arguing that, although it belongs to "the theory of cognition", Plato "had to express it by that clumsy apparatus", that is, as an allegory (ibid., 367).[3]

Hence, for Jung, the importance of the category of *revelation*. On a later occasion on 3 June 1936, he reminded his audience that "there is no real life without archetypal experiences", citing "religious systems" as an example of this principle (Jung 1989, vol. 2, 970). According to Jung, a religious system (such as the Hīnayāna and the Mahāyāna, the two schools of Buddhism)[4] is "like a safe form, a body of teaching, of principles, of advice and so on, which is destined to help [humankind] to navigate over the troubled waters of the unconscious" (ibid., 970). Hence the image of the "small vehicle" and the "great vehicle" in Buddhism, or the Christian allegory of Christ at the tiller of the ship of the Church; in fact, Jung explicitly highlights the image of the ship (ibid., 970).[5] From where, however, do these teachings come? Usually we assume that religious systems are invented by human beings: Moses as the inventor of the law, for example, or Christ as "a sort of moral philosopher who had very good ideas, like Socrates" (!), or the Old Testament prophets as "people who were just bothered with the fate of their nation and tried to help people by good advice" (ibid., 970). In Jung's view, however, this kind of account—which we could describe as a kind of *anthropological reductionism*—is simply wrong; he dismisses it as a sort of euhemerism (named after the Greek mythographer Euhemerus, who believed mythological accounts originated from real historical events or persons) that does not explain the facts. For in Jung's view the "real facts" are that "all these methods [...] are not inventions, but are revelations", expressing "a revealed truth or a perceived truth which has been thought before [humankind] has thought [it]" (970–971). Here we find a deeply Platonic resonance within Jung's thinking:

> Before I had that thought it had already been thought, and I merely happened to perceive it once in time; it has been there since eternity, is always there, has always lived, and I just happened in a certain moment to perceive it. [...] So these things have been thought by an invisible thinker—we don't know where they come from. But I should call this the "Holy Ghost": that gives the helpful thought, personified in many forms in many times [...].
> (Jung 1989, vol. 2, 971)

Jung gives us several examples of how the "helpful thought" is "personified in many forms in many times": as Oannes (in Sumerian) or Uanna (in Akkadian), the first of the Apkallu or seven demi-gods, part man and part fish, associated in ancient Mesopotamia with human wisdom; or as Tages, a founding prophet of Etruscan religion, whose view of divinity and techniques for divination are recorded in the *Etrusca Disciplina*[6]; or as the *puer aeternus* in Roman antiquity[7]; or as the "Holy Spirit" in the Christian tradition; or as *any other helpful god who reveals the truth*. For Jung, "all these different personifications are always one and the same thing, the revelation of the thought that existed before [the human being] had the thought" (ibid., 971).[8]

Subsequently various commentators have examined the question of Jung's relation to Plato. In 1977, a diploma thesis submitted to the C.G. Jung Institute in Zurich by Charles Kent Dominey under the title *Archetype and Idea* undertook to consider the points of correspondence between Jung's theory of the archetypes and Plato's theory of the Forms, with particular reference to Platonic ontology and epistemology. In his introduction, Dominey states clearly that he is not attempting to "turn Jung into a Platonist or to portray Plato as an ancient precursor of Analytical Psychology", while adding (somewhat archly): "In fact, I have been impressed too many times with the experience of people, sometimes even professional and academic psychologists who, having neither read, much less understood, either Plato or Jung, nevertheless assured me that Jung was in fact a Platonist" (Dominey 1977, 6)!

Some twenty years later, in two lectures given in 1997 at the Philosophical Research Society (and subsequently released as DVDs in the series *Wisdom Literature and the Platonic Tradition*), Pierre Grimes b. 1925) examined the structure of the dialectic in Platonic and Jungian thought with reference to the allegory of the divided line (Grimes 1997a). Here, however, the main point of contact was identified as being the *Liber Platonis quartorum*, an alchemical work to which Jung makes repeated reference in his lectures "Religious Ideas in Alchemy" (1937) and "Transformation Symbolism in the Mass" (1942; 1954)—but one that can be only loosely associated with the historical Plato (see Singer 1946; Hasse 2002, 58–64).

In an extensive paper entitled "Materialistic Psychology: Jung's Essay on the Trinity" (published in 2013 but based on an unpublished long manuscript written in German in 1993) Wolfgang Giegerich (b. 1942) tackled head-on many of the issues connected with Jung's use of Plato and the problem of the Third and the Fourth (Giegerich 2020, 85–163). Giegerich questions the way Jung interprets as exemplifying "the subtle modes by which an archetype influences our actions" an episode when, while travelling in Africa near Mount Elgon, the governor of Uganda requested Jung's party of three men take with them a fourth person (a woman) (Jung 1963, 289); suggests that, rather than "the archetype of the triad […] call[ing] for the fourth to complete it, as we have seen again and again in the history of this archetype", it is Jung who calls for the Fourth; and wonders whether one archetype from within itself can *call for* the other at all (Giegerich 2020, 86–87). Moreover, Giegerich points to "strong evidence" for the self-display of "Three" as complete, citing Aristotle's *De caelo* (268a 1–13), the triadic thinking of Neoplatonism (e.g. the three hypostases of the One, Mind, and Soul in Plotinus and Porphyry, or the dynamic dialectical triad of *monê* = "remaining", "indwelling", *prohodos* = "proceeding forth", "emanation", and *epistrophê* = "reversion", "returning into itself" in Plotinus and Proclus), and the triad in German Idealism (J.G. Fichte's triad of *Grundsätze* and Hegel's dictum in his *Habilitation Theses* of 1801 that "the square is the law of nature, the triangle that of the mind") (ibid., 88–90). And he makes the important point that the 3 + 1 structure is from the outset a type of *quaternity* and that "one must not confuse the *quaternity-internal* three of the 3 + 1 structure with the wholly different and self-sufficient three of the Trinity" (ibid., 90).

On the specific question of Jung's reading of the *Timaeus*, Giegerich reminds us that, according to W.K.C. Guthrie (1906–1981), Plato "does not say that two elements by themselves cannot mix: the emphasis is on *kalôs*", that is, on the beautiful (Guthrie 1978, 277), and that what counted for Plato was "a rational bond, the *most beautiful* (the harmonious and most lasting) of bonds (δεσμῶν κάλλιστος), 31c" (Giegerich 2020, 100). Then again, the description of the creation of the World Soul (35a) (see below), which Jung himself was surely not wrong to describe as "far from simple" (Jung 1969b, §189), has been interpreted in various ways, but in the judgement of T.M. Robinson, the one that makes the most sense is that of Proclus, championed in more recent times by G.M.A. Grube and Francis Cornford (Robinson 1970, 70; cited in Giegerich 2020, 109); by contrast, Giegerich looks askance at Jung's interpretation, describing it as "altogether idiosyncratic"—not *in itself* a reason to reject it, since it *could* mean that Jung "all alone had a deeper insight than all the experts" and that, "on the basis of his psychological knowledge", he had "access to a level of understanding that remained closed to the other interpreters", but this would nevertheless mean that, in order to be plausible, his view would require corroboration by "cogent arguments"... (Giegerich 2020, 110). Yet, as we shall see (in Chapter Four), there is evidence that, on at least one occasion, Jung believed that he had "understood the Platonic myth" and experienced how, in Guthrie's words, "the cosmos, though not perfect, is the best and most lasting of all created living things"; that it "cannot therefore have been thrown together haphazard, but was planned as an organism in which the various components are blended with the most exquisite delicacy and precision"; and that, because "this proportionate blending ensures its wholeness and unity (32d9-33a1), knitting its parts together in bonds of amity indissoluble save by its author", the binding force of the world can be expressed "in terms of *analogia*, geometrical proportion" (Guthrie 1978, 277–278).

Standing fully within the Jungian tradition as a practising psychoanalyst, in 2017 Jane Weldon made the case for a "Platonic Jung" on the basis of striking similarities, as she saw them, between their respective conceptions of the structure of the cosmos and the psyche and of the nature of the self. In Platonic and Jungian thought alike, she argued, the individual self is identified as a "soul", located in a "third" level of being between the divine Self (or One) and the ego (or sense-based self). For both thinkers, she concluded, individuation consists of uniting these opposites in the lower self, thereby healing conflicts within the ego and developing consciousness in a transformative way (Weldon 2017).

Most recently, in his wide-ranging discussion of Jung's life and work in *Catafalque* (2 vols, 2018), Peter Kingsley (b. 1953) touches several times on the relation between Jung and Plato. When, for instance, Jung remarks in his foreword to Daisetz Teitaro Suzuki's *Introduction to Zen Buddhism* (1939) that even such works as Goethe's *Faust* and Nietzsche's *Zarathustra*—"these most promising of all products of the Western mind"—are "overlaid [...] with the materiality and concreteness of our thinking, as moulded by the Greeks", adding in a footnote that "the genius of the Greeks lay in the break-through of consciousness into the materiality of the world, thus robbing the world of its original dreamlike quality" (Jung 1969b, §905 and n. 42), Kingsley's response is surprisingly frank, even scathing. In so writing, he declares, Jung is "just parroting the bastard wisdom endlessly churned by the German textbooks of philosophy he had been devouring since he was a child—textbooks which mindlessly projected the rampant rationalism of the eighteenth, nineteenth, twentieth centuries back onto the ancient world" (Kingsley 2018, vol. 2, 201). Yet Kingsley also points to a more fruitful aspect of the Plato-Jung connection, applying to the case of Jung himself the words attributed to Socrates by Plato, "the gift of prophecy comes most readily to men—at the point of death" (*Apology*, 39c; Plato 1989, 24), and describing the function of Jung's visions shortly before his death in 1961 and indeed the entire project of analytical psychology as essentially prophetic (Kingsley 2018, vol. 1, 425; cf. vol. 2, 792–795).

Tellingly, perhaps, one of Jung's most detailed discussions of Plato takes place in the context, not of a pagan, but of a Christian concept, namely: the concept of the Trinity. In 1940, Jung gave a lecture entitled "On the Psychology of the Idea of the Trinity" at the celebrated Eranos conferences held annually in Ascona since 1933. Initially published in the *Eranos-Jahrbuch* for 1940–1941 (Jung 1942), he later revised and expanded this lecture into a longer essay published in *Symbolik des Geistes* in 1948 (Jung 1948); it is this later version that is published in volume 11 of Jung's *Gesammelte Werke* or *Collected Works*, and that provides the basis for the discussion here in this study.

At key points in his paper on a psychological approach to the dogma of the Trinity, Jung refers to the *Timaeus*, classed (along with the *Sophist*, the

Statesman, the *Critias*, the *Philebus*, and the *Laws*) among Plato's late dialogues, that is, in a period roughly dateable as between 367 and 347 BCE (the latter date being the date of Plato's death at the age of eighty or eighty-one).[9] Before turning to Jung's reading of this work, it might be helpful to say a few words about the structure and some of the main ideas of this dialogue.[10]

PLATO'S "TIMAEUS"

In his commentary on the *Timaeus*, Proclus cites the "divine" Iamblichus as saying that "the whole theory of Plato" is comprehended in two dialogues, the *Parmenides* and the *Timaeus* (Proclus 1998a, 22). On this account, the whole of philosophy is divided into the theory of intelligibles and sensibles, corresponding to the twofold world of the intelligible and the sensible. The relation between the *Parmenides* and the *Timaeus* may be summarized as follows (ibid., 22; Plato 1996, 380):

Parmenides	*Timaeus*
Through Parmenides, Plato presents a theory of intelligibles	Through Timaeus, Plato presents a theory of sensibles (or "mundane natures")
An account of the divine orders	An account of the progression of sensible essences
Shows how sensibles are contained in intelligibles paradigmatically	Shows how intelligibles are contained in sensibles according to similitude
Theological speculations	Physical speculations
A book on true beings	A book on the universe
The whole doctrine of supermundane natures	The whole doctrine of mundane natures
Suspends the progression of all things from the One	Refers the cause of everything in the world to the first artificer or the Demiurge
Exhibits beings as participating of a uniform essence (i.e. an "hyparxis"[a] which has the form of the One)	Represents all things as participating of demiurgic providence
Prior to theology, Parmenides presents an investigation of immaterial forms	Prior to physiology, Timaeus extends through images the theory of mundane natures

[a] By *hyparxis* (υπαρξις), Proclus means both the first principle (or foundation) of a thing's essence and the summit of essence itself, in this case, the One.

In other words, these two dialogues have the same subject, albeit approached from opposing angles: in the *Parmenides*, from the aspect of the intelligible or ideal world, and in the *Timaeus* from the aspect of the physical and physiological world. As Proclus put it in his commentary on the *Parmenides*, "as Timaeus does not simply inquire about nature in the usual manner of the natural scientist, but in so far as all things get their cosmic ordering from the one Demiurge, so also Parmenides, we may say, in conducting an inquiry about beings, is himself examining these beings in so far as they are derived from the One" (641; Proclus 1987, 36). These two aspects, Proclus assures us in his *Timaeus* commentary, are complementary: "For it is requisite after having been exercised in discussions about the best polity, to be led to the knowledge of the universe; and after having contended with strenuous doubts about forms [or ideas], to be sent to the mystic theory of the unities of beings [or the 'Henads']" (Proclus 1998b, 22–23; cf. Proclus 2006, 107–108).[11]

The *Timaeus*—so named after one of the four speakers in the dialogue, Timaeus of Locri, a wealthy aristocrat with Pythagorean views (who may or may not have actually existed)—connects with Plato's works in two other ways: it looks back to the *Republic*, the subject of the previous day's discussion, which centres on the discussion of justice;[12] and it looks forward, inasmuch as it is the first part of a planned, but never complete trilogy (of which the others parts were the *Critias*, which breaks off in an unfinished sentence, and the *Hermocrates*, which was never written). These dialogues have clear thematic links: the cosmology presented by Timaeus, that is, his account of the world as a kosmos (κόσμος), a place of universal order, shows how the good (τὸ ἀγαθόν) is present in nature (φύσις), and this natural order is represented as extending into the realm of politics, for the just city as presented by Socrates in the *Republic* finds its counterpart in Critias's account of the island state of Atlantis.[13] (In *Timaeus*, Socrates takes a back seat, and lets Timaeus do most of the talking; his role in the *Sophist* and the *Statesman* is similarly peripheral, and in the *Laws* he is entirely absent.)

In order for the *Timaeus* and the *Critias* to present the world as a place where the good prevails, from the planets down to the human realm, the prefatory function of the *Timaeus* is to offer nothing less than an account of the creation of the physical world and of the birth of humankind. Or as Francis Cornford (1874–1923) (following the Italian classicist Giuseppe Fraccaroli [1849–1918]) puts it, the purpose of this cosmological introduction is "to link the morality externalised in the ideal society to the whole organisation of the world": whereas the *Republic* "had dwelt on the structural analogy between the state and the individual soul", now Plato "intends to base his conception of human life, both for the individual and for society, on the inexpugnable foundation of the order of the universe", and so "the parallel of macrocosm and microcosm runs through the whole discourse" (Cornford 1997, 6). Thus the ambition of this dialogue is vast; not surprisingly, therefore, after an introductory conversation about the number of participants (17a-20c)—which caught Jung's attention and appears to have been a source of ceaseless fascination for him (see Chapter Three)—and an initial account given by Critias of the story of Atlantis as learned by Solon from an Egyptian priest (20c-27b), which constitute a prologue, Timaeus's first move is a methodological one. For he concludes his opening remarks about the nature and scope of physics (rehearsing the distinctions between being and becoming, between becoming and its cause, and between the model and its copy), by admitting that he cannot provide certainties, but only a "likely story":

> Wherefore, Socrates, if in our treatment of a great host of matters regarding the Gods and the generation of the Universe we prove unable to give accounts that are always in all respects self-consistent and perfectly exact, be not thou surprised; rather we should be content if we can furnish accounts that are inferior to none in likelihood, remembering that both I who speak and you who judge are but human creatures, so that it becomes us to accept the likely account of these matters and forbear to search beyond it. (29c-d; Plato 1929, 53)

The discourse that ensues is divided into three parts: first, a section on the works of reason or intellect (27c-47e); second, a section on the works of necessity (47e-69a); and third, a section on the combined workings of rationality and necessity, and it is in this context that Timaeus discusses humankind—the human frame, the working of the organs, and disorders of body and soul (69a-92c). (As a "creation narrative", therefore, the *Timaeus* corresponds to the opening chapter of Genesis: God's initiative to create the world as a place that is "good", and the decision to create humankind "in the image" of God; the creation of the physical universe; and the creation of Adam and Eve. In fact, in the form of its translations into Latin by Cicero and in the fourth century by Calcidius, the *Timaeus* was one of the most influential of Plato's works on the Church Fathers and on mediaeval theology, especially thinkers associated with the School of Chartres.)[14]

The opening of this third section briefly recapitulates what has been established in the previous two: namely in the account of the works of reason, how the rational souls was created by the Demiurge (Plato's name for the creator god, and not to be confused with its Gnostic counterpart); and, in the account of the works of necessity, how the bodily can be analysed down to its foundation in space, the Receptacle of all becoming (i.e. the *chôra* or χώρα), and built up through the elements of regular geometrical shape. Now Timaeus considers further the point of contact through sense perception between the individual soul and the external world, and how the co-operation of reason and necessity can be found in the work of the created gods. Although Timaeus discusses the bodily seats of the moral parts of the soul, the spirited part in the heart and the appetitive part in the stomach (69d-72d), various diseases (including those affecting the soul [86b-89d]), and indeed "the care of the soul" (89d-90d)—famously hailed by the Scottish classicist, John Burnet (1863–1928), as lying at the core of Socrates's teaching (Burnet 1916)— Jung never refers to this part of the dialogue.[15] The dialogue closes with the following words:

> And now at length we may say that our discourse concerning the Universe has reached its termination. For this our Cosmos has received the living creatures both mortal and immortal and been thereby fulfilled; it being itself a visible Living Creature embracing the visible creatures, a perceptible God made in the image of the Intelligible, most great and good and fair and perfect in its generation—even this one Heaven sole of its kind. (92c; Plato 1929, 253)

Now in itself the *Timaeus* is a remarkable work, and Cornford is surely right to speculate that "Plato's trilogy, had it been finished, would have stood out as his masterpiece, throwing even the *Republic* into the shade" (Cornford 1997, 363). Of its numerous themes, however, perhaps its central one is this: an attempt to explain, not so much how the world was created, as how we can be in a universe in which we can know both ourselves *and* that universe, in much the same way as Hegel's philosophy is an attempt to determine to what extent we can as subjects be satisfied in this world or the world meets what Frederick Neuhouser calls "the basic aspirations of subjectivity" (Neuhouser 2000, 306; cf. Grimes 1997b).

This theme is reflected in Timaeus's opening words in the section on the works of reason about the motive of the creation. In other words, why did the Demiurge create the world at all? As Timaeus explains, the real reason or cause (αἰτία) for the creation of an ordered world in the realm of Becoming has to do with the essential goodness of the creator:

> Let us now state the Cause wherefor[e] He that constructed it constructed Becoming and the All. He was good, and in him that is good no envy ariseth ever concerning anything; and being devoid of envy He desired that all should be, so far as possible, like unto Himself. This principle, then, we shall be wholly right in accepting from men of wisdom as being above all the supreme originating principle of Becoming and the Cosmos. For God desired that, so far as possible, all things should be good and nothing evil; wherefore, when He took over all that was visible, seeing that it was not in a state of rest but in a state of discordant and disorderly motion, He brought it into order out of disorder, deeming that the former state is in all ways better than the latter. (29d–30a; Plato 1929, 55)

On this account, the desire of the Demiurge was primarily for order and, as a result, beauty (i.e. *kallos*, κάλλος):

> For Him who is most good it neither was nor is permissible to perform any action save what is most fair. As He reflected, therefore, He perceived that of such creatures as are by nature visible, none that is irrational will be fairer, comparing wholes with wholes, than the rational; and further, that reason cannot possibly belong to any apart from Soul. So because of this reflection He constructed reason within soul and soul within body as He fashioned the All, that so the work He was executing might be of its nature most fair and most good. (30a–b; Plato 1929, 55)

The link between order and beauty is, of course, a core Platonic theme, and on Timaeus's account a key importance accrues to the soul (i.e. *psykhē* or ψυχή), as something imparted to the universe as a whole—a world that is characterized by reason, hence order, hence beauty, and hence goodness: "Thus, then, in accordance with the likely account, we must declare that this Cosmos has verily come into existence as a Living Creature endowed with soul and reason owing to the providence of God" (30b–c; Plato 1929, 55).[16]

On this account, the entire world is "ensouled", inasmuch as reason is spread throughout the whole of it.[17] In fact, within the *Timaeus* we can identify six different kinds of soul in the universe: four of which are immortal (the World Soul, the star souls, the souls of the inferior gods, and the human soul), two of which are mortal (the *thymos* and the *epithymêtikon*, i.e., its spirited and its appetitive parts).[18] Further on, in his discussion of the nature of the soul which begins at 34a–c, Timaeus describes the composition of the World Soul out of three elements (i.e. Existence, Sameness, and Difference), in a passage which (as we shall see) attracted the attention of Jung:

> Midway between the Being which is indivisible and remains always the same and the Being which is transient and divisible in bodies, He blended a third form of Being compounded out of the twain, that is to say, out of the Same and the Other; and in like manner He compounded it midway between that one of them which is indivisible and that one which is divisible in bodies. (35a; Plato 1929, 65)

On this account (which has provoked much critical commentary), the Demiurge creates a mixture of Sameness (or indivisible Existence) and Difference (or divisible Existence) and thereby creates a compound,[19] which he remixes into a unity and blends with Existence (or Being, i.e. *ousia* or οὐσία) in order to create the soul (35a).[20] In this way Timaeus explains how the soul is able to partake both of Being *and* Becoming, or of both eternity and time (since, in the famous phrase from the *Timaeus*, time is the moving likeness of eternity [37c–38c].)[21]

In fact, the notion of likeness, proportion, or analogy (*analogia* or ἀναλογία) plays a central role in the argument of the *Timaeus*: "And the fairest of bonds", Timaeus declares, "is that which most perfectly unites into one both itself and the things which it binds together; and to effect this in the fairest manner is the natural property of proportion" (31c; Plato 1929, 59); or, as Thomas Taylor (1758–1835) translates this passage, "And that is the most beautiful of bonds which renders both itself and the natures which are bound remarkably one. But the most beautiful analogy naturally produces this effect" (Plato 1996, 433). This principle marks the starting-point of an argument about planes and solids that causes Jung much puzzlement, as we shall also see.

The idea of proportion is evident in the account that follows of the division of the World Soul. Having created the soul out of a mixture of Difference, Sameness, and Existence, and thus having made a unity of the three, the Demiurge takes the resulting cosmic material or "soul-stuff" and turns it into a strip which he divides into divisions measured by two, four-term geometrical proportions, viz. 1 – 2 – 4 – 8 and 1 – 3 – 9 – 27 (35b–c). Having thus divided the cosmic soul-stuff, the Demiurge slits it lengthwise into two strips, which he fixes together in their middle, like the letter X (*chi*), and bends round until their ends connect, so as to form two crossing circles[22] (Fig. 2.1):

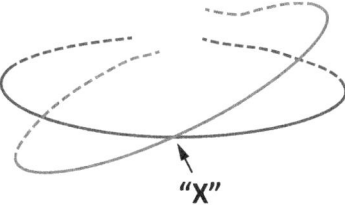

Fig. 2.1 How the Demiurge arranges the fabric of the universe. (Diagram reproduced with the kind agreement of Dr Barbara J. Becker, Department of History, University of California, Irvine. https://faculty.humanities.uci.edu/bjbecker/ExploringtheCosmos/week1c.html)

These circles are now set in motion: the outer circle is associated with Sameness (and is equivalent to the celestial or sidereal equator), while the inner circle is associated with Difference (and is equivalent to the ecliptic or the Zodiac) (Fig. 2.2):

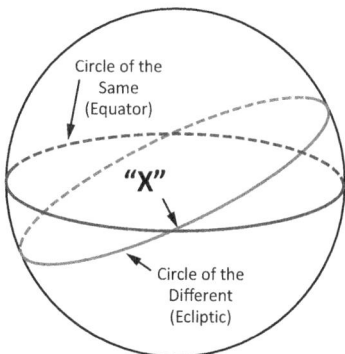

Fig. 2.2 How the Demiurge structures the universe. (Diagram reproduced with the kind agreement of Dr Barbara J. Becker, Department of History, University of California, Irvine. https://faculty.humanities.uci.edu/bjbecker/ExploringtheCosmos/week1c.html)

While the outer circle of Sameness is left undivided, the inner circle of Difference is divided into six parts, creating seven unequal circles. These circles move in opposite directions from each other, three at equal speeds and four at unequal (but proportionate) speeds (39d). On one reading (proposed by Proclus in his commentary on the *Timaeus* and, subsequently, by R.G. Bury [1869–1951] and Cornford), these circles correspond to the orbits of the sun, Venus, and Mercury as well as to the orbits of the moon, Mars, Jupiter, and Saturn, respectively: their movements in relation to each other repeat after the period known as the Platonic year.[23] As Barbara J. Becker has explained to me, however, what Timaeus calls the intersection of the circle of the Same and the circle of the Different refers to the alignment of the celestial equator and the ecliptic, and Plato's focus is on explaining the origins of the motions of the fixed celestial bodies (i.e. the stars) and the unfixed (i.e. the sun, the moon, and the planets).[24] (As Becker reminded me, in the so-called myth of Er in the *Republic*, Socrates talks about the heavens even more fancifully, describing how a larger outer circle moves the whole together at a uniform pace, while inner circles move, each at its own individual rate, while being swept along by the overriding power of the outer circle [*Republic*, 616b–617c].)[25]

Closely related to this model is the notion of the *musica universalis* or the "harmony of the spheres", a kind of application of the Pythagorean notion of harmonious proportion. In *De caelo* (*On the Heavens*), Aristotle explicated (but did not endorse) this theory as follows:

> Some thinkers suppose that the motion of bodies of that size must produce a noise, since on our earth the motion of bodies far inferior in size and in speed of movement has that effect. Also, when the sun and the moon, they say, and all the stars, so great in number and in size, are moving with so rapid a motion, how should they not produce a sound immensely great? Starting from this argument and from the observation that their speeds, as measured by their distances, are in the same ratios as musical concordances, they assert that the sound given forth by the circular movement of the stars is a harmony. Since, however, it appears unaccountable that we should not hear this music, they explain this by saying that the sound is in our ears from the very moment of birth and is thus indistinguishable from its contrary silence, since sound and silence are discriminated by mutual contrast. What happens to men, then, is just what happens to coppersmiths, who are so accustomed to the noise of the smithy that it makes no difference to them. (Book 2, §9; Aristotle 1984, vol. 1, 479)

(He did not endorse, inasmuch as he argued in favour of silent, frictionless spheres.)[26] Subsequent commentaries, such as that of Macrobius on Cicero's *Somnium Scipionis* (*The Dream of Scipio*) (see Bullock 1983), link the notion of scale or proportion in the *Timaeus* with Socrates's description in the myth of Er of how a Siren sits, perched, on each of the spheres (617b) (Macrobius 1990, 193–194). More recently, the Neoplatonic scholar Donna M. Altimari Adler has argued in considerable detail that the *Timaeus* does, in fact, articulate "a musical paradigm of the cosmos": not only is the primary musical scale "hidden within Plato's recipe for constructing the world soul", but "the exact 'fabric' that [the Demiurge] cut to form the χ ('chi') figure instrumental to making the world soul" is "a particular matrix of numbers intimately connected with Plato's musical cosmology" (Adler 2019, xi). (By describing this cosmology as "far more extensive than ancient or modern commentators have allowed", Adler has in her sights such contemporary scholars as Luc Brisson and Walter Meyerstein (see Brisson 1974; Brisson and Meyerstein 1995)—but also Francis Cornford.) As we shall see (in the fourth chapter), the notion attributed by Aristotle to the Pythagoreans that we should suppose "the elements of numbers to be the elements of all things, and the whole of heaven to be a musical scale and a number" (*Metaphysics*, book 1, §5, 986a; Aristotle 1984, vol. 2, 1559) recurs in Jung's (and Wolfgang Pauli's) notion of synchronicity and of a "universal number".

On yet another reading, the construction of the circles of the Same and the Different should be read in conjunction with the conclusion of the dialogue quoted above (92c) and its reference to a "perceptible" or "visible" god: drawing on a range of evidence (from such Roman writers as Marcus Manilius and his *Astronomica*; such early Christian writers as St Justin Martyr, Lactantius, and Eusebius of Caesaria; and Imperial coins minted during the reigns of Antonius Pius, Marcus Aurelius, Macrinus, and other emperors), George Latura has argued that such a visible god could only refer to the phenomenon known as zodiacal light, which at certain times of the year and in certain zones of the earth rises from the horizon, envelops planets along the ecliptic, and intersects the Milky Way—thus revealing a "visible" god in the form of a celestial X, reflecting the World Soul in the heavens (Latura 2012). As photographs in journals of astronomy testify, this is a stunning visual effect (and one that Jung himself claimed to have seen). On Latura's account, the dramatic visual impact of this intersection in the heavens would help explain why this Platonic account played such an important role in Hellenistic cosmology and soteriology.

Now that the description of the World Soul is complete—its composition out of the three intermediate kinds of Existence, Sameness, and

Difference; its division into proportions, corresponding to the intervals of cosmic harmony; and its fashioning into two circles, within which (on one account) the heavenly bodies are set in motion—what remains is for the Demiurge to create all that is corporeal or bodily, and to connect it to the soul. The soul is diffused and extends throughout the entire universe, "from the centre to the extremity", spread out through everything and invisibly enveloping all that is visible. Because the soul has *ousia* or Being, it is capable of turning around on itself, or in other words it begins to rotate, initiating "a divine beginning of unceasing and intelligent life lasting throughout time" (36e; Plato 1929, 73).

As Proclus puts it, "since [...] the soul consists of three parts, essence [i.e., Existence], same [i.e., Sameness] and different [i.e., Difference], and has these genera, as media between impartible [i.e., indivisible] and partible [i.e., divisible] natures, it knows both [orders of things] through them. [...] For all knowledge derives its completion through a similitude [i.e., likeness] of that which knows to the thing known" (2. 298; Proclus 1998b, 706; cited Cornford 1997, 94). (Earlier Proclus had made the same point when he said that "the soul is the medium between beings and non-beings, and that it knows all beings, both intelligibles and sensibles", adding that Plato "constitutes the soul, as being allied to intelligibles, from the genera of being, which primarily subsist in them; but [...] he gives figure to the soul, as being allied to sensibles" (2. 135 and 136; Proclus 1998b, 562).) Hence the soul stands at the intersection of the eternal and the changing, and to it accrues the following remarkable status:

> And whereas the body of the Heaven is visible, the Soul is herself invisible but partakes in reasoning and in harmony, having come into existence by the agency of the best of things intelligible and ever-existing as the best of things generated. Inasmuch, then, as she is a compound, blended of the natures of the Same and the Other and Being, these three portions, and is proportionately divided and bound together, and revolves back upon herself, whenever she touches anything which has its substance dispersed or anything which has its substance undivided she is moved throughout her whole being and announces what the object is identical with and from what it is different, and in what relation, where and how and when, it comes about that each thing exists and is acted upon by others both in the sphere of the Becoming and in that of the ever-uniform. (36e–37b; Plato 1929, 73–75)

This moving discourse on the World Soul and how, in Cornford's words, its cognitive activity of its ceaseless and intelligent life is based on the fundamental principle of likeness (proportion, analogy), that is, that "like knows like", is followed by a more polemical point about methodology: "When [the soul] is concerned with the rational, and the circle of the Same, spinning truly, declares the facts, reason and knowledge of necessity result. But should anyone assert that the substance in which these two states arise is something other than Soul, his assertion will be anything rather than the truth" (37b–c; Plato 1929, 75). Or in other words, *noús* (νοῦς) is something that can, thanks to its unique status and its triple essence of *ousia*, energy, and power, exist only in soul (Cornford 1997, 96).

As this brief overview shows, the *Timaeus* is a work of remarkable scope and depth, even if (or perhaps because) Plato never completed the trilogy of which it was intended to be the first part. At the same time, it is a work of ceaseless fascination, and it is therefore perhaps not surprising that it is the work by Plato to which Jung most frequently makes reference and hence made his own, much as Freud repeatedly referred to the *Symposium*.[27] For Jung, *Timaeus* represented a "familiar world to me" (*die mir vertraute Welt*), a view of the world that had been "a sacrosanct authority for medieval science"—"and rightly so!", he added, and a world-view which was, he believed, in the process of being rediscovered in "modern form" (*in moderner Form*), as he suggested in a letter of 22 March 1957 to the mineralogist Werner Nowacki (Jung 1973–1975, vol. 2, 352). (For Jung, this was no throw-away remark: as he put it in the conclusion to *Liber secundus* in his *Red Book*, "I must catch up with a piece of the Middle Ages—within myself. We have only finished with the Middle Ages of—others" [Jung 2012, 457].) And, as we shall see (below and in the fourth chapter), Jung's interest in the *Timaeus* goes back at least as far as the 1920s and the time when he was working on his *Black Books*, the precursor to his legendary *Red Book*.

A bibliographical note: Jung seems to have known the text of the *Timaeus* in various translations, quoting in his essay on the dogma of the Trinity from the translation by Otto Apelt (1845–1932) (see Plato 1922), while also referring to the translations into English by Francis Cornford and Thomas Taylor (both of which are in his library) (C.G. Jung-Bibliothek Katalog, 58). Jung's library also contains, however, a translation into German of the *Timaeus*, the *Crito*, and book 10 of the *Laws* published by Otto Kiefer (1846–1912) in 1909 (see Plato 1909), as well as a three-volume selection of Plato's writings translated by Ludwig von Georgii (1810–1896), Franz Susemihl (1826–1901), Julius Deuschle (1828–1861), W.S. Teuffel (1820–1878), and Wilhelm Wiegand (1803–1881), containing (in volume 1) an account of Plato's life, the

Symposium, the *Apology of Socrates*, the *Crito*, and the *Phaedo*; (in volume 2) the *Phaedrus*, the *Protagoras*, and the *Gorgias*; and (in volume 3) the *Laws* (see Plato 1854–1859); a translation of the *Symposium* by Rudolf Kassner (1873–1959) (see Plato 1906); Kiefer's translation of the *Parmenides* and the *Philebus* (see Plato 1925); a selection of Plato's political writings translated by Edgar Salin (1892–1974) entitled *Von Mensch und Staat* (see Plato 1942); and Salin's translation of the *Apology*, the *Crito*, and the *Phaedo* (see Plato 1945). And in terms of the Neoplatonists, they are represented in Jung's library by Greek and German editions of Plotinus's *Enneads* and a translation of "On the Nature of the Soul" (*Enneads*, IV) by Stephen Mackenna (1872–1934) (see Plotinus 1905; Plotinus 1951/1959; and Plotinus 1924); and Proclus's *Select Theorems on the Perpetuity of Time*, extracted from Thomas Taylor's translation of Ocellus Lucanus's *On the Nature of the Universe* and other works (Taylor 1831, 85–96).

TRANSFORMATIONS AND SYMBOLS OF THE LIBIDO (1911–1912)

Jung's interest in the Platonic dialogue called the *Timaeus* has a long history and can be traced back to his first major work of 1911–1912, entitled *Transformations and Symbols of the Libido*. Here Jung had noted in the context of his discussion of the symbolism of the mother and of rebirth that "the thought of 'union,' expressed by the symbol of the cross, is met with in the *Timaios* of Plato, where the world soul is conceived as stretched out between heaven and earth in the form of an X (Chi)" (and hence, he added, "in the form of a 'St Andrew's cross'") (Jung 1991, §406). He went on to cite the following passage from the preceding section where Timaeus introduces the World Soul:

> And in the midst thereof He set Soul, which He stretched throughout the whole of it, and therewith He enveloped also the exterior of its body; and as a Circle revolving in a circle He [e]stablished one sole and solitary Heaven, able of itself because of its excellence to company with itself and needing none other beside, sufficing unto itself as acquaintance and friend. And because of all this He generated it to be a blessed God. (34b; Plato 1929, 65)

On the basis of this passage Jung argues that "this highest degree of inactivity and freedom from desire, symbolized by *being enclosed within oneself*", signifies "divine blessedness" (*göttliche Seligkeit*), a conception for which the only human prototype is the child in the mother's womb or the adult in a perpetual embrace and entwinement with the mother as the origin (Jung 1991, §407). (The decision of Diogenes the Cynic to live in a tub, as reflected in the famous painting, *Diogenes Sitting in His Tub* by Jean-Léon Gérôme (1860), is, for Jung, a means of giving mythological expression to the blessedness and resemblance to the divine in his lack of needing anything, that is, the fantasy of the womb.) Turning to Timaeus's account of how the soul is prior to the body, Jung cites the following passage:

> Now as regards the Soul, although we are essaying to describe it after the body, God did not likewise plan it to be younger than the body; for, when uniting them, He would not have permitted the elder to be ruled by the younger; but as for us men, even as we ourselves partake largely of the accidental and casual, so also do our words. God, however, constructed Soul to be older than Body and prior in birth and excellence, since she was to be the mistress and ruler and it the ruled [...]. (34b–c; Plato 1929, 65)

On Jung's reading, Timaeus is suggesting that the very concept of the "soul" itself is a derivative of the mother-imago, or in other words "a symbolic designation for the amount of libido remaining in the mother-imago" (Jung 1991, §408). (As an analogous example, Jung cites the Christian representation of the soul as "the bride of Christ".)

At this point Jung refers to Timaeus's account of the composition of the World Soul and its division into harmonic intervals (35a-c), describing it as a development "tak[ing] place in an obscure fashion in mystic numerals" (ibid., §408). Once this is complete, the Demiurge constructs the Circles of the Same and the Different and the planetary circles in the passage cited above from which Jung highlights two sentences. First, citing the passage: "Next, He split all this that He had put together into two parts lengthwise; and then He laid the twain one against the other, the middle of one to the middle of the other, like a great cross" (36b), Jung comments that this account "approaches very closely the division and union of Atman who, after the division, is compared to a man and a woman who hold each other in an embrace" (ibid., §409). Jung is thinking here of a passage in the Brihadāraṇyaka Upanishad (I, 4),[28] whose notion of the original state of Ātman he had earlier in chapter 3 of *Transformations and Symbols of the Libido* compared to Plato's conception of the World Soul (ibid., §251).²⁹ And second, citing the passage: "And when the construction of the Soul had all been completed to the satisfaction of its Constructor, then He fabricated within it all the Corporeal, and uniting them center to center He made them fit together" (36d–e), Jung refers the reader back to his comments on the maternal meaning of the World Soul as found in Plotinus in chapter 2 of *Transformations and Symbols of the Libido*.

There, in his discussion of the conception and the genetic theory of the libido, Jung moves from Arthur Schopenhauer's notion of the libido via the "cosmogonic meaning" of Eros in Plato (in the *Symposium* [180b], *Cratylus* [398d], and *Phaedrus* [252b and 255c-e]) and in Hesiod (in his *Theogeny*) to the Orphic figure of Phanes or the "shining one": Phanes is the first created, the "father of Eros"; signifies, in Orphic terms, Priapus; and is the bisexual god of love similar to Dionysos Lysios, whose sanctuary was in Thebes (Jung 1991, §223).³⁰ At this point Jung turns to Plotinus and the Neoplatonic conception of the World Soul as the energy of the intellect. As Jung makes clear, in so doing he is drawing in part on the study by the Monist philosopher Arthur Drews (1865–1935), *Plotin und der Untergang der antiken Weltanschauung* (1907),³¹ and Drews is the source of the formulation that the World Soul is "the energy of the intellect" (Drews 1907, 127).

In his *Enneads*, Plotinus compared the One (or the creative primordial principle) to light; the intellect, to the sun (♂); and the soul, to the moon (♀), "which gets its light from the sun".³² Elsewhere Plotinus suggests that the relation of the One to the intellect is like that of a father to a son.³³ Inasmuch as the One as Ouranos is transcendent,³⁴ the son as Kronos has dominion over the visible world, and the World Soul (as Zeus) appears as subordinate to him.³⁵ Plotinus describes the One or οὐσία as the first hypostasis, one of three metaphysical principles or forms of emanation (i.e. the Soul, the Intellect, and the One), and therefore as "one being in three hypostases"; hence comparable, as Drews argued, with the formula "three hypostases in one ousia" (μία ουσία ἐν τρισίν υποστάσεσιν) that came to be accepted as the orthodox formulation of the doctrine of the Trinity (God as Father, Son, and Holy Spirit) at the Councils of Nicaea (325) and Constantinople (381) (Drews 1907, 134–135).³⁶ At this point, Jung notes that some early Christian sects attributed a material significance to the Holy Spirit (as the World Soul or the moon), and cross-refers to his later comments about the chi in the *Timaeus*.

On Jung's account, Plotinus argues that the World Soul "has a tendency towards a divided existence and towards divisibility" (see *Enneads*, IV.2, §1, "On the Essence of the Soul"),[37] something which Jung regards as "the *conditio sine qua non* of all change, creation, and procreation" (and hence as a "maternal quality") (Jung 1991, §223). (It is "in its nature to be divided", Plotinus argues, because in this world souls are "in bodies and are divided by bodies" [IV.2, §1].) Drawing again on Drews, Jung describes the soul as "an 'unending all of life' and wholly energy [...] a living organism of ideas, which attain in it effectiveness and reality [*Wirksamkeit und Wirklichkeit*]" (ibid., §223).[38] What is the relation of the (world) soul to intellect? On Jung's reading of Plotinus, "the intellect is its procreator, its father, which, having conceived it, brings it to development in thought"; although Jung refers the reader to *Enneads*, IV.8, §3, in reality he is adopting Drew's account, according to which the soul distinguishes itself from the intellect precisely in this respect—that it unfolds what it intuits into reality and brings it into appearance in the sensible (i.e. as opposed to the intelligible) realm.[39] Or in other words, the inward "effectiveness" of the intelligible (*Wirksamkeit* [...] *nach innen*) that takes place in the intellect corresponds to that of the soul as an outward "effectiveness" (*Wirksamkeit nach außen*) (Drews 1907, 138).

Although Jung appears to be citing Plotinus, he is in fact citing directly from Drews when he quotes the following passage: "What lies enclosed in the intellect, comes to development in the world-soul as Logos, fills it with meaning [*Inhalt*] and makes it as if intoxicated with nectar" (Jung 1991, §223).[40] Pointing to the analogy between nectar (as the drink of fertility and life) and sperma, Jung argues that the soul is *fructified* by the intellect (or, in other words, by the father—as found in analogous Egyptian representations) (ibid., §224). Following Drews's account of the Plotinian doctrine of the duality of the World Soul, that is, an upper soul (represented by the heavenly Aphrodite) and a lower soul (represented by the earthly Aphrodite), Jung cites Drews's allusion to how the soul "knows the birth pangs",[41] before noting that it is not for nothing that the dove as the bird of Aphrodite is also the symbol of the Holy Spirit (ibid., §224). What this fragment of the philosophy of history teaches us, Jung concludes, is "the significance of the endopsychic"—or as we might now say, "intrapsychic"—"perception of the libido and its symbols for human thought" (ibid., §225).

Jung's *Transformations and Symbols of the Libido* marked his break with Freud and, in effect, launched the project of analytical psychology—a project described by Sonu Shamdasani as the "dream of a science"

(Shamdasani 2003). Looking back at this work in his foreword to its substantially revised version of 1952, *Symbols of Transformation*, Jung described it—intellectually and professionally—as "a landmark, set up on the spot where two ways divided" (Jung 1967, xxiv). Yet the book was also written in 1911, in Jung's thirty-sixth year: a "critical" time, for it marks "the beginning of the second half of life, when a metanoia, a mental transformation, not infrequently occurs"—inwardly and privately (ibid., xxvi). If *Transformations*, with its dense network of references and allusions, represents the *intellectual* source of analytical psychology, his work in the *Black Books* and in the *Red Book* (beginning in 1913 and continuing, with interruptions, until 1928) represents its *intuitive*, or even *spiritual* source. Jung's work now took him in new, cultural-historical directions: into typology in *Psychological Types* (1921), into alchemy (see *Psychology and Alchemy* [1944] among other works), into Gnosticism (see *Aion* [1951]), and into religion in both its Western and Eastern forms. In 1937, Jung delivered the Terry Lectures at Yale on psychology and religion; and the Eranos conferences held in Ascona in Switzerland,[42] Jung lectured on various topics, including in 1940 on transformation symbolism in the Mass and on the psychology of the Trinity.

Notes

1. Elsewhere in the alchemical tradition, Jung pointed to the *Tractatus aureus* attributed to Hermes Trismegistus, according to whom "God [contains] all the treasure of his godhead [...] hidden in himself as in an archetype [*in se tanquam archetypo absconditum*]", and to the notion in the *Tractatus de igne et sale* of Vigenerus (Blaise de Vigenère) that the world is "made after the likeness of its archetype" (*ad archetypi sui similitudinem factus*)—both highly Platonic formulations (Jung 1969a, §5, fn 8).
2. For good measure Jung added that, although the actual *term* "archetype" is not found in St Augustine, the *idea* of it is in his notion of "*ideae principales*" (*Eighty-Three Different Questions*, §46), and he went on to compare the "archaic or [...] primordial types" or "universal images that have existed since the remotest times" with the *représentations collectives* of Lucien Lévy-Bruhl (1857–1939), and with myth and fairytale (Jung 1969a, §5–§6).
3. The same point applied, Jung added, to the "very elegant" Latin of the Stoics or the Neoplatonists, as well as the "unspeakably heavy and difficult [...] original German". In the case of (ancient) Greek, the problem was "much subtler", but compared with a modern language it was still "exceed-

ingly archaic". As Jung put it, the ancient Greeks (including Plato) were "always under the pressure of spirit, which made it as very real thing to them, and they felt the word as the visible face of the spirit"—and "therefore it was to them divine" (Jung 1989, vol. 1, 367).
4. Nowadays the term Hīnayāna is considered pejorative, and instead the term Nikaya Buddhism is used to refer to early Buddhist schools.
5. Intriguingly, in book 7 of Plato's *Laws*, the Athenian Stranger uses precisely the image of ship-building in respect of designing education when he says that what he is doing is "much the same as what a shipwright does in the beginning of build ships, when he sketches the shape of ships in outline by laying down the keels" (803a; Plato 1988, 192).
6. The legendary figure of Tages is said to have appeared at plough-time and, according to Cicero (in *On Divination*, book 2, §23), to have taught the Etruscans the art of divination (Cicero, *On Divination* in Cicero 1923, pp. 427–429). The origins of Tages are mysterious: for some, such as Festus (in *De significatu verborum*, 359.14), Tages was the son of Genius and the grandson of Jupiter; for others, such as Ovid (*Metamorphoses*, book 15, ll. 553–559), "[a] man, / Ploughing one day Etruscan fields, [...] saw / The fateful clod of its own accord / Move, though no one had touched it, and assume / A human form and lose its earthy shape, / And open its new mouth in prophecies. / The people called him Tages. He first taught / The Etruscans to discover things to come" (Ovid 1987, 368).
7. The phrase *puer aeternus* is applied by Ovid in his *Metamorphoses* (book 4, ll. 18–29), to Iacchus and other figures associated with the Eleusinian cults: "For you / Have youth unfading; you're a boy for ever; / You shine the fairest in the firmament. / When you lay by your horns, your countenance / Is like a lovely girl's" (Ovid 1987, 74). C.G. Jung wrote a study on the *puer aeternus* entitled "The Psychology of the Child Archetype" (1941), later collected with a monograph by Carl Kerényi and published under the title *Einführung in das Wesen der Mythologie* (1941), translated by R.F.C. Hull in 1949 (Jung and Kerényi 1969), while Marie-Louise von Franz delivered a series of lectures on the *puer aeternus* at the C.G. Jung Institute in Zurich during the winter semester 1959–1960 (von Franz 2000).
8. This view forms the basis for the therapeutic aspect of Jung's analytical psychology: "You can have all the experiences of those hermits in the desert. What are a thousand years? Just nothing. [...] Of course the indispensable condition is that you have an archetypal experience, and to have that means you have surrendered to life. If your life has not three dimensions, if you don't live in the body, if you live on the two-dimensional plane in the paper world that is flat and printed, as if you were only living your biography, then you are nowhere. You don't see the archetypal world, but live like a pressed flower in the pages of a book, a mere memory of yourself" (Jung 1989, vol. 2, 972).

9. As William Altman has argued, the order of composition of Plato's dialogues is not necessarily the order in which they should be read; on this account, the *Timaeus* stands at the beginning of a second group of seventeen interconnected dialogues, after the pivotal dialogue of the *Republic* which separates a first group of dialogues (Altman 2010, 44).
10. In preparing this section, I have referred to Cornford (1997, 1–8), Johansen (2011, 2015), and Zeyl and Sattler (2019). For a detailed treatment, the reader is advised to consult Taylor (1928) (reprinted 1967), which highlights the influence of fifth-century Pythagoreanism on the *Timaeus*; and, more recently, the essays in Wright (2000) and Mohr and Sattler (2010), as well as Altman (2016).
11. Within Plotinus's Neoplatonism there are three principles or hypostases, namely: the Soul (*psychê*), the Intellect or Intelligence (*nous*), and the One: in its abundance the One overflows and turns back on itself, giving rise to the Intellect—the "home" of the Ideas or Forms. In turn, the Intellect engenders the third hypostasis, the Soul or the creative principle. The doctrine of the Henads, developed in Proclus's *Elements of Theology* and *Platonic Theology*, seeks to mediate between the hypostases of the Divine Triad, that is, between the unknowable unity of the One and the lower realities. The Henads—identifiable with the gods—are arranged in the following hierarchical order: Intelligible Henads, Intellectual Henads, Supercosmic Henads, and Intracosmic Henads, thus mediating Being, divine Intelligence, divine Soul, and divine Body (Wallis 1995, 147–153). For further discussion, see Riel (2017).
12. On the question of whether the speech on the previous day *was* the *Republic* and the opposing views of, among others, Proclus, A.E. Taylor, Erwin Rohde (1845–1898), and Seth Bernadete (who think it was) and Gilbert Ryle (1900–1976), Francis Cornford, and Paul Friedländer (1882–1968) (who argue against this view), see Lampert and Planeaux (1998, 90). A compromise position is taken by Thomas Taylor, who argues that on the day of the Bendidia festival, celebrating the Thracian goddess Bendis and held on the nineteenth day of the month of Thargelion, that is, prior to the Panathenaia, Socrates went down to the Piraeus and held a discourse about the republic with Polemarchus, Cephalus, Glaucon, Adeimantus, and Thrasymachus (and thus the dialogue called the *Republic*); on the following day, he related this discourse in the city to Timaeus, Critias, Hermocrates, and a nameless fourth person; and now Timaeus resumes this discussion with his discourse on the creation of the universe (and thus the dialogue called *Timaeus* itself) ("Introduction", in Plato 1996, 378–379).
13. As Proclus notes, one of the earliest commentators on Plato, Crantor, regarded Critias's account of Atlantis as "mere history", while others inter-

preted it as an allegory or fable (1,76; Proclus 1998a, p. 77). As Thomas Taylor notes, however, Proclus highlights how Critias describes his account as "a tale which, though passing strange, is yet wholly true" (20d; Plato 1929, 29; cf. "Introduction", in Plato 1996, 393). For further discussion, see Rosenmeyer (1956), Dušanic (1982), Morgan (1998), and Vidal-Naquet (2007). For his part, Jung demonstrated a refreshing scepticism about the historicity of the Atlantis myth, reacting caustically to its appropriation by "legions of theosophical enthusiasts" (Jung 1971, §594; and Jung 1969a, §471). Compare with Jung's remark in his letter to a correspondent called Frau Patzelt of 29 November 1935: "I have read a few books by Rudolf Steiner and must confess that I have found nothing in them that is of the slightest use to me. [...] So long as Steiner is or was not able to understand the Hittite inscriptions yet understood the language of Atlantis which nobody knows existed, there is no reason to get excited about anything Herr Steiner has said" (Jung 1973–1975, vol. 1, 203–204). (For a collection of material on the anthroposophical approach to Atlantis, see Steiner 2001.) In the Twenties, interest in the myth of Atlantis was also revived by the ethnologist Leo Frobenius (1873–1938), an important thinker for Jung because of his study of the night-sea journey; Jung's library possesses a couple of the volumes in a twelve-volume series exploring the hypothesis of Atlantis, including *Die Atlantische Götterlehre* (Frobenius 1926). (It would be fair to describe Frobenius's concept of *Kulturmorphologie* as ripe for decolonization.) In a letter to Heinrich Boltze of 13 February 1951, Jung dismissed Atlantis as "a mythical phantasm" and described Frobenius as "an imaginative and somewhat credulous original" (*ein phantasiebegabtes und etwas gutgläubiges Original*): "Great collector of material. Less good as a thinker" (*Großer Materialsammler. Als Denker weniger gut*) (Jung 1973–1975, vol. 2, 4). And for an example of how the Atlantis myth apparently still possesses a remarkable imaginative vitality, see Cooper and Hutton (2005).

14. For a detailed discussion of the reception of *Timaeus* in the Latin tradition, notably Cicero, Apuleius, Calcidius, and St Augustine, see Hoenig (2018).
15. Nor, surprisingly enough, does Jung discuss the passage where Timaeus highlights the significance of dreams or visions: "And that God gave unto man's foolishness the gift of divination a sufficient token is this: no man achieves true and inspired divination when in his rational mind, but only when the power of his intelligence is fettered in sleep or when it is distraught by disease or by reason of some divine inspiration. But it belongs to a man when in his right mind to recollect and ponder both the things spoken in dream or waking vision by the divining and inspired nature, and all the visionary forms that were seen, and by means of reasoning to discern about them all wherein they are significant and for whom they portend evil

or good in the future, the past, or the present" (71e–72a; Plato 1929, 187). Cf. *Republic*, 364b; *Laws*, 772d; and *Phaedrus*, 244a ff.

16. For an overview of Plato's conception of *psychê*, see Lorenz (2011); and Robinson (2015).
17. For an alternative account of the Demiurge as a creator figure who alternately governs the universe and abandons it to its fate, see the *Statesman*, 269c–270a and 271e–274e (Plato 1984, III.18–III.24).
18. For further discussion of the relation between individual soul and World Soul, see Lisi (2007); Finamore and Kutash (2017); Bertozzi (2021, 92–94); and Wilberding (2021).
19. As Cornford points out, understanding of these terms appears to presume prior knowledge of these terms as used in another dialogue, the *Sophist* (Cornford 1997, 61). On Existence, Sameness, and Difference as Forms, see the *Sophist*, 254b–255e (in Cornford 1960, 273–285).
20. In the *Philebus*, Socrates distinguishes between four "elements" or kinds of being: (1) the infinite (or the limitless); (2) the finite (or the limited); (3) the union of the two (or a mixed kind of being); and (4) the cause of this union (or the cause of this mixture)—this last being identified with reason (*Philebus*, 30a–b; Plato 1989, p. 1107). For further discussion of this dialogue, see Bernadete (1993) (and esp. 162–165); and for a polemical, anti-Platonic reading, see Onfray (2006, 147–157).
21. In the *Phaedo*, 78b, Socrates distinguishes between something mortal, multiform, unintelligible, dissoluble (because a composite), and perpetually changing (i.e. the body) and something similar to the divine, immortal, intelligible, simple, and indissoluble (because not composite) (i.e. the soul) (cf. Cornford 1997, 63).
22. On Timaeus's description of the circle as the most perfect of all figures and its indebtedness to Parmenides, see Ballew 1974.
23. For further diagrams and discussion, see Bury's notes in Plato (1929, 71–73); and Cornford (1997, 72–93); for Proclus's interpretation, see Proclus (1998b, 654).
24. Barbara J. Becker, personal communication via email, 28 April 2022.
25. For further discussion of the myth of Er, see Halliwell (2007). Oddly, apart from the Atlantis myth (*Timaeus* 21e–26d, *Critias*) (and then only negatively) and the myth of the androgyne (*Symposium*, 189d–193d) (and then only in passing), Jung has nothing to say about the myth of Er (*Republic*, 614a–621d), nor about many of the other Platonic myths, such as the Gorgias myth (523a–527a), the Phaedo myth (107c–115a), the myth of the winged soul (*Phaedrus*, 246a–249d), the myth of Theuth (*Phaedrus*, 274c–275e), the cosmological myth of the Statesman (268–274e), and the *Laws* myth (903b–905b). For further discussion, see Stewart (1960); Brisson (1998, 2004); Plato (2004); and Collobert et al. (2012).

26. For an overview of the notion of the "music of spheres", see Haar (1980); and for a survey of Plato's contribution to musicology, see Anderson (1980).
27. See Freud (1999), vol. 7, 456; vol. 13, 62; vol. 14, 105; and vol. 16, 20. For his part, Jung's interest in the *Symposium* relates to:

    - the problem of universals as existing "in a heavenly place" and Diotima's discourse on beauty (211b; see Jung 1971, §36);
    - the bisexuality of the Original Man (190a–191e; see Jung 1969a, §138, n. 26, etc.);
    - Diotima's description of Eros as a "mighty daimon" (202d–e; see Jung 1967, §242);
    - the motif of a precious substance hidden in a "statue", reflected in Alcibiades's comparison of Socrates to the figures of Silenus in statuaries' shops (215a; see Jung 1970, §564);
    - the Neoplatonist commentary on the *Symposium* by Marsilio Ficino (1433–1499); and, above all:
    - the "daimon" of Socrates, comparable to Asclepius and the Cabir Telesphorus, to Faust and Mephistopheles, and to the "voice of conscience" (Jung 1954, §300; and Jung 1964, §843 and §853).

28. Here Ātman is described as "of the size of a man and a woman in close embrace": "He split (*pat-*) this Self in two: and from this arose husband (*pati*) and wife (*patnī*). [...] He copulated with her, and thence were human beings born" (Zaehner 1992, 42).
29. "For of eyes it had no need, since outside of it there was nothing visible left over; [...] For nothing went out from it or came into it from any side, since nothing existed" (33c; Plato 1929, 63).
30. The figure of Phanes had special associations for Jung, given the role played by this deity in his *Red Book*, where he is depicted as "the image of the divine child" who is "the newly appearing god" (Jung 2012, 358), but his full significance is clearer in the *Black Books*, where he appears in the entry for 28 September 1916 as "a golden bird" who emerges from "the tree of light" (Jung 2020, vol. 5, 260); and on 20 February 1917 as "the one above" (ibid., 280). On 11 September and 11 October 1917, Philemon sings the praises of Phanes in two hymns (vol. 7, 158–159), while on 31 July 1918 and on 2 August 1918 Phanes himself speaks: "The one voice of all beings speaks in you. / The sun of all suns shines in you. / You go the way of all ways, alone with all. / [...] He who is perfect [*Der Vollendete*] knows male and female, but I am the human [*ich bin der Mensch*], his father and son beyond masculine and feminine, beyond child and the aged. / He who is perfect knows rise and fall, but I am the center beyond dawn and dusk [*der Mittelpunkt jenseits von Morgenröthe und Abendröthe*]. / He who is perfect knows me and hence he is different from me" (vol. 7, 192–194; cf. Jung 2012, 358–359, fn. 211).

31. In this study (a copy of which is in Jung's library), Drews used the translations of Plotinus by Hermann Friedrich Müller (1843–1919) (see Müller 1878–1880) and by Otto Kiefer (1846–1912) (see Kiefer 1905). Jung owned a copy of the latter translation; his copies of Plotinus's works in Greek date from the Fifties.
32. *Enneads*, V.6, §4 (in Plotinus 1966–1988, vol. 5, 211); cf. Drews (1907, 132).
33. *Enneads*, V.8, §13 (ibid., vol. 5, 279) and *Enneads*, V.9, §8 (ibid., vol. 5, 307) (where κόρος = "fullness", "satiety" is read as equivalent to "son" or "boy"; cf. Drews 1907, 133). For the word-play on Χρόνος (*khrónos*) and κόρος (*kóros*), see the notes to V.1, §4 (ibid., 23) and to V.1, §7 (ibid., 38).
34. *Enneads*, III.5, §2 (ibid., vol. 3, 177); cf. Drews (1907, 133).
35. *Enneads*, V.1, §7 (ibid., vol. 5, 37–39); cf. Drews (1907, 133).
36. There are, however, important differences between this Plotinian Trinity and the Christian: first, because it is not three *persons*; and second, because the three principles involved are unequal (Kreeft 2018, 45).
37. Plotinus (1966–1988, vol. 4, 21–23); cf. Drews (1907, 137).
38. Drews (1907, 138); cf. *Enneads*, II.5, §3.
39. Drews (1907, 138); cf. *Enneads*, IV.8, §3; and IV.8, §6.
40. Although Jung cites this as "*Enneads*, III.5, §9", he is quoting Drews's summary of the passage (Drews 1907, 138).
41. Drews (1907, 140–141). The motif is a common one in Platonic thought and constitutes the starting-point of "philosophical midwifery" (see Grimes and Uliana 1998).
42. For further discussion of the significance of the Eranos conferences, see Wasserstrom (1999), Bernardini (2011), and Hakl (2013).

Bibliography

Adler, Donna M. Altimari. 2019. *Plato's "Timaeus" and the Missing Fourth Guest: Finding the Harmony of the Spheres*. Leiden and Boston: Brill.

Altman, William H.F. 2010. The Reading Order of Plato's Dialogues. *Phoenix* 64 (1/2): 18–51.

———. 2016. *The Guardians in Action: Plato the Teacher and the Post-"Republic" Dialogues from "Timaeus" to "Theatetus"*. Lanham, ML: Lexington Books.

Anderson, Warren. 1980. Plato. In *The New Grove Dictionary of Music and Musicians*, ed. Stanley Sadie, vol. 14, 853–857. London, New York, Hong Kong: Macmillan.

Aristotle. 1984. *The Complete Works of Aristotle*. Ed. by Jonathan Barnes, 2 vols. Princeton, NJ: Princeton University Press.

Ballew, Lynne. 1974. Straight and Circular in Parmenides and the 'Timaeus'. *Phronesis* 19 (3): 189–209.

Bernadete, Seth. 1993. *The Tragedy and Comedy of Life: Plato's "Philebus"*. Chicago and London: University of Chicago Press.
Bernardini, Riccardo. 2011. *Jung a Eranos: Il progetto della psicologia complessa*. Milan: FrancoAngeli.
Bertozzi, Alberto. 2021. *Plotinus on Love: An Introduction to His Metaphysics through the Concept of "Eros"*. Leiden and Boston: Brill.
Brisson, Luc. 1974. *Le même et l'autre dans la structure ontologique du "Timée" de Platon: Un commentaire systématique du "Timée" de Platon*. [Publications de l'Université de Paris X Nanterre, Lettres et Sciences Humaines, Série A : Thèses et Travaux, No 23]. Paris: Klincksieck.
———. 1998. *Plato the Myth Maker* [*Platon, les mots et les mythes: Comment et pourquoi Platon nomma le mythe?*]. Ed. and trans. by Gerard Naddaf. Chicago and London: University of Chicago Press.
———. 2004. *How Philosophers Saved Myths: Allegorical Interpretation and Classical Mythology* [*Introduction à la philosophie du mythe*, vol. 1, *Sauver les mythes*]. Trans. by Catherine Tihanyi. Chicago and London: University of Chicago Press.
Brisson, Luc, and Walter Meyerstein. 1995. *Inventing the Universe: Plato's "Timaeus", the Big Bang, and the Problem of Scientific Knowledge*. Albany, NY: State University of New York Press.
Bullock, Percy, trans. 1983. *The Dream of Scipio (Somnium Scipionis)* [1894]. Wellingborough: The Aquarian Press.
Burnet, John. 1916. *The Socratic Doctrine of the Soul*. [British Academy: Second Annual Philosophical Lecture, Henriette Hertz Trust]. London: Published for the British Academy by H. Milford, Oxford University Press.
Cicero. 1923. *Works, Vol. 20, On Old Age; On Friendship; On Divination*. Trans. by W.A. Falconer. Cambridge, MA: Harvard University Press.
Collobert, Catherine, Pierre Destrée, and Francisco J. Gonzalez, eds. 2012. *Plato and Myth: Studies on the Use and Status of Platonic Myths*. Leiden and Boston: Brill.
Cooper, Diana, and Shaaron Hutton. 2005. *Discover Atlantis: A Guide to Reclaiming the Wisdom of the Ancients*. London: Hodder & Stoughton.
Cornford, Francis MacDonald. 1960. *Plato's Theory of Knowledge: The "Theaetetus" and the "Sophist" of Plato Translated with a Running Commentary* [1935]. London: Routledge & Kegan Paul.
———. 1997. *Plato's Cosmology: The "Timaeus" of Plato* [1935]. Indianapolis, IN: Hackett.
Dominey, Charles Kent. 1977. *Archetype and Idea: Some Points of Correspondence between Jung's Theory of Archetypes and Plato's Theory of Forms*. Diploma Thesis, C.G. Jung Institute, Zurich.
Drews, Arthur. 1907. *Plotin und der Untergang der antiken Weltanschauung*. Jena: Diederichs.

Dušanic, Slobodan. 1982. Plato's Atlantis. *L'Antiquité Classique* 51: 25–52.
Finamore, John F., and Emilie Kutash. 2017. Proclus on the *Psyché*: World Soul and the Individual Soul. In *All From One: A Guide to Proclus*, ed. Pieter d'Hoine and Marije Martijn, 122–137. New York: Oxford University Press.
Franz, Marie-Louise von. 2000. *The Problem of the Puer Aeternus*. 3rd ed. Toronto: Inner City Books.
Freud, Sigmund. 1999. *Gesammelte Werke: Chronologisch geordnet*. Ed. by Anna Freud, Edward Bibring, and Ernst Kris. 18 vols. Frankfurt am Main: Fischer.
Frobenius, Leo, ed. 1926. *Die Atlantische Götterlehre [Atlantis: Volksmärchen und Volksdichtungen Afrikas*, Vol. 10]. Jena: Diederichs.
Giegerich, Wolfgang. 2020. "Dreaming the Myth Onwards": C.G. Jung on Christianity and on Hegel: Part 2 of "The Flight into the Unconscious" [*Collected English Papers*, Vol. 6] [2013]. London and New York: Routledge.
Grimes, Pierre. 1997a. Jung: The Dialectic and Plato's Divided Line. *Wisdom Literature and the Platonic Tradition*. NSPRS 075 and 076, 2 DVDs. Los Angeles, CA: Opening Mind Academy.
———. 1997b. 1997-06-23 NSPRS 063—Plato's *Timaeus*. https://archive.org/details/19970623NSPRS063.
Grimes, Pierre, and Regina L. Uliana. 1998. *Philosophical Midwifery: A New Paradigm for Understanding Human Problems*. Costa Mesa, CA: Hyparxis Press.
Guthrie, W.K.C. 1978. *A History of Greek Philosophy, Vol. 5, The Later Plato and the Academy*. Cambridge: Cambridge University Press.
Haar, James. 1980. Music of the Spheres. In *The New Grove Dictionary of Music and Musicians*, ed. Stanley Sadie, vol. 12, 835–836. London, New York, Hong Kong: Macmillan.
Hakl, Hans Thomas. 2013. *Eranos: An Alternative Intellectual History of the Twentieth Century* [2001]. Trans. Christopher McIntosh. Montréal, QC: McGill-Queen's University Press.
Halliwell, Stephen. 2007. The Life-and-Death Journey of the Soul: Interpreting the Myth of Er. In *The Cambridge Companion to Plato's "Republic"*, ed. G.R.F. Ferrari, 445–473. New York: Cambridge University Press.
Hasse, Dag Nikolaus. 2002. Plato Arabico-Latinus: Philosophy—Wisdom Literature—Occult Sciences. In *The Platonic Tradition in the Middle Ages: A Doxographic Approach*, ed. Stephen Gersh and Maarten J.F.M. Hoenen, 31–65. Berlin and New York: de Gruyter.
Hoenig, Christina. 2018. *Plato's "Timaeus" and the Latin Tradition*. Cambridge: Cambridge University Press.
Johansen, Thomas K. 2011. The *Timaeus* on the Principles of Cosmology. In *The Oxford Handbook of Plato*, ed. Gail Fine, 463–483. New York: Oxford University Press.
———. 2015. *Timaeus* and *Critias*. In *The Bloomsbury Companion to Plato*, ed. Gerald A. Press, 99–100. London: Bloomsbury.

Jung, C.G. 1942. Zur Psychologie der Trinitätsidee. In *Eranos Jahrbuch 1940–41*, 31–64. Zurich: Rhein-Verlag.

———. 1948. Versuch zu einer psychologischen Deutung des Trinitätsdogmas. In *Symbolik des Geistes: Studien über psychische Phänomenologie*, 321–446. Zurich: Rascher.

———. 1954. *The Development of Personality*. Trans. by R.F.C. Hull = *Collected Works*, Vol. 17. London and Henley: Routledge & Kegan Paul.

———. 1963. *Memories, Dreams, Reflections*. Ed. by Aniela Jaffé. Trans. by Richard and Clara Winston. London: Collins; Routledge & Kegan Paul.

———. 1964. *Civilization in Transition*. Trans. by R.F.C. Hull = *Collected Works*, Vol. 10. London and New York: Routledge.

———. 1967. *Symbols of Transformation: An Analysis of the Prelude to a Case of Schizophrenia*. Trans. by R.F.C. Hull = *Collected Works*, Vol. 5, 2nd ed. Princeton, NJ: Princeton University Press.

———. 1969a. *The Archetypes and the Collective Unconscious*. Trans. by R.F.C. Hull = *Collected Works*, Vol. 9/i. Princeton, NJ: Princeton University Press,

———. 1969b. *Psychology and Religion: West and East*. Trans. by R.F.C. Hull = *Collected Works*, Vol. 11, 2nd ed. London: Routledge & Kegan Paul.

———. 1970. *Mysterium coniunctionis: An Inquiry into the Separation and Synthesis of Psychic Opposites in Alchemy*. Trans. by R.F.C. Hull = *Collected Works*, Vol. 14, 2nd ed.. Princeton, NJ: Princeton University Press.

———. 1971. *Psychological Types*. Trans. by H.G. Baynes, rev. by R.F.C. Hull = *Collected Works*, Vol. 6. Princeton, NJ: Princeton University Press.

———. 1973–1975. *Letters*. Ed. by Gerhard Adler and Aniela Jaffé, trans. by R.F.C. Hull, 2 vols. Princeton, NJ: Princeton University Press.

———. 1989. *Nietzsche's "Zarathustra": Notes of the Seminar Given in 1934–1939*. Ed. by James L. Jarrett, 2 vols. London: Routledge.

———. 1991. *Psychology of the Unconscious: A Study of the Transformations and Symbolisms of the Libido: A Contribution to the History of the Evolution of Thought* [1916]. Trans. by Beatrice M. Hinkle. London: Routledge.

———. 2012. *The Red Book: Liber Novus* [Reader's Edition]. Ed. by Sonu Shamdasani, trans. by Mark Kyburz, John Peck, and Sonu Shamdasani. New York and London: Norton.

———. 2020. *The Black Books, 1813–1932: Notebooks of Transformation*. Ed. by Sonu Shamdasani, trans. by Martin Liebscher, John Peck, Sonu Shamdasani, 7 vols. New York and London: Norton.

Jung, C.G., and Carl Kerényi. 1969. *Essays on a Science of Mythology: The Myth of the Divine Child and the Mysteries of Eleusis*. Trans. by R.F.C. Hull. Princeton, NJ: Princeton University Press.

Kiefer, Otto. 1905. *Plotin: Enneaden in Auswahl*. 2 vols. Jena and Leipzig: Diederichs.

Kingsley, Peter. 2018. *Catafalque: Carl Jung and the End of Humanity*, 2 vols. London: Catafalque Press.
Kreeft, Peter. 2018. *The Platonic Tradition*. South Bend, IN: St. Augustine's Press.
Lampert, Laurence, and Christopher Planeaux. 1998. Who's Who in Plato's *Timaeus-Critias* and Why. *The Review of Metaphysics* 52 (1): 87–125.
Latura, George. 2012. Plato's Visible God: The Cosmic Soul Reflected in the Heavens. *Religions* 3: 880–886.
Lisi, Francisco. 2007. Individual Soul, World Soul and the Form of the Good in Plato's *Republic* and *Timaeus*. *Études platoniciennes* 4: 105–118.
Lorenz, Hendrik. 2011. Plato on the Soul. In *The Oxford Handbook of Plato*, ed. Gail Fine, 243–266. New York: Oxford University Press.
Macrobius. 1990. *Commentary on the Dream of Scipio*. Ed. and trans. by William Harris Stahl. New York: Columbia University Press.
Mohr, Richard D., and Barbara M. Sattler, eds. 2010. *One Book, The Whole Universe: Plato's "Timaeus" Today*. Las Vegas, Zurich, Athens: Parmenides Publishing.
Morgan, Kathryn A. 1998. Designer History: Plato's Atlantis Story and Fourth-Century Ideology. *The Journal of Hellenic Studies* 118: 101–118.
Müller, Hermann Friedrich. 1878–1880. *Die Enneaden des Plotin*. 2 vols. Berlin: Weidmann.
Neuhouser, Frederick. 2000. *Foundations of Hegel's Social Theory*. Cambridge, MA: Harvard University Press.
Onfray, Michel. 2006. *Les Sagesses antiques* [*Contre-histoire de la philosophie*, Vol. 1]. Paris: Grasset.
Ovid. 1987. *Metamorphoses*. Trans. by A.D. Melville. Oxford and New York: Oxford University Press.
Plato. 1854–1859. *Platons ausgewählte Schriften in deutscher Übersetzung*. Trans. by Ludwig von Georgii, Franz Susemihl, Julius Deuschle, W.S. Teuffel, and Wilhelm Wiegand, 3 vols (Vol. 1: *Platon's Leben, Gastmahl, Apologie, Kriton, Phaidon*; Vol. 2, *Phaidros, Protagoras, Gorgias*; Vol. 3, *Die Staatsverfassung*). Stuttgart: Metzler.
———. 1906. *Platons Gastmahl ins Deutsche übertragen*. Trans. by Rudolf Kassner, 2nd ed. Leipzig: Diederichs.
———. 1909. *Timaios, Kritias, Gesetze X*. Trans. Otto Kiefer. Jena: Diederichs.
———. 1922. *Platons Dialoge "Timaeus" und "Kritias"*. Trans. by Otto Apelt [Philosophische Bibliothek, Vol. 179]. Leipzig: Meiner.
———. 1925. *Parmenides; Philebos*. Trans. by Otto Kiefer. Jena: Diederichs.
———. 1929. *Plato with an English Translation, Vol. 7, Timaeus; Critias; Cleitophon; Menexenus; Epistles*. Trans. by R.G. Bury. London; New York: Heinemann; Putnam.

———. 1942. *Von Mensch und Staat: Sokrates und Platon: Die antike Botschaft der Gerechtigkeit*. Ed. and trans. by Edgar Salin [Sammlung Klosterberg Europäische Reihe]. Basel: Schwabe.

———. 1945. *Apologie, Kriton, Phaidon*. Trans. by Edgar Salin. Basel: Schwabe.

———. 1984. *The Being of the Beautiful: Plato's "Theaetetus", "Sophist", and "Statesman"*. Trans. by Seth Bernadete. Chicago and London: Chicago University Press.

———. 1988. *The Laws of Plato*. Ed. and trans. by Thomas L. Pangle. Chicago and London: University of Chicago Press.

———. 1989. *Collected Dialogues of Plato*. Ed. by Edith Hamilton and Huntington Cairns. Princeton, NJ: Princeton University Press.

———. 1996. *Works of Plato in Five Volumes*, Vol. 2. Trans. by Thomas Taylor and Floyer Sydenham [TTS, Vol. 10]. Sturminster Newton: Prometheus Trust.

———. 2004. *Selected Myths*. Ed. by Catalin Partenie. New York: Oxford University Press.

Plotinus. 1905. *Enneaden in Auswahl übersetzt*. Trans. by Otto Kiefer, 2 vols. Jena: Diederichs.

———. 1924. *On the Nature of the Soul, Being the Fourth Ennead*. Trans. by Stephen MacKenna. London and Boston: The Medici Society.

Plotinus. 1951/1959. *Opera*, Vol. 1, *Porphyrii vita Plotini; Enneades I–III*; Vol. 2, *Enneades IV–V*, ed. by Paul Henry and Hans-Rudolf Schwyzer. Paris; Brussels: Desclée de Brouwer; L'Édition universelle.

Plotinus. 1966–1988. *Works*. Trans. by A.H. Armstrong. 7 vols. Cambridge, MA, and London: Harvard University Press; Heinemann.

Proclus. 1987. *Commentary on Plato's "Parmenides"*. Trans. by Glenn R. Morrow and John M. Dillon. Princeton, NJ: Princeton University Press.

———. 1998a. *Commentary on the "Timaeus" of Plato*, Vol. 1. Trans. by Thomas Taylor [TTS, Vol. 15]. Sturminster Newton: Prometheus Trust.

———. 1998b. *Commentary on the "Timaeus" of Plato*, Vol. 2. Trans. by Thomas Taylor [TTS, Vol. 16]. Sturminster Newton: Prometheus Trust.

———. 2006. *Commentary on Plato's "Timaeus", Vol. 1, Book 1: Proclus on the Socratic State and Atlantis*. Trans. by Harold Tarrant, ed. by Dirk Baltzly and Harold Tarrant. New York: Cambridge University Press.

Riel, Gerd Van. 2017. The One, the Henads, and the Principles. In *All From One: A Guide to Proclus*, ed. Pieter d'Hoine and Marije Martijn, 73–97. New York: Oxford University Press.

Robinson, T.M. 1970. *Plato's Psychology*. Toronto: University of Toronto Press.

———. 2015. Soul (*psyché*). In *The Bloomsbury Companion to Plato*, ed. Gerald A. Press, 247–249. London: Bloomsbury.

Rosenmeyer, T.G. 1956. Plato's Atlantis Myth: 'Timaeus' or 'Critias'? *Phoenix* 10 (4): 163–172.

Shamdasani, Sonu. 2003. *Jung and the Making of Modern Psychology: The Dream of a Science*. Cambridge: Cambridge University Press.

Singer, Dorothea Whaley. 1946. Alchemical Texts Bearing the Name of Plato. *Ambix* 2 (3–4): 115–128.

Steiner, Rudolf. 2001. In *Atlantis: The Fate of a Lost Land and its Secret Knowledge*, ed. Andrew Welburn. Forest Row: Sophia Books.

Stewart, J.A. 1960. *The Myths of Plato* [1905]. Ed. by G.R. Levy. London: Centaur Press.

Taylor, A.E. 1928. *A Commentary on Plato's "Timaeus"*. Oxford: Clarendon Press (Reprinted New York: Garland, 1967).

Taylor, Thomas, ed. and trans. 1831. *Ocellus Lucanus, "On the nature of the universe;" Taurus, the Platonic philosopher, "On the eternity of the world"; Julius Firmicus Maternus, "Of the thema mundi; in which the positions of the stars at the commencement of the several mundane periods is given"; "Select theorems on the perpetuity of time", by Proclus*. London: Printed for the Translator.

Vidal-Naquet, Pierre. 2007. *The Atlantis Story: A Short History of Plato's Myth* [*L'Atlantide: Petite histoire d'un mythe platonicien*]. Trans. by Janet Lloyd. Exeter. University of Exeter Press.

Wallis, R.T. 1995. *Neoplatonism*. 2nd ed. London: Bristol Classical Press.

Wasserstrom, Steven M. 1999. *Religion after Religion: Gershom Scholem, Mircea Eliade, and Henry Corbin at Eranos*. Princeton, NJ: Princeton University Press.

Weldon, Jane. 2017. *Platonic Jung and the Nature of Self*. Asheville, NC: Chiron.

Wilberding, James, ed. 2021. *World Soul: A History*. New York: Oxford University Press.

Wright, M.R., ed. 2000. *Reason and Necessity: Essays on Plato's "Timaeus"*. London: Duckworth and The Classical Press of Wales.

Zaehner, R.C. 1992. *Hindu Scriptures* [1938]. New York, London, Toronto: Knopf.

Zeyl, Donald, and Barbara Sattler. 2019. Plato's *Timaeus*. In *The Stanford Encyclopedia of Philosophy* (Summer 2019 Edition), ed. Edward N. Zalta. https://plato.stanford.edu/archives/sum2019/entries/plato-timaeus/.

CHAPTER 3

Jung on the Doctrine of the Trinity

Abstract This chapter examines Jung's essay on the psychology of the doctrine of the Trinity, first delivered as a lecture at the Eranos conferences. In this paper Jung approaches Plato's via Pythagoras's theory of number and the numerology of Gerhard Dorn, before turning to the account in the *Timaeus* of why the body of the world consists of four primary bodies. In a highly compressed form, Jung alludes to Plato's career not just as a political thinker but as a political actor, which we examine in a bit more detail. We consider Jung's discussion of the motif of the Three and the Four in the *Timaeus*, which Jung goes on to link to the Cabiri scene in Goethe's *Faust*, Part Two. Jung argues that the Three "yearns" to become a Four, although he curiously neglects to consider the symbolism of three, four, and indeed five in other parts of the *Timaeus*.

Keywords Jung • Trinity • Eranos • Pythagoras • Gerhard Dorn • Goethe • *Faust*

In his introduction to the first published form of "On the Psychology of the Idea of the Trinity", Jung acknowledged that the original lecture had provoked a strong reaction and that discussion of Christian symbols had been considered objectionable—"even when it carefully avoided any infringement of their religious value" (Jung 1969, §170).[1] Such a reaction

© The Author(s), under exclusive license to Springer Nature Switzerland AG 2022
P. Bishop, *Reading Plato through Jung*,
https://doi.org/10.1007/978-3-031-16812-3_3

is perhaps not surprising, considering that the group had been established by the Dutch spiritualist and theosophist, Olga Fröbe-Kapteyn (1881–1962), at the suggestion of the Lutheran theologian and comparative religionist, Rudolf Otto (1869–1937). Shrewdly, Jung nevertheless suggests that his critics would have been a good deal less vocal if he had interpreted, not Christian, but Buddhist symbols, whose "sacredness" is "just as indubitable" (ibid., §170).

And Jung—someone whom critics frequently take to task for his alleged lack of rationality—goes on to make a plea precisely for the use of "thoughtful understanding" when approaching Christian symbols as opposed to consigning them to "a sphere of sacrosanct unintelligibility". Indeed, he continues, such symbols risk becoming "so remote" that "their irrationality turns into preposterous nonsense" (Jung 1969, §170)! And he makes the important declaration that "faith is a charisma not granted to all; instead, humankind has the gift of thought, which can strive after the highest things" (*sich um die höchsten Dinge bemühen*) (ibid., §170). Jung situates this position in the context of the ancient sources of Christianity, noting that the "timid defensiveness" displayed by "certain moderns" was emphatically not shared by St Paul, nor by such Church Fathers as Clement of Alexandria or Origen, nor by Pseudo-Dionysius the Areopagite. Rather than as a sign of confidence, Jung interprets such "timidity and anxiety" about Christian symbols as a sign of disbelief, for "wherever belief reigns, doubt lurks in the background". In contrast, he argues, "thinking people welcome doubt", for it can serve as "a valuable stepping-stone to higher knowledge" (*zu verbesserter Erkenntnis*) (ibid., §170).

The particular dogmatic symbol chosen for Jung in this paper is, as is evident from the title, the Trinity. The classic definition of this dogma can be found, as Jung points out, in the so-called Athanasian Creed; that is, the statement of faith attributed to Athanasius of Alexandria, who is said to have composed it when in exile from Alexandria in Rome and to have presented it in the latter half of the fourth century to Pope Julius I as a sign of his orthodoxy. (Its attribution to Athanasius was, however, questioned by the Dutch Protestant theologian Gerardus Vossius in 1642.) The doctrinal argument of the creed can be represented diagrammatically as follows (Fig. 3.1):

3 JUNG ON THE DOCTRINE OF THE TRINITY   53

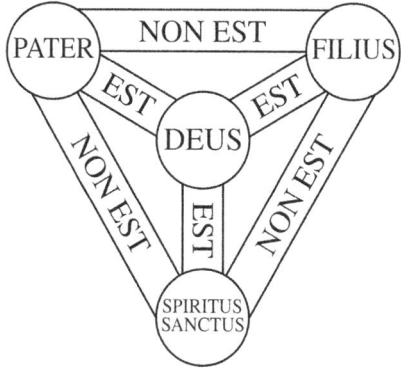

Fig. 3.1 Schematic representation of the Trinity. (A compact version of a basic minimal (equilateral triangular) version of the "Shield of the Trinity" or "Scutum Fidei" diagram of traditional Christian symbolism, with original Latin captions. In the public realm and available at https://en.wikipedia.org/wiki/Shield_of_the_Trinity#/media/File:Shield-Trinity-Scutum-Fidei-compact.svg)

Far from trying to "psychologize" (*in einen Psychologismus auflösen*) this dogma, Jung describes his purpose as being to uncover its "archetypal foundation" and, in this way, to "understand the dogmas *as a symbol* in the psychological sense" (Jung 1969, §171; my emphasis). His reason for doing so is based on the premise that the dogma stands to the psyche (*Seele*) from which it originated "in a relationship of living reciprocity" (*in lebendigister Wechselbeziehung*) (ibid., §171).

Jung's paper on the Trinity is rich, dense, and learned; in fact, it is a masterclass in erudition.[2] Much as he did in *Psychological Types* (1921), where he began with a consideration of the psychology of types in the history of classical and medieval thought, in his lecture on the Trinity Jung takes the historical long view. Hence it is beyond the scope of this study to discuss in full all the various aspects of Jung's exercise in intellectual history. After briefly examining the pre-Christian parallels to the Trinity in Babylonia (in the form of the divine triad of Anu, Bel, and Ea, and the secondary triad of Sin, Shamash, and Ishtar) and in Egypt (in the form of the myth of Osiris, Horus, and Isis), Jung turns to Greece—and to Plato. Jung's approach to Plato is, however, indirect and via Pythagoras's theory of number.

Number in Pythagoras and Gerhard Dorn

This section of Jung's paper begins by noting that the "mathematical speculations" of the Greek philosophers hold an important place in the "pre-Christian sources" of the dogma of the Trinity, as evidenced by the "philosophizing temper"—indeed, the "Gnostic inspiration"—of the Gospel according to John.[3] In due course, Jung adds, this philosophical cast of mind amplified the "archetypal content" of Christianity and interpreted it in "Gnostic terms" (Jung 1969, §179). One of the driving forces behind this development was, Jung suggests, the school of Pythagoras and, in particular, the Pythagorean system of numbers. For his discussion of Pythagoras, Jung relies on the history of Greek philosophy written by Eduard Zeller (1814–1908), a philosopher and theologian who belonged to the Tübingen School of theology. Of the numbers 1, 2, and 3, Zeller writes: "One is the first from which all other numbers arise, and in which the opposite qualities of numbers, the odd and the even, must therefore be united; two is the first even number; three the first that is uneven and perfect, because in it we first find beginning, middle, and end" (Zeller 1876, 368–369; 1881, vol. 1, 429). As a source of confirmation for this statement, Jung cites *On the Heavens* (book 1, §1; 268a), where Aristotle says the following about the number 3:

> As the Pythagoreans say, the universe and all that is in it is determined by the number three, since beginning and middle and end give the number of the universe, and the number they give is the triad. And so, having taken these three from nature as (so to speak) laws of it, we make further use of the number three in the worship of the gods. (Aristotle 1984, vol. 1, 447)

In line with the argument proposed by the British idealist philosopher A.E. Taylor (1869–1945), Jung suggests that fifth-century Pythagoreanism was an important influence on Plato, particularly on the *Timaeus* (Taylor 1928, 18–19; cited in Cornford 1997, vi–vii). Yet Jung's account of the Pythagorean system of numbers turns out to rely not so much on Pythagoras as on the work of the Belgian (or rather Flemish) alchemical philosopher Gerhard Dorn (c. 1530–1584).

Jung proceeds by first noting the "exceptional position" occupied by the number 1, found also in the natural philosophy of the Middle Ages. For this system, he remarks, one (i.e. 1) was not, in fact, a number at all; rather, the first number was 2. Jung is right: the ancient Greeks, and subsequent thinkers, argued over whether one was really a number or not.

(The basis of this dispute is its unique status as a multiplier: 4 multiplied by 1 is 4, but 2573 multiplied by 1 is also 2573. Equally, the square root of one is one. In mathematical terms, one is called "unity", and because it is so unlike other numbers, it was considered by such thinkers as Aristotle and Euclid not as an actual number so much as the *fons et origo* from which all other numbers flowed [Caldwell and Xiong, 2002].) For instance, in his *Etymologiae* (c. 636) that was highly influential in the fifteenth century, Isidore of Seville (c. 560–636) explained that "number is a multitude made up of units", for "one is the seed of number but not number" (Grant 1974, 4–5). However, the source for this idea as given by Jung is Macrobius, who argues in his *Commentary on the Dream of Scipio* (book 1, chapter 6, §7–§8):

> [...] One is called *monas*, that is Unity, and is both male and female, odd and even, itself not a number, but the source and origin of numbers. This monad, the beginning and ending of all things, yet itself not knowing a beginning or ending, refers to the Supreme God, and separates our understanding of him (the One, without number) from the number of things and powers following; you would not be so rash as to look for it in a sphere lower than God. It is also that Mind, sprung from the Supreme God, which, unaware of the changes of time, is always in one time, the present; and although the monad is itself not numbered, it nevertheless produces from itself, and contains within itself, innumerable patterns of created things. (Macrobius 1990, 100–101)

On Jung's account, 2 is the first number because it enables separation and multiplication, without which counting is not possible. At the same time, something happens on the psychological level: with the number 2, the idea of alterity or *otherness* appears. This development is reflected, Jung suggests, in language—given that "in many languages 'the other' and 'the second' are expressed by the same word" (Jung 1969, §180).

At the same time, there is a *moral* dimension to this alterity or otherness, for the ideas of "right and left", of "favourable and unfavourable", and of "good and bad" are associated with the number 2 (Jung 1969, §180). In support of this statement, Jung cites the passage in Plato's *Timaeus* where Timaeus speaks about "the movement of the Different to the left" (36c), a passage to which we shall return; but the unnamed, yet easily identifiable, "medieval alchemist" who is the source for the notion that "the 'other' can have a 'sinister' significance—or one feels it, at least, as something opposite and alien" is, of course, Dorn (ibid., §180).

In two treatises, *De tenebris contra naturam, et Vita brevi* ("On the Shadows that are Against Nature, and on the Brevity of Life") and *De duello animi cum corpore* ("On the Conflit between Mind and Body"), Dorn pointed out that, in the Biblical account of the Creation, God said on the evening of every day that what he had done was good—except for one, the evening of the second day, when he had separated the upper waters from the lower. The reason, Dorn argued, why God omitted to say on the evening of the *second* day that what He had done was "good" was because, in so separating upper from lower, God had created the *binarius*, the cause of "confusion, division, and strife".[4] Even worse than the binary is the binary of the binary, that is to say, the quaternity, hence Dorn's description of the Devil as the *quadricornutus binarius*, the "four-horned devil". Thus, on Dorn's account, from the *binarius* there issued *sua proles quaternaria*, "its quaternary offspring", and hence number 2 is associated with Eve, number 3 with Adam, and number 2 × 2 = 4 with the Devil.

For his part, however, Jung pursues a different numerological argument. For him, the dialectic between the One and the Other gives rise to the Third, revealing an essential logical (and psychological) dynamic:

> In the third, the tension [between the One and the Other] is resolved and the lost unity is restored. Unity, the absolute One, cannot be numbered, it is indefinable and unknowable; only when it appears as unit, the number one, is it knowable, for the "Other" which is required for this act of knowing is lacking in the conditions of the One. Three is an unfolding of the One to a condition where it can be known—unity become recognizable; had it not been resolved into the polarity of the One and the Other, it would have remained fixed in a condition devoid of every quality. (Jung 1969, §180)

Behind Jung's language here it is hard not to hear an echo of the so-called Axiom of Maria, that is, "One becomes two, two becomes three, and out of the third comes the one as the fourth", attributed to the third-century alchemist Maria Prophetissa (Patai 1995, 60–91).[5] Indeed, Jung will later explicitly refer to this axiom in relation to the problem of the union of opposites and its two possible solutions—either a self-subsistent, but purely intellectual triad, or what he calls the "real" solution, that is, the quaternity (Jung 1969, §184).

On Jung's account, Three therefore appears as "a suitable synonym for a process of development in time, and this forms a parallel to the self-revelation of the Deity as the absolute One unfolded into Three" (Jung

1969, §180). Echoing a passage in the second volume of the *Dogmengeschichte* of the Lutheran theologian and Church historian, Adolf von Harnack (1851–1930), in which the Scholastic conception of the Trinity is compared to an equilateral triangle,[6] Jung argues that the relation of Threeness to Oneness can be expressed as a triangle, or as the formula A = B = C, that is, by "the identity of the three, threeness being contained in each of the three angles" (ibid., §180). As a consequence, he concludes, "this *intellectual* idea of the equilateral triangle is a *conceptual* model for the *logical* image of the Trinity" (ibid., §180). Whether these three categories (intellectual, conceptual, logical = *intellektuell, denkerisch, logisch*) are equivalent or different in significance remains at this point unclear, but this discussion of Pythagoras turns out to be a mere prolegomenon to a more detailed analysis of Plato's *Timaeus*, a text which Jung with good reason describes as "mystery-laden" (ibid., §181).

Timaeus's Account of the Body of the World

At this point Jung's discussion jumps over the introductory conversation between Socrates, Timaeus, Hermocrates, and Critias (17a–27b), as well as the prelude to the discourse of Timaeus with its account of the nature and scope of physics (27c–29d), and starts instead with Timaeus's argument about the body of the world and why it consists of four primary bodies, that is, fire, air, water, and earth (31a–34a). Jung quotes in its entirety the following section from the *Timaeus*:

> Hence, in beginning to construct the body of the All, God was making it of fire and earth. But it is not possible that two things alone should be conjoined without a third; for there must needs be some intermediary bond to connect the two. And the fairest of bonds is that which most perfectly unites into one both itself and the things which it binds together; and to effect this in the fairest manner is the natural property of proportion. For whenever the middle term of any three numbers, cubic or square, is such that as the first term is to it, so is it to the last term,—and again, conversely, as the last term is to the middle, so is the middle to the first,—then the middle term becomes in turn the first and the last, while the first and last become in turn middle terms, and the necessary consequence will be that all the terms are interchangeable, and being interchangeable they all form a unity. (31b–32a; Plato 1929, 59)

In his commentary on this passage, Jung underscores the mathematical nature of Timaeus's argument and its emphasis on proportion, drawing on *Plato's Cosmology* (1937), a translation of the *Timaeus* with an extensive commentary by the English classical scholar F.M. Cornford (1874–1943), which in turn draws on the *History of Greek Mathematics* (2 vols, 1921) by the classicist and mathematician Sir Thomas Heath (1861–1940).[7] On this account, "in a geometrical progression, the quotient (q) of a series of terms remains the same", thus—$2 : 1 = 4 : 2 = 8 : 4 = 2$, or expressed algebraically—a, aq, aq^2, that is, in this proportional relationship, 2 is to 4 as 4 is to 8, or a is to aq as aq is to aq^2 (Jung 1969, §181). When applied to "square" numbers this quotient or proportion takes the form of a mean analogy,[8] thus—$a^2 : ab :: ab :: b^2$; conversely, $b^2 : ab :: ab :: a^2$; alternately, $ab : a^2 :: b^2 : ab$.

In Plato's dialogue, this argument is followed by a reflection which has, Jung suggests, "far-reaching psychological implications": "Now if the body of the All had had to come into existence as a plane surface, having no depth, one middle term would have sufficed to bind together both itself and its fellow-terms; but now it is otherwise: for it behoved it to be solid of shape, and what brings solids into unison is never one middle term alone but always two" (32a–32b). In mathematical terms, this means that, for a continuous proportion of "solid" (or cubic) numbers, two mean terms are required,[9] for example, $a^3 : a^2b :: a^2b : ab^2 :: ab^2 : b^3$. In psychological terms, Jung spells out the following implications:

> If a simple pair of opposites, say fire and earth, are bound together by a mean (μέσον), and if this bond is a geometrical proportion, then *one* mean can only connect plane figures, since two means are required to connect solids. [...] Accordingly, the two-dimensional connection is not yet a physical reality, for a plane without extension in the third dimension is only an *abstract thought*. If it is to become a physical reality, three dimensions and therefore two means are required. (Jung 1969, §182)

(In so arguing, Wolfgang Giegerich believes, Jung "succumbs to a momentous mistake": the transition from a two-dimensional plane to a three-dimensional solid "has nothing whatsoever to do with the 'realization' of something that is merely thought"—"as if a solid in geometry did not also lack weight" [Giegerich 2020, 94–95]!) Indeed: "mathematics is not physics", yet Giegerich also rightly emphasizes that "Plato, here all Pythagorean, argues *mathematically* from the outset" (ibid., 94); likewise

Heath points out that the mathematics of the *Timaeus* is "essentially Pythagorean" (Heath 1908, vol. 2, 294), and he explains (in a way that Jung takes over into his own account) how it can be expressed as algebraic formulae:

- in the union in two dimensions of earth (p^2) and fire (q^2), $p^2 : pq = pq : q^2$ (i.e. the mean is pq)
- in the physical union of earth and fire, represented by p^3 and q^3, $p^3 : p^2q = p^2q : pq^2 = pq^2 : q^3$ (i.e. the two means are p^2q and pq^2, corresponding to water and air). (Jung 1969, §182; cf. Heath 1921, vol. 1, 89)

What is "Pythagorean" about this argument is the idea that mathematical or numerical relations can tell us something about the organization of the physical world,[10] but what Plato presents in terms of *cosmology* is reinterpreted by Jung in terms of *psychology*. For at this point, Jung returns to the text of the *Timaeus*, and cites the next part of its argument:

> Thus it was that in the midst between fire and earth God set water and air, and having bestowed upon them so far as possible a like ratio one towards another—air being to water as fire to air, and water being to earth as air to water,—he joined together and constructed a Heaven visible and tangible. For these reasons and out of these materials, such in kind and four in number, the body of the Cosmos was harmonized by proportion and brought into existence. These conditions secured for it Amity, so that being united in identity with itself it became indissoluble by any agent other than Him who had bound it together. (32b–32c; Plato 1929, 59–61)

On the basis of this passage, Jung's argument moves in the following direction. If the union of *one pair of opposites* produces only a two-dimensional triad (i.e. $p^2 + pq + q^2$) which, being a plane figure, is "not a reality but a thought", then *two pairs of opposites*, or a *quaternio* (i.e. $p^3 + p^2q + pq^2 + q^3$), are needed to "represent physical reality" (Jung 1969, §183).[11] For Jung, this algebraic representation of this passage in its triadic and quaternary formulae, respectively, thus presents us with "the dilemma of three and four" to which the opening of the dialogue alludes when Socrates asks, "One, two, three—but where, my dear Timaeus, is the fourth of those guests of yesterday who were to entertain me today?" (17a), and to which, in turn, Goethe gestures in the Cabiri scene of *Faust*,

Part Two.[12] These opening words will, Jung suggests, "fall familiarly upon the ears of the psychologist and alchemist", and for him (as for Goethe) Plato will be seen as "alluding to something of mysterious import" (ibid., §184).

For Jung takes this dilemma of the Third and the Fourth, understood as the difference between a self-subsistent triad (i.e. the union of opposites in two-dimensional terms as an *intellectual* problem to be solved by thinking) and a quaternity (i.e. the solution of this problem in physical reality), and translates it into his own psychological terms. Now alluding explicitly to the "axiom of Maria Prophetissa" (see above), Jung introduces his system of psychic functions as set out in *Psychological Types* (1921), that is, thinking, feeling, sensation, and intuition. For Jung, it is axiomatic that if three functions are well differentiated, the fourth (or "inferior") function will become "undomesticated, unadapted, uncontrolled, and primitive"; it will become "contaminated" by the collective unconscious and possess "archaic and mystical qualities" (Jung 1969, §184). (To take one example: if, say, the most differentiated function is thinking, then the inferior, fourth function will be feeling.)[13] And Jung pursues his approach of translating what is, for Plato, *metaphysical* into something that is, for Jung, *psychological*—albeit a "problem of the first order":

> [What Plato is alluding to] was nothing less than the dilemma as to whether something we think about is a mere thought or a reality, or at least capable of becoming real. And this, for any philosopher who is not just an empty babbler, is a problem of the first order and no whit less important than the moral problems inseparably associated with it. (Jung 1969, §184)

Indeed, for Jung the problems Plato is here facing are not just *moral*, but also *political*,[14] inasmuch as "in this matter Plato knew from personal experience how difficult is the step from two-dimensional thinking to its realization in three-dimensional fact":

> Already with his friend Dionysius the Elder, tyrant of Syracuse, he had so many disagreements that the philosopher-politician contrived to sell him as a slave, from which fate he was preserved only because he had the good fortune to be ransomed by friends. His attempts to realize his political theories under Dionysius the Younger also ended in failure, and from then on Plato abandoned politics for good. Metaphysics seemed to him to offer more prospects than this ungovernable world. (Jung 1969, §184)

Here Jung is presenting in highly compressed form a number of significant moments in Plato's career as a political thinker—and indeed as a political actor, and it is a career we should briefly review.

Plato and Politics

As a member of an influential aristocratic family, Plato had naturally considered entering public life. In the turbulent political scene toward the end of the Peloponnesian War, Plato was in his twenties and was handed a golden opportunity when the Thirty Tyrants, a pro-Spartan oligarchy, overthrew the democratic constitution and took control of Athens after its defeat in the Peloponnesian War in 404 BCE. They invited Plato to join them, and he did (as he recalled in his *Seventh Letter*) (Klosko 2012, 58–60). The reign of justice the Thirty had promised and for which Plato hoped never materialized; instead it degenerated into a reign of terror, at which Plato was appalled. In a short time, he wrote, "these men made the former government look in comparison like an age of gold" (324d), and the worst of their deeds was the execution of Socrates. Observing all this, Plato "withdrew in disgust from the abuses of those days" (325a). The descent into political chaos lead to the overthrow of the Thirty, to the restoration of democracy, and to the return of Plato's desire to "take part in public life and in politics" (325b). Reflecting in particular on the circumstances surrounding the death of Socrates, Plato drew some sobering conclusions:

> Now as I considered these matters, as well as the sort of men who were active in politics, and the laws and the customs, the more I examined them and the more I advanced in years, the harder it appeared to me to administer the government correctly. […] In regard to action, I kept waiting for favorable moments, and finally saw clearly in regard to all states now existing that without exception their system of government is bad. Their constitutions are almost beyond redemption except through some miraculous plan accompanied by good luck. (325d–e and 326a; Plato 1989, 1575–1576)

The remedy or the "miraculous plan" that Plato had conceived was the convergence of political power and philosophical insight in the figure of the philosopher-king: "The human race will not see better days until either the stock of those who rightly and genuinely follow philosophy acquire political authority, or else the class who have political control be led by some dispensation of providence to become real philosophers" (326a–b; cf. *Republic*, 473d). One should note the emphasis on a *miraculous plan* and a *dispensation of providence*, for elsewhere Plato reaffirms his scepticism about whether the philosopher can successfully take part in politics (330c–331d) (Klosko 1981, 383).

But for now, Plato kept trying: and his focus shifted from Athens to Syracuse in the island of Sicily (see Marcuse 1947). According to Diogenes Laërtius, Plato first visited Syracuse in 389-388 while it was under the rule of Dionysius the Elder. When Plato maintained that "the interest of the ruler alone was not the best end" (*Lives and Opinions*, 3.1 §18), Dionysius turned against Plato and wanted to have him executed. Thanks to the intervention of Dion of Syracuse (Dionysius's brother-in-law, whom Plato had befriended and converted to Platonism) and Aristomenes, Dionysius I was persuaded instead to have Plato sold into slavery; on the island of Aegina, Anniceris (possibly the Cyrenaic philosopher of this name) recognized Plato and ransomed him for twenty minas. After the death of Dionysius I in 367, his son, Dionysius II assumed power, under the supervision of his uncle, Dion. In 366-365 Plato visited Syracuse a second time, persuaded by Dion to try and educate the new tyrant, Dionysius II, into becoming a philosopher-king. This experiment also failed; while Dionysius II seemed to accept Plato's teachings, he became suspicious of Dion, whom he expelled while keeping Plato in Syracuse against his will. Eventually Plato was allowed to leave; but he returned for a third and final occasion in 361-360.

In order to test whether Dionysius II's attachment to philosophy was genuine, Plato explained to him "what preliminary steps and much hard work it will require" if someone is "genuinely devoted to philosophy" and has "a natural affinity and fitness for the work" (*Seventh Letter*, 340b-c; see Edelstein 1966). Perhaps unsurprisingly, it turned out that Dionysius II's devotion was not sufficiently genuine, and he expelled Plato from the palace and forced him to lodge in the soldiers' barracks; escaping accusations that he was plotting with others to overthrow Dionysius II, Plato fled Syracuse for the third and final time.

In 357, Dion put together a fleet and sailed to Syracuse to overthrow Dionysius II; although his rebellion was successful and Dion became ruler in Syracuse, in 354 he was assassinated, and power was seized by Calippus (an Athenian disciple of Plato), who was himself overthrown a year later and exiled from Syracuse. On Diogenes Laërtius's account, Plato "returned to his own country without achieving anything" and there he "refrained from meddling with politics, although his writings show that he was a statesman" (*Lives and Opinions*, 3.1 §23), reflecting on the failure of his political interventions in his *Seventh Letter*. Or in Jung's words, Plato "abandoned politics for good" and "metaphysics seemed to him to offer more prospects than this ungovernable world" (Jung 1969, §184).

On Jung's account, this failure was inevitable, given Plato's "main emphasis" on the "two-dimensional world of thought"; and nowhere was this more true, Jung believed, than in the case of the *Timaeus*, written in c. 360, that is, after his third visit to Syracuse and his "political disappointments", and generally reckoned as belonging to his late works (Jung 1969, §184).[15] Yet at the same time, Jung claims to discover in precisely this dialogue important insights about the relation between intellectual thought and physical reality; in other words, Jung wants to use Plato against Plato! In order to do so, Jung returns to the opening scene of the dialogue and to Socrates's riddling question, "One, two, three,—but where, my dear Timaeus, is the fourth of our guests of yesterday, our hosts of today?" (17a).

THE THIRD AND THE FOURTH IN THE "TIMAEUS"

The *Timaeus* dialogue takes place on the day of the Panathenaia, a festival in honour of the goddess Athena, the protectress of the city of Athens. The previous day, Socrates had been discoursing with Critias, a leading Athenian figure, and his two guests from Italy and Sicily, Timaeus of Locri and Hermocrates of Syracuse, on topics related to the themes of the *Republic*; now Timaeus explains that the fourth guest is absent because "some sickness has befallen him" (17a). (The identity of the fourth figure, perhaps another visitor from Italy or Sicily, or perhaps even Plato himself, remains a matter for conjecture.)[16] Timaeus's remark lends, Jung suggests, a somewhat "mournful significance" to this introductory scene, and he goes on (in a way that sets the tone for his ensuing argument) to discuss its significance in "symbolic" terms of the four classical elements (Jung 1969, §185). In these "symbolic" terms, then, which of the four elements is missing? Is it air (in which case there is no connecting link with fire, i.e. "spirit") or is it water (in which case there is no link with earth, i.e. "concrete reality")? In the case of Plato, Jung argues, there is certainly no lack of spirit (*Geist*), so the missing element must be, in psychological terms, the "concrete realization of ideas" (*konkrete Verwirklichung der Ideen*), which becomes the basis for an *ad hominem* critique of Plato as someone who had contented himself with "the harmony of airy thought-structures that lacked weight, and with a paper surface that lacked depth" (Jung 1969, §185). (As Giegerich—rightly—protests, to claim that Plato desired concrete realization and felt ideas to be deficient is itself "an entirely unplatonic assertion" and "contradicts everything that Plato wanted to achieve with his doctrine of Ideas […] as the *ontôs on*, the really real" [Giegerich 2020, 95–96].)

On Jung's reading, the opening step in the *Timaeus* of the move from three to an absent fourth brought Plato sharply up against "something unexpected and alien to his thought, something heavy, inert, and limited"—a problem that the philosophical category of μὴ ὄν (i.e. "not being") or the doctrine of *privatio boni* cannot solve (Jung 1969, §185). In Jung's words, this problem is one that corrupts "even God's fairest creation", and is reflected in the presence of "idleness, stupidity, malice, discontent, sickness, old age and death" in the world, this "blessed god" (34b); in this "grievous spectacle", even what Timaeus calls the World Soul itself is sick. Yet in the *Timaeus* dialogue itself, this insight is overlooked or suppressed or repressed, for to Plato's "inner eye" (at least, as voiced by Timaeus) the World Soul appears as follows:

> Such, then, was the sum of the reasoning of the ever-existing God concerning the god which was one day to be existent, whereby He made it smooth and even and equal on all sides from the centre, a whole and perfect body compounded of perfect bodies. And in the midst thereof He set Soul, which He stretched throughout the whole of it, and therewith He enveloped also the exterior of its body; and as a Circle revolving in a circle He [e]stablished one sole and solitary Heaven, able of itself because of its excellence to company with itself and needing none other beside, sufficing unto itself as acquaintance and friend. And because of all this He generated it to be a blessed God. (34a–34b; Plato 1929, 65)

At this point, Jung turns to a closer consideration of Timaeus's account of the World Soul and its composition.

On this account, the world, "created by a god, is itself a god, a son of the self-manifesting father" (Jung 1969, §186). Thanks to the Demiurge, that is, the notion introduced by Plato into philosophy of the universal fashioner, divine craftsman or creator god (29d–30c),[17] the world is furnished with a soul which is "prior" to the body (cf. 34b) and is fashioned as follows: as a mixture of the indivisible (ἀμερές) and the divisible (μεριστόν), thus producing a third form existence having a nature independent of the "Same" (το αύτον) and the "Different" (το έτεον) (ibid., §186). Relying on the second volume of *Griechische Denker* (3rd edn, 1912) by the Austrian classical scholar Theodor Gomperz (1832–1912) (who resigned from his professorial chair in Vienna to work on this *magnum opus*), Jung recalls that, in the *Philebus*, two primary substances are mentioned and designated as the limit and the unlimited; the same and the other; or the divisible and the indivisible (Gomperz 1909, vol. 2, 487–488; Gomperz (1901–1912), vol. 3, 215). On this basis Jung identifies the Same with the indivisible and the Different with the divisible, and (switching in his paper from following Cornford's English translation to citing the German translation offered by Otto Apelt) he cites the following passage from the *Timaeus* (given here in the translation by R.G. Bury):

> Midway between the Being which is indivisible and remains always the same and the Being which is transient and divisible in bodies, He blended a third form of Being compounded out of the twain, that is to say, out of the Same and the Other; and in like manner [κατὰ ταὐτὰ] He compounded it midway between that one of them which is indivisible and that one which is divisible in bodies. And He took the three of them, and blent them all together into one form, by forcing the Other into union with the Same, in spite of its being naturally difficult to mix. And when with the aid of Being [οὐσία] He had mixed them, and had made of them one out of three [...] each portion was a mixture of the Same, of the Other, and of Being. (35a–35b; Plato 1929, 65–67)

On this basis, Jung concludes that the World Soul, inasmuch as it represents "the governing principle of the whole physical world", possesses "a triune nature", and that "since, for Plato, the world is a δεύτερος θεός [*deuteros theos*] (second god), the World Soul is a revelation or unfolding of the God-image" (Jung 1969, §187). In a footnote, Jung points to this later passage in which the first god is described as "the Father" and the creation is the copy of an original "Model" or "pattern", which is himself (ibid., §187, n. 21): "And when the Father that engendered it perceived it in motion and alive, a thing of joy to the eternal gods, He too rejoiced; and being well-pleased He designed to make it resemble its Model still more closely" (37c; Plato 1929, 75).

Next Jung moves to a consideration of the "actual process of creation", which he describes as "very curious" and requiring "some elucidation"

(Jung 1969, §188). To begin with, Jung notes the repetition of the expression "he mixed" (συνεκεράσατο): why, he asks, should this mixing be repeated, since (a) the mixture consists of three elements at the beginning of the process and three at end, and (b) Same and Different seem to correspond to the indivisible and the divisible (ibid., §188)? Why indeed? The answer proposed by Jung is that this mixture combines, in fact, *two* separate pairs of opposites, the first involving οὐσία (i.e. being) and the second φύσις (i.e. nature). Correspondingly this mixture can be presented in the form of a diagram of the *quaternio* (Fig. 3.2):

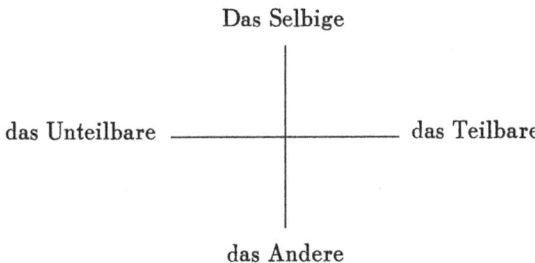

Fig. 3.2 Plato's elements arranged as a quaternity

What appears in the form of this simple diagram as static should, however, be thought of as a dynamic, as Jung makes clear. For the indivisible and the divisible form, together with their mean, a simple triad, mirroring the the Same and the Different and corresponding to the condition of being thought but not actually existing. For "thought" to become "reality", a second mixture is required—one in which the "Other" (or the Different) is "forcibly" (*»gewaltsam«*) incorporated as *a fourth* element whose nature is "adversarial" (*sich als »Widersacher« auszeichnet*) and "resistant" to harmony (*der Harmone widerstrebt*).[18] As the *Timaeus* itself suggests (35a), this fourth element is intimately bound up with the desire for Being—or at least with Plato's desire for being, linking back to what Jung had said earlier about Plato as a failed politician: "One thinks, not unnaturally, of the impatience the philosopher must have felt when reality proved so intractable to his ideas", he remarks, and he adds: "That reasonableness might, under certain circumstances, have to be imposed by force is a notion that must sometimes have crossed his mind" (Jung 1969, §188).

Yet Jung does not leave his interpretation there, commenting that the passage as a whole is "far from simple" (Jung 1969, §189) (and, in his commentary, Cornford devotes over six pages to the explication of 35a!). Jung returns to a phrase in the middle of the passage, συνέστησεν ἐν μέσῳ τοῦ τε ἀμεροῦς, that is, "he compounded (a form of the nature of sameness and difference) *in the middle* (ἐν μέσῳ) of the indivisible (and the divisible)". Because the middle term of the second pair of opposites coincides with the middle term of the second pair, the resultant diagram of these relations takes the form of a quincunx (i.e. an arrangement of four points at the corners of a square with a fifth at its centre), since these two pairs of opposites have in common a mean or "third form" (τρίτον ... εἶδος) (Fig. 3.3):

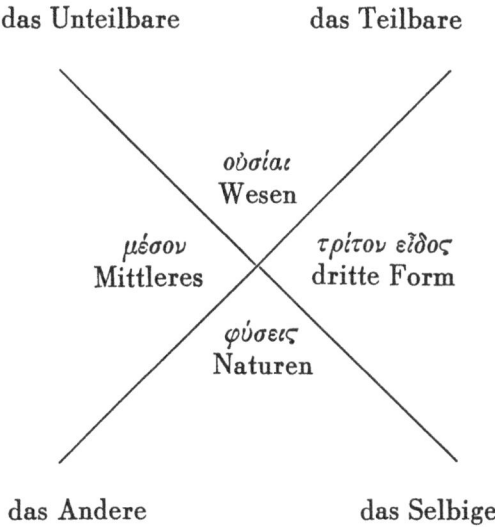

Fig. 3.3 Plato's elements arranged as a quincunx

Whereas, in the previous diagram, the opposites are presented facing each other, in this diagram the opposites are placed *side by side*, representing their union in a single mean. Since the mean is called the "third form", each pair of opposites represents the first forms, so that the Indivisible = the first form, the Divisible = the second form, and the mean = the third form, and their union in a quincunx signifies the "union of the four elements in a world-body" (Jung 1969, §190).

In support of this interpretation, Jung cites the view of the nineteenth-century English Platonist Thomas Taylor (1758–1835), who, in his introduction to his translation of the *Timaeus*, notes of the mundane (or World) soul: "For those which are connected with her essence in a following order, proceed from her [the *anima mundi*] according to the power of the fourth term (4), which possesses generative powers; but return to her according to the fifth (9) which reduces them to one" (in Plato 1996, 402). (As Jung notes, Taylor's commentary was strongly influenced by Proclus, whose own substantial commentary on the *Timaeus* was also translated in full by Taylor [see Proclus 1998a and 1998b].) For further confirmation of the essentially quaternary nature of the World Soul and the world's body, Jung cites the passage where the Demiurge takes this compound of three ingredients (i.e. Sameness, Difference, and Existence) as if it were a long strip of soul-stuff, splits it lengthwise into two strips, binds them at their middles, and bends round into two circles or rings:

> Next, He split all this that He had put together into two parts lengthwise; and then He laid the twain one against the other, the middle of one to the middle of the other, like a great cross + ; and bent either of them into a circle, and joined them, each to itself and also to the other, at a point opposite to where they had first been laid together. And He compassed them about with the motion that revolves in the same spot continually, and He made the one circle outer and the other inner. And the outer motion He ordained to be the Motion of the Same, and the inner motion the Motion of the Other. And He made the Motion of the Same to be toward the right along the side, and the Motion of the Other to be toward the left along the diagonal [...]. (36b–c; Plato 1929, 71–73)

Proclus records that, according to Porphyry, an X in a circle was, for the Egyptians, a symbol of the World Soul (Jung 1969, §190), explaining that (in Taylor's words) its right lines signified "its biformed progression", and its circle "its uniform life and intellective progress, which is of a circular nature" (in Plato 1996, 405). In addition, Jung notes, a circle in a cross was an Egyptian hieroglyph for "city" (see Griffith 1898, 34B, fig. 142); again, a political dimension to this discussion makes itself felt. As an example, Jung cites in a footnote an example where the symbol represents the plan of a village with cross-streets. And Jung even goes so far as to suggest that, in this passage, Plato was trying to constellate the mandala structure that later appeared in the *Critias* (115c–117e) in his account of the capital of Atlantis (Jung 1969, §190).[19]

Although Jung draws on such scholarly commentators as Thomas Taylor and Cornford (and while Taylor might have been considered out-of-date at the time when Jung was writing, Cornford's work was very much cutting-edge), he is by no means entirely reliant on them. For instance, in his commentary Cornford suggests that the *Timaeus* (35a) refers to three "intermedia" (i.e. Intermediate Existence, Intermediate Sameness, and Intermediate Difference), and he offers the following diagram of the composition of the soul (Cornford 1997, 61) (Fig. 3.4):

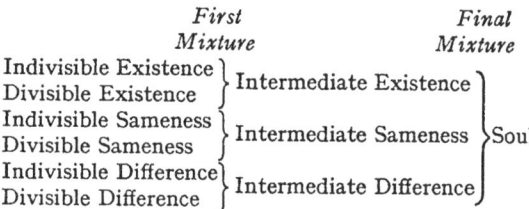

Fig. 3.4 Cornford's "full scheme" of the composition of the soul

Jung raises two objections to this interpretation. First, he questions whether the assumption that Indivisible and Divisible are opposite attributes of each of the three principles, that is, Existence, Sameness, and Difference, is valid. Does the text, Jung asks, "permit of such an operation?" (Jung 1969, §191, n. 27). And second, he objects to Cornford's emphasis on "three *intermedia*" and a "threefold procedure" rather than on "four substances", and Jung reminds the reader that the Middle Ages recognized the so-called *quatuor elementa* (A, B, C, D) and the *tria regimina* (three procedures) which united them as follows: as A-B, B-C, or C-D. In the light of this schema, Jung is so bold as to suggest that Cornford "fails to catch Plato's subtle allusion to the recalcitrance of the fourth [*die Widerspenstigkeit des Vierten*]" (ibid., §191).

Of course, both critiques beg the very question to which Jung devotes himself in the penultimate paragraph, namely: to what extent do "the thought-processes [...] deduced from the text of the *Timaeus* represent Plato's conscious reflections" (Jung 1969, §192)? After all, Jung reflects, however "extraordinary" the genius of Plato may have been, it "by no means follows that his thoughts were all conscious ones" (ibid., §192).

For Jung, everything hinges on this question of the fourth term. As a problem, he suggests, it is both "an absolutely essential ingredient of totality", yet it is something that "can hardly have reached [Plato's] consciousness in complete form" (ibid., §192). In effect, Jung is placing Plato on the analyst's couch when he suggests that, if Plato had been conscious of the problem of the fourth, he would have been "repelled by the violence with which the elements were to be forced into a harmonious system", and he would not have been so "illogical" as to "insist on the threefoldedness of his world-soul" (ibid., §192).

In the end, Jung comes to the somewhat wistful conclusion that, while the opening words of the *Timaeus* are not necessarily "a conscious reference to the underlying problematic of the recalcitrant fourth [*des widerstrebenden Vierten*]", nevertheless everything suggests that "the same unconscious *spiritus rector* was at work which twice impelled the master to write a tetralogy" (Jung 1969, §192). In so writing, Jung is picking up a suggestion found in Gomperz's *Griechische Denker*, volume 3, that Plato harboured the ambition to write a dialogical tetralogy, and twice abandoned this ambition (Gomperz 1909, vol. 2, 475–476; Gomperz 1901–1912, vol. 3, 200): the two unfinished tetralogies being (a) the *Republic*, the *Timaeus*, the *Critias* (left incomplete), the *Hermocrates* (never written); and (b) the *Theatetus*, the *Sophist*, the *Statesman*, the *Philosopher* (never written). Indeed, Jung traces the failure of this ambition to the very heart of Plato's personal life, explaining the fact Plato remained a bachelor to the end of life as in some way affirming "the masculinity of his triadic God-image" (Jung 1969, §192).

Jung concludes his review of the pre-Christian parallels to the Trinity in Babylonian religion, Egyptian mythology, and Platonic philosophy by observing that, "as history draws nearer to the beginning of our era", so "the gods become more and more abstract and spiritualized"—a transformation reflected, Jung adds, in the changing conception of Yahweh (Jung 1969, §193). For the Christian triad of Father, Son, and Holy Spirit is prefigured in the emergence, next to Yahweh, of Logos and Sophia (ibid., §193). Yet this is by no means Jung's last word about Platonism in his lecture on a psychological approach to the Trinity. After having explored the dogma of the Trinity as it is expounded in the Apostles' Creed, the creed of St Gregory Thaumaturgus, the Nicene Creed, and the Nicene-Constantinopolitan, Athanasian, and Lateran Council Creeds (ibid., §207–§221) and after having investigated its archetypal dimension

(§222–§242), Jung returns for a second time to the *Timaeus* and its "problem of the fourth", which he now approaches from a very different angle.

THE THIRD AND THE FOURTH IN GOETHE'S "FAUST"

This time, Jung makes—as he had done in an earlier Eranos lecture of 1936 entitled "Individual Dream Symbolism in Relation to Alchemy"— an audacious leap by linking this opening exchange in the *Timaeus* to the Cabiri scene in Goethe's *Faust*, Part Two. This scene belongs to that part of the "Classical Walpurgis Night" in Act 2 set in the "rocky inlets of the Aegean Sea", in which the Sirens, the Nereids, and the Tritons introduce the equally mythical figures of the Cabiri, raising as they do so various numerological questions about them. If, for Jung, the second part of *Faust* fell—along with the *Shepherd of Hermas*, Dante's *Divine Comedy*, Nietzsche's "Dionysian experience", Wagner's *Ring*, *Tristan*, and *Parsifal*, Spitteler's *Olympian Spring*, Blake's painting and poetry, the *Hypnerotomachia* of Francesco Colonna, E.T.A. Hoffmann's *Der goldne Topf*, and Jacob Boehme's "poetic-philosophic stammerings"—into the category of the mode of artistic creation he described as "visionary" and as exemplifying a "primordial experience which surpasses human understanding and to which in their weakness humans may easily succumb" (Jung 1966, §142 and §141), then no part of *Faust*, Part Two, is arguably more "visionary" or more expressive of "primordial experience" than is its Classical Walpurgis Night.

In fact, the scene attracted the attention of Karl Kerényi (1897–1973), a classical scholar with whom Jung collaborated on two papers, published together under the title *Essays on a Science of Mythology* (1941) (Jung and Kerényi 1969), and whom Jung described in his address on the occasion of the founding of the C.G. Jung Institute on 24 April 1948 as "one of the most brilliant philologists of our time" and as having "supplied such a wealth of connections [of psychology] with Greek mythology that the cross-fertilization of the two branches of science can no longer be doubted" (Jung 1976, §1131 and §1132). In 1941, Kerényi published a study of the Aegean Festival,[20] and he sent a copy to Jung. For his part, Jung avowed he was deeply impressed by Kerényi's essay, later claiming that the book had been the stimulus behind his *own* decision to write *Mysterium coniunctionis* (see Jung 1970, xiii). In that late, great work

Jung argued that the sea journey as described by Christian Rosencreutz with its essential motif of the royal marriage was an alchemical motif that had been taken up by Goethe in *Faust II*, notably in the Aegean Festival scene, whose "archetypal content" had been elaborated by Kerényi in "a brilliant amplificatory interpretation" (ibid., §658). On Kerényi's account, the bands of nereids on Roman sarcophagi reveal "the epithalmic and the sepulchral element", inasmuch as "the identity of marriage and death on the one hand, and of birth and the eternal resurgence of life from death on the other" is "basic to the antique mysteries" (ibid., §658).[21]

Now the Cabiri have rightly been seen in the light of two earlier discussions of them on which Goethe is known to have drawn, namely: *Symbolik und Mythologie der alten Völker, besonders der Griechen* (1810–1812; ²1819; ³1837) by Friedrich Creuzer (1771–1858) and *On the Deities of Samothrace* (1815) by F.W.J. Schelling (1775–1854). Since the publication of the *Red Book*, however, it is impossible to overlook the specific significance the figures of the Cabiri had for Jung in relation to the construction (in the chapter entitled "The Magician" in *Liber secundus*) of Jung's Tower (Jung 2012, 425–429). (Not found in *Black Book 4*, the earliest manuscript with a dialogue between Jung's "I" and the Cabiri is the *Handwritten Draft* (1914–1915), leading Sonu Shamdasani to surmise that it may have been written separately, prior to the summer of 1915 [ibid., 425, n. 310; cf. Jung 2020, vol. 4, 244].) What, however, is their function for Goethe in *Faust*, Part Two, and what is their numerological significance?

On the level of narrative action, the Cabiri—in the form of mysterious, silent idols—are carried by a procession of Nereids and Tritons, held in the gigantic tortoise shell of Chelone (a nymph transformed by Hermes into a sea tortoise), to the festival in honour of Neptune, the god of the sea (and the Roman counterpart to the Greek god, Poseidon). As the *Faust* commentator Albrecht Schöne notes, the function of these passages is by no means satirical, even if Goethe once described F.W.J. Schelling's *Über die Gottheiten von Samothrake* as a "going-off on the wrong dark, poetic, philosophical, clerical track",[22] for it is precisely Schelling who supplies Goethe with crucial details about these figures, especially their hungry yearning (cf. *Sehnsuchtsvolle Hungerleider*; ll. 8204–8205). Schelling explains that the name of one of the Cabiri, Axieros, means in the Phoenician dialect "'hunger,' 'poverty,' and in consequence 'yearning,' 'seeking'" (*den Hunger, die Armuth, und was daraus folgt, das Schmachten, die Sucht*) (Brown [ed.] 1974, 18; Schelling 1815, 11). He notes that, of the diverse fragments of the Phoenician cosmogony that have been preserved, one of them "locates time above all the gods, which time itself has no number because it is the common context and bearer of all numbers; next to it, however, and therefore as the first number, it mentions the wistful longing" (*die schmachtende Sehnsucht*) (ibid., 19; ibid., 15). Indeed, Schelling argues that "the representation of longing as the beginning, as first ground of creation, was indigenous to Phoenician cosmogony" (*die Vorstellung der Sehnsucht als Anfangs, als ersten Grundes zur Schöpfung*), and on the evidence of a text by Pliny he extends this principle to the cult at Samothrace (ibid., 19–20; ibid., 16). Identifying another of the Cabiri, Axiokersa, with Persephone or Ceres, Schelling claims that Ceres, "as [the pining for reality, as] the hunger for being which we recognize as the most inward aspect of all of [longing-filled] nature" (*als [das Schmachten nach Wirklichkeit, als] der Hunger nach Wesen, den wir noch als das Innerste der ganzen [sehnsuchtsvollen] Natur erkennen*), is "the moving power through whose ceaseless attraction everything, as if by magic, is brought from the primal indeterminateness to actuality or formation" (ibid., p. 20; ibid., p. 17). Or as the Nereids and Tritons in *Faust II* describe the Cabiri:

> Far horizons they beseech,
> Peerless, distance-cherishers,
> Ever-famished perishers
> For the out-of-reach.[23]

Yet while these Proteus-like Samothracian deities thus appear in the context of this cultic festival essentially as embodiments of "Faustian" desire, Jung focuses instead on the numerological aspects of this scene.

True, Jung notes their broader mythological significance, describing the Cabiri as "the mysterious creative powers, the gnomes who work under the earth, i.e., below the threshold of consciousness, in order to supply us with lucky ideas", yet adding that "as imps and hobgoblins, however, they also play all sorts of nasty tricks, keeping back names and dates that were 'on the tip of the tongue,' making us say the wrong things, etc." (Jung 1969, §244). Thus seen, these deities could be regarded as an embodiment of what Freud (in *The Psychopathology of Everyday Life* [1901]) called parapraxes, although for Jung their significance goes much further, as he argues that "deeper insight will show that the primitive and archaic qualities of the inferior function conceal all sorts of significant relationships and symbolic meanings, and instead of laughing off the Cabiri as ridiculous Tom Thumbs [one] may begin to suspect that they are a treasure-house of hidden wisdom" (ibid., §244). (Based on a figure from English folklore, a work called *The History of Tom Thumb* was published in 1621, narrating how the eponymous Tom, whose size is no larger than his father's thumb, experiences various remarkable adventures.) But it is the question of how many Cabiri there are that really interests Jung.

As Jung notes (ibid., §243), the question of the Fourth is stated by the Nereids and the Tritons when they say:

> Three we took off beside us,
> The fourth of them denied us,
> He told us he had the call,
> And thought for one and all.[24]

In these lines, Goethe is following the argument found in Schelling's treatise on the Cabiri about the hierarchy of these deities.[25]

As Jung equally notes (ibid., §244), not only does the fourth think "for them all", but there is disagreement among the Sirens, the Nereids, and Tritons as to exactly how many Cabiri there are in total. According to the Nereids and the Tritons (who are, after all, carrying them in the procession), "Seven we know them to be" (l. 8194), yet in response to the Sirens' question, "Where are the other three?" (l. 8195), they reply:

> That's asking more than we know.
> Enquire on Olympus, though;
> That's where the eighth, too, must be sought
> Whom no one yet has given thought!
> Aware of us in grace,
> But none as yet in place.[26]

As Schöne notes, these lines playfully allude to the speculative analogies detected by such mythologists as Schelling in the hierarchy of the Cabiri, in which a particular significance accrues to the Eighth. As Schelling put it, these Samothracian deities are arranged "as links of a chain ascending from the depths into the heights, or as rungs of a ladder" (*wie Glieder einer vom Tiefsten in's Höchste aufsteigenden Kette, oder wie Sprossen einer Leiter*), with Axieros as "certainly the first in nature, but not the highest" and Kadmilos as "the last among the four, but the highest" (Brown [ed.]

1974, 23 and 22; Schelling 1815, 22). Schelling is keen to point out that "this insight at once transforms the whole sequence into one which is living and progressing" and opens up the prospect of "a further development of the series [...] through which the sequence of personalities continues up to a total of seven *or eight*" (ibid., 23; my italics).

On these lines from *Faust II* Jung puts his own, psychological gloss, claiming that the mysterious fourth could only have been Goethe's own "thinking function", along the lines of the principle enunciated by Faust that "Feeling is all; / Names are sound and smoke" (ll. 3455–3456). According to Jung, Goethe "showed great insight in not underestimating his inferior function, thinking", even if it was "in the hands of the Cabiri and thus undoubtedly mythological and archaic" (Jung 1969, §244). Hence the line, "The fourth would not come", can read as hinting that it wanted "for some reason to stay behind or below" (ibid., §244), and as confirming Jung's insight that each human has four orienting psychological functions, three of which are available to consciousness while the fourth is not. Accordingly Jung interprets the line, "The fourth would not come", as referring to the inferior function, the function that "remain[s] down below—or up above—in the unconscious realm" (ibid., §245).

This quasi-numerological, quasi-psychological reading of the Cabiri scene in *Faust* forms the basis of Jung's discussion of the concept of quaternity, which possesses for him a peculiarly psychological dimension. He begins by offering a survey of quaternary as opposed to trinitarian thinking—a kind of thinking he associates above all with Plato (Jung 1969, §246). Although the quaternity itself is "an archetype of almost universal occurrence", the origin of a quaternary type of thought "lies far back in the dark prehistory of Greek thought" (ibid., §246), notably the Pythagorean school. Here the role played, not by three, but by four, is reflected in the Pythagorean oath, according to which the tetractys (with its triangular arrangement of 1 + 2 + 3 + 4 = ten points in four rows), thus:

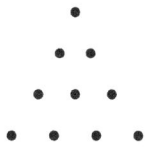

"contains the fount and root of eternal nature" (echoed in the four *rhizōmata*, i.e. roots or elements, of Empedocles),[27] and in the belief that the soul is a square, not a triangle (ibid., §246). And Jung lists numerous other examples: four elements, four prime qualities, four colours, four castes in India, four ways of spiritual development in Buddhism (or the four Noble Truths); four psychological functions; and even Schopenhauer's fourfold root of the principle of sufficient reason (ibid., §246). But what does four have that three apparently lacks? According to Jung, this "fourfold aspect" is the *logical* basis for any "whole judgment" (*Ganzheitsurteil*), and while "the ideal of completeness is the circle or sphere", its "natural minimal division" is a quaternity (ibid., para. 246).

Now the implications of this assertion are swiftly spelt out by Jung. In the *Timaeus*, the basic geometrical structure of earth as an element is said to be a cube (55d–e) (whereas fire = tetrahedron, air = octahedron, water = icosahedron, and aether as the fifth element or quintessence = dodecahedron).[28] Yet there is a tension between this symbolic recognition of the fourth and other aspects of Plato's thought. If Plato had insisted on his triadic structure of thought, he would (Jung argues) have been unable to arrive at "a whole judgement" (*Ganzheitsurteil*), for the "necessary fourth" would be "left out" (Jung 1969, §247); and if Plato had taken the three-sided figure as "symbolic of the Beautiful and the Good" and endowed it with all "positive qualities", he would (Jung further argues) have had to deny "evil and imperfection" to the Beautiful and the Good (ibid., §247). (As, indeed, Plato does.) In terms of Christian theology, this position is known as the doctrine of *privatio boni*, that is, that evil is a lack, absence, or privation of good,[29] and it is a position that Jung decisively rejects. So what, then, *is* this fourth element?

What Is the Fourth?

Jung variously (and highly problematically) suggests that this fourth element is (in terms of Christian theology) the Devil or Lucifer (Jung 1969, §248, §252, §256–§258), the Virgin Mary (§251–§252), or indeed the feminine more generally. Or as Jung puts in, albeit with a gesture of recognition toward the *Timaeus*, in strikingly theological terms:

> Ever since the *Timaeus* the "fourth" has signified "realization" [»*Verwirklichung*«], i.e., entry into an essentially different condition, that of worldly materiality, which, it is authoritatively stated, is ruled by the Prince of this world—for matter [*der Stoff*] is the diametrical opposite of spirit [*zum Geiste*]. It is the true abode of the devil, whose hellish hearth-fire

burns deep in the interior of the earth, while the shining spirit soars in the aether, freed from the shackles of gravity. (Jung 1969, §251)

In other words, "the dark weight of the earth must enter into the picture of the whole" (*zum Bild des Ganzen gehört die dunkle Schwere der Erde*) (§264).

This kind of theological rhetoric has, in terms of Jung's reception, been the cause of much opprobrium, ever since Freud accused Jung of mysticism—or mystification.[30] Yet Jung nevertheless insists that the origins of the Fourth are actually pre-Platonic (or Presocratic) inasmuch as they are Pythagorean, and he is at pains to trace a subterranean tradition from Pythagoreanism to Hermetic philosophy:

> The Pythagorean quaternity was a natural phenomenon, an archetypal image, but it was not yet a moral problem, let alone a divine drama. Therefore it "went underground" [*»untergegangen«*]. It was a purely naturalistic, intuitive idea born of the nature-bound mind. The gulf that Christianity opened out between nature and spirit enabled the human mind to think not only beyond nature but in opposition to it, thus demonstrating its divine freedom, so to speak. This flight from the darkness of nature's depths culminates in trinitarian thinking, which moves in a Platonic, "supracelestial" realm. But the question of the fourth, rightly or wrongly, remained. It stayed down "below" [*»unten«*], and from there threw up the heretical notion of the quaternity and the speculations of Hermetic philosophy. (Jung 1969, §261)

Here again Jung draws support for this position from one of his favourite mediaeval thinkers, Gerhard Dorn, and his notion of the *binarius* as "the devil of discord and, what is worse, of feminine nature" (Jung 1969, §262; cf. §256 and §262). (As a contribution to gender studies, this and other problematic remarks by Jung clearly deserve close interrogation.)

In the following section on the psychology of the quaternity, Jung advances the quasi-Hegelian proposition that the three persons of the Trinity—Father, Son, Holy Spirit—correspond to different stages of psychological development. (There are more than shades of Joachim of Fiore (c. 1135–1202) and his mystical theory of the three ages in the model Jung proposes here.) On this account, the Father corresponds to "the earlier state of consciousness [....] a passive, unreflecting condition, a mere awareness of what is given, without intellectual or moral judgment" (Jung 1969, §270); the Son corresponds to the stage when the son puts himself in the place of the father, a change which, "according to the archaic pattern, [...] takes the form of quasi-father-murder—in other words, violent identification with the father followed by his liquidation"; and the Spirit corresponds to a third step and to "a living activity [...] which raises the subsequent stages of consciousness to the same level of independence as that of 'Father' and 'Son'", described by Jung as "something like a recognition of the unconscious, if not actual subordination to it" (ibid., §271–§273). The Spirit is represented by such theriomorphic symbols as the lamb, the dove, and the snake; in addition, the snake symbolizes the Gnostic *nous* (and the Agathodaimon has a pneumatic significance, for "the devil, too, is a spirit") (ibid., §276).

Yet about what lies beyond this third stage, which involves "articulating one's ego-consciousness with a supraordinate totality" (Jung 1969, §276), it turns out that Jung has tantalizingly little to say: for all his emphasis on the quaternio, this developmental pattern seems to be governed by three, not by four! Unless, that is, we are to understand that the fourth stage itself corresponds to the totality envisaged by Jung as the outcome of this process, represented by the figure of the Cosmic Man, the Anthropos, as well as by different kinds of alchemical symbolism such as geometrical configurations (e.g. the sphere, circle, square, or octagon) or chemical symbols (e.g. the Philosophers' Stone, the ruby, the diamond, quicksilver, gold, water, fire, or spirit) (ibid., §276)? It is by no means clear how the symbolism of the *complexio oppositorum* necessarily fits the pattern of the quaternity rather than a triadic pattern.

Just before Jung turns to his conclusion, he offers some general remarks on symbolism, once again taking Plato's *Timaeus* as his starting-point. Although he regards it as "extremely improbable" that the Christian notion of the Trinity derives from the triadic World Soul (i.e. made up of Sameness, Difference, and Existence) of the *Timaeus*, he believes that both are "rooted in the same archetype" (Jung 1969, §280). He restates his earlier analysis that the number three represents "an intellectual schema only" while noting that just as the second mixture (i.e. the divisible, or the Different) reveals "the resistance of the fourth ingredient [*den Widerstand des vierten Ingrediens*]", so we meet it here "as the 'adversary' [*Widersacher (Diabolus)*] of the Christian Trinity" (ibid., §280). And he states more radically and clearly than previously that "*without the fourth* the three would have no reality [*die Wirklichkeit*] as we understand it"; indeed, "they even *lack meaning* [*ein Sinn*]" (ibid., §280; my emphasis). For a "thought" can only have meaning, Jung argues, if it "refers to a possible or actual reality", and he applies this principle to the idea of the Trinity itself, suggesting that "people nowadays tend to lose sight of it altogether, without even noticing the loss" (ibid., §280)! For what the Trinity lacks is, of course, its "incommensurable 'fourth'" (*mit dem inkommensurabeln Vierten*). Nevertheless, this loss makes itself felt, he asserts, when we run up against the problem of "reconstruction" (*Rekonstruktion*), that is, those clinical cases where a "dissociation" separates the conscious part of the psyche from its unconscious part. In order to heal this split, consciousness must be able to formulate conceptions (*Anschauungen*) which give "adequate expression" to unconscious contents. In short, this is what Christian theology with its doctrine of the Trinity plus an "incommensurable fourth" is trying to do (ibid., §280).

Yet although this doctrine is said to have a "redeeming, whole-restoring effect", Jung declares that ultimately it must fail, because it is trying to express something that, in the end, exceeds the possibilities of discursive thought. Or as he puts it, "rational formulae may satisfy the present and the immediate past, but not the experience of humankind as a whole"—an experience which calls for "the all-embracing vision of the myth, as expressed in symbols" (Jung 1969, §280). What is this mythical vision; where are its symbols to be found? As Jung claims to have demonstrated in *Psychology and Alchemy*, they can frequently be found in dreams and in their symbols of triads and quaternities. Paying attention to dreams can, Jung claims, uncover numerous examples of motifs of three or four. In such cases, banal dream-motifs can, on closer inspection, turn out to be "an allusion to [one's] total personality", in which the fourth figure is, "as a rule, particularly instructive", inasmuch as it shows itself to be "incompatible, disagreeable, frightening, or in some way odd, with a different sense of good and bad, rather like a Tom Thumb beside his three normal brothers" (ibid., §281).

In Jung's view, the figure of the Trinity is full of archetypal yearning— the yearning for the wholeness of, not three, but four.[31] After all, this is what an archetype (in Jung's view) *does*: it serves, first, as "an organizing schema and a criterion for judging the quality of an individual psychic structure"; and it functions, second, as "a vehicle of the synthesis in which the individuation process culminates" (Jung 1969, §281). So Jung can point, in his typical intercultural way, to various examples of the quaternity as a symbol of the self, for example, those found in Indian philosophy; in the Middle Ages, such quaternities as the *Rex gloriae*, the tympanum (c. 1150) above the central portal of Chartres cathedral, showing Christ in majesty surrounded by the symbols of the four evangelists (three theriomorphic, one anthropomorphic); and in Gnosticism, the figure of Barbēlō (whose name, in Hebrew, means "God is four"), from whom emerges (according to the *Apocryphon of John*) Foreknowledge, Incorruptibility, Eternal Life, and Truth. At this juncture, a tricky question arises: is the archetypal image of God identical to the archetypal image of the self? And, if not, what is the relation between them? On this question, Jung's response demonstrates a kind of creative ambiguity that is the hallmark of his subtle thinking.

To begin with, he states that it is "psychologically true" to say that the "God-image aspect" of the quaternity is a reflection of the self, as well as that the self is an *imago Dei* in humankind,[32] arguing that "the self, which can only be perceived subjectively as a most intimate and unique thing, requires universality as a background, for without this it could not manifest itself in its absolute separateness" (Jung 1969, §282). Then he changes tack, adding that, "strictly speaking, the self must be regarded as the extreme opposite of God" (ibid., §282). Then he brings in the German mystic Angelus Silesius (1624–1677) and his maxim, "I am as great as God, / He is as small as me, / He cannot be without me, / Nor I without him be" (*Ich bin so groß als Gott, / Er ist als ich so klein, / Er kann nicht ohne mich / Ich ohne ihn nicht sein*).[33] Finally Jung reaches the following conclusion: "Although the empirical symbol requires two diametrically opposed interpretations, neither of them can be proved valid"—and so "the symbol means both and is therefore a paradox" (ibid., §282). Here as elsewhere we encounter Jung's preference for paradox as "one of our most valuable spiritual possessions", on the grounds that "only the paradox comes anywhere near to comprehending the fulness of life" (Jung 1968, §18).

Other Numerical Schemes in the "Timaeus"

Strangely enough, Jung neglects to mention the symbolism of three, four, and indeed five in other parts of the *Timaeus*. For instance:

- the introduction into the initial distinction between the two orders of existence, that is, the intelligible and unchanging model and the changing and visible copy, of a third factor (*triton genos*, 48e), described as "the Receptacle" (i.e. "as it were, the nurse—of all Becoming") (49a).[34] These three factors of the Form, the Copy, and

Space as the Receptacle (χώρα or *chôra*) are summarized by Timaeus in 51e–52d. In fact, at this juncture Plato touches briefly on the question of dreams (52b-c), but this passage is nowhere mentioned by Jung;
- the four kinds of living creature: (1) the heavenly race of gods; (2) winged things whose path is in the air; (3) all that dwells in the water; (4) all that goes on foot on the dry land (39e–40a);
- the ideal models of Fire, Air, Water, Earth (51b-e);
- the actual construction of the figures of the four primary bodies, that is, the pyramid (or tetrahedron), the octahedron, the icosahedron, and the cube (53c–55c), the first three of which have equilateral triangular faces, while the cube alone has square faces;
- the detailed description in 54d–55c of how the three bodies of the pyramid, the octahedron, and the icosahedron are composed of elementary triangles (i.e. the triangle whose hypotenuse is double of the shorter side in length), while the second elementary triangle (the half-square) is used to construct the square face of the cube;
- the assignment of these regular figures to the four primary bodies, that is, earth = the cube, fire = the pyramid, air = octahedron, water = icosahedron (55d–56c);
- the construction in 55c of a *fifth* body, that is, the dodecahedron, constructed from an isosceles triangle having each of its base angles double of the vertical angle (Cornford 1997, 218–219). This figure, Timaeus suggests, was used by the Demiurge "for the whole" (55c), on the basis that this figure approaches most nearly in volume the sphere, recalling Jung's comments about the circle or the sphere as the "ideal of completeness" (Jung 1969, §246).
- the suggestion at 55c-d of the possibility of the existence of *five* worlds, on the basis (as explained by Plutarch in his treatise *On the E at Delphi*, §11) that there are five "perfect figures" in Nature, that is, earth, water, air, fire, and a fifth element called "the heavens" or "light" or "aether", described as "a substance [...] which alone of the bodies has by nature a circular motion that is not the result of any compelling power or any other incidental cause".[35]

Instead of considering these passages, Jung focuses uniquely (if repeatedly) on Timaeus's account (34b) of how the Demiurge fashions the world out of the indivisible = the Same, the divisible = the Different, and existence = Being (Jung 1969, §186), an account from which Jung then tries to uncover a *soi-disant* "recalcitrant" fourth, turning a triadic relation into a quaternity (§188) or even a quincunx (§189). The "Third" *must* become a "Fourth", because Jung is trying to convert Plato's cosmology into the terms of his *own* psychology, and whether or not this succeeds on *conceptual* grounds is, for him, less important than whether it succeeds on *clinical* or *therapeutic* grounds. Through his constellation of Plato, Goethe and (among others) Gerhard Dorn on the problem of the Fourth, Jung was also seeking to acknowledge (as he put it in 1928 in *The Relations between the Ego and the Unconscious*) that what had kept mediaeval thinkers passionately attached to alchemy had been its "liveliest intuition of profound truths", adding (in a barely disguised autobiographical aside) that "no one who has undergone the process of assimilating the unconscious"—as in the *Red Book* he himself had undertaken to do—would deny that it "gripped his very vitals and changed him" (Jung 1953, §361). Is there an experiential dimension to Jung's reading of Plato that we should also consider?

NOTES

1. Jung's paper provoked a response not just within the Eranos circle, but more widely; for instance, see Leibrand (1951).
2. For discussion of Jung as an exponent of erudition, particularly of the Gnostic and Neoplatonic variety, see Rieff (1966, 108–111).
3. In two papers in 1923 and 1925, "Der religionsgeschichtliche Hintergrund des Prologs zum Johannesevangelium" and "Die Bedeutung der neu erschlossenen mandäischen und manichäischen Quellen für das Verständnis des Johannesevangeliums", the German Lutheran theologian Rudolf Bultmann (1884–1976) had argued for the close connection between the Gospel of John and Gnosticism.
4. Dorn, "De tenebris contra naturam, et vita brevi", in *Theatrum chemicum*, vol. 1; cited in "Psychology and Religion: The Terry Lectures" (1938/1940) (Jung 1969, §104, fn. 47; cf. §180).
5. Even earlier than Maria Prophetissa, the Taoist philosopher Lao Tzu, an older contemporary of Confucius, observed in *Tao Te Ching*, book 2, §42: "The way begets one; one begets two; two begets three; three begets the myriad creatures" (Lao Tzu 1963, 103).
6. See Adolf von Harnack, *Lehrbuch der Dogmengeschichte*, vol. 2, *Die Entwickelung des kirchlichen Dogmas I*, 4th and revised edition: "Geometrically one can quite accurately represent the Western conception by an equilateral triangle, the Eastern one by a line with two lines emerging

from it at right angles" (*Geometrisch kann man das abendländische Bild ganz zutreffend durch ein gleichseitiges Dreieck, das morgenländische durch einen Strich mit zwei von ihm ausgehenden Seitenstrichen darstellen*) (von Harnack 1909, 303, n. 1). For his assistance with sourcing this reference, I am grateful to Peter Kingsley.

7. For further discussion of the principle of proportionality or analogy, see Taylor, *The Theoretic Arithmetic of the Pythagoreans*, book 2, chapters 23–25 (Taylor 2006, 97–102).

8. Cf. the footnote to *Timaeus*, 31c in the Loeb edition (Plato 1929, 58).

9. Cf. the footnote to *Timaeus*, 32b in the Loeb edition (Plato 1929, 59). For further discussion of the principle that plane numbers are conjoined by one mean but solid numbers by two, see Taylor, *The Theoretic Arithmetic of the Pythagoreans*, book 2, chapter 26 (Taylor 2006, 103–104), which refers to the passage in the *Republic*, book 8, where Socrates introduces the Muses with reference to the geometrical number known as the "nuptial number" (546b–547a; Bloom [ed.] 1991, 467–468).

10. Explaining the "physical" (as opposed to the "ethical") Pythagorean dogmas, Proclus records in his *Commentary on the "Timaeus" of Plato* that "they said that every physical production was held together by numbers, and that all the fabrications of nature subsisted conformably to numbers" (Proclus 1998a, vol. 1, 25).

11. To support this reading, Jung might have turned to the way that, in book 9 of the *Republic*, Socrates turns the difference between the pleasure of the tyrant and that of the king into a solid figure, in order that can be perceived by Glaucon: "There are [...] three pleasures—one genuine, and two bastard. The tyrant [...] dwells with a bodyguard of certain slave pleasures; and the extent of his inferiority isn't at all easy to tell, except perhaps as follows. [...] The tyrant, of course, stood third from the oligarchic man; the man of the people was between them. [...] Then wouldn't he dwell with a phantom of pleasure that was respect to truth is third from that other, if what went before is true? [...] And the oligarchic man is in his turn third from the kingly man, if we count the aristocratic and the kingly man as the same. [...] Therefore, [...] a tyrant is removed from true pleasure by a number that is three times three. [...] Therefore, [...] the phantom of tyrannic pleasure would, on the basis of the number of its length, be a plane? [...] But then it becomes clear how great the distance of separation is on the basis of the square and the cube. [...] Then if one turns it around and says how far the king is removed from the tyrant in truth of pleasure, he will find at the end of the multiplication that he lives 729 times more pleasantly, while the tyrant lives more disagreeably by the same distance" (587b–e; Bloom [ed.] 1991, 270). Glaucon is convinced by this argument—"You've poured forth [...] a prodigious calculation of the differ-

ence between the two men—the just and the unjust—in pleasure and pain" (ibid.)—but should we be? In his commentary, Bloom explains Socrates's thinking as follows: "The first step is the 'line,' derived from the distance between the two pleasures. The line is paradoxically called a 'plane' because its length is a number (9) formed of the two elements (3 × 3), which could represent length and width. Square numbers were technically called 'plane numbers.' Then the 'plane line' is squared and cubed and results in a solid, the number of which is 729", that is, 9 × 9 × 9 (Bloom [ed.] 1991, 470). Even so, Bloom questions this argument, adding that "why Socrates chooses the value he does, or why he uses multiplication rather than addition, or why a solid must be produced are all unclear, unless he wishes to make the result as large as possible in this prototypical attempt to mathematize human beings" (ibid.).

12. For the connection between the *Timaeus* and the Cabiri scene in Goethe's *Faust*, see Jung (1969, §243–§245) (discussed below); and "Individual Dream Symbolism in Relation to Alchemy" (1936) in Jung 1968, §204–§210 (discussed in the fourth chapter).

13. For definitions of psychological functions and of the inferior function, see Jung (1971, §731 and §763–§764).

14. The *political* nature of this problem is underscored in a footnote with a quotation from Friedrich Schiller's plays in his trilogy about the great Bohemien general of the Thirty Years' War (1618–1648), *Wallensteins Tod* (Act 2, scene 2).

15. In the 1950s a debate between G.E.L. Owen (1922–1982) and Harold F. Cherniss (1904–1987) turned precisely on the controversial question of whether stylometric analysis could show whether the *Timaeus* belonged to the middle or late works; see Owen (1953) and Cherniss (1957).

16. On the identity of the speakers and on the question of the fourth, see Lampert and Planeaux (1998); and Altman (2013).

17. See Matthias Vorwerk, "Maker or Father? The Demiurge from Plutarch to Plotinus", in Mohr and Sattler (2010, pp. 79–100).

18. In a footnote, Jung recalls how, in Part One of Goethe's *Faust*, Mephistopheles talks about how "The Something, this coarse world, this mess, / Stands in the way of Nothingness" (*Was sich dem Nichts entgegenstellt, / Das Etwas, diese plumpe Welt*) (ll. 1363–1364; Goethe 1987, 43).

19. Thus, of the various possible ways of reading the myth of Atlantis—historico-politically (as a polemic against the existing political structures in Athens); archaeologically (as evidence or otherwise of the existence of the island); or cosmogonically (by depicting the war of the Athenians against the Atlanteans as a parallel to the struggle of the cosmos against chaos)—Jung seems to incline to the third.

20. Karl Kerényi, *Das Ägäische Fest: Die Meergötterszene in Goethes Faust II* [Albae Vigiliae, XI] (Amsterdam and Leipzig: Pantheon, 1941; third edn, Wiesbaden: Limes-Verlag, 1950); see Kerényi (1978, 116–149).
21. See Kerényi (1978, p. 128). For further discussion, see the unpublished page proofs of "Mysteria: Jung and the Ancient Mysteries" (Noll 1994).
22. Goethe, letter to Meyer of 25 August 1819; cf. Schöne (2005, 567).
23. *Faust II*, ll. 8202–8205; Goethe (2001, 232).
24. *Faust II*, ll. 8186–8189; Goethe (2001, 232).
25. Drawing on a scholium on Apollonius of Rhodes's *Argonautica* (I.916), Schelling argues that the four names of the Cabiri as recorded at Samothrace, that is, Axieros, Axiokersa, Axiokersos, and finally Kadmilos, correspond to Demeter, Persephone, Hades (or in its place, Osiris or Dionysos), and finally Hermes (who leads the other gods from the underworld and into heaven), and thus represent a process of spiritual ascent. Because this process involves recapitulating its earlier three stages at a higher heavenly level with Kadmos/Hermes serving as a mediator between the highest of the gods, Zeus, and the first three gods of the Cabiri, this brings the total number of the Cabiri to seven (although Goethe jokingly suggests in ll. 8194–8199 that there might be an eighth!).
26. *Faust II*, ll. 8196–8201; Goethe (2001, 232).
27. See Hippolytus, *Refutation of All Heresies*, book 1, §2; book 4, §51. Walter Burkert describes the tetractys as "the epitome of Pythagorean wisdom", for "the 'tetrad' of the numbers 1, 2, 3, and 4 which add up to 10 (the 'perfect triangle'), contains within itself at the same time the harmonic ratios of fourth, fifth, and octave. The Sirens produce the music of the sphere, the whole universe is harmony and number, Ἀριθμῷ δὲ τὲ πάντ ἐπέοικεν [Everything is given order by numbers]. The tetractys has within it the secret of the world" (Burkert 1972, 186–187). For further discussion of the tetractys, see Taylor, *The Theoretic Arithmetic of the Pythagoreans*, book 3, chapter 6 (Taylor 2006, 161–166).
28. These figures are composed of triangles, confirming the Platonic principle that "the ternary alone is the principle of breadth and superficies" (see Taylor, *The Theoretic Arithmetic of the Pythagoreans*, book 2, chapter 5; Taylor 2006, 74–76). The significance of the number 5 from a Jungian perspective has been explored by Christine Driver in her recent study of the self and the quintessence (Driver 2020), illuminatingly reviewed by David Henderson in the *British Journal of Psychotherapy* (Henderson 2021).
29. For St Augustine's argument that evil is the absence (or privation) of good, see *Enchiridion* (or *Handbook on Faith, Hope, and Love*), §4 ("The Problem of Evil"); and *The City of God*, book 11, §9 and §22; cf. Plotinus, *Enneads*, 3.2 ("On Providence (1)"), §5.

30. In his *On the History of the Psycho-Analytic Movement* (1914), Freud accused Jung (along with Adler) of "court[ing] a favourable opinion by putting forward certain lofty ideas, which view things, as it were, *sub specie aeternitatis*" and of substituting for sexual libido an "abstract concept [...] of which one may safely say that it remains mystifying and incomprehensible to wise men and fools alike" (Freud 1993, 119 and 123).
31. The notion of wholeness is, however, itself problematic in the Platonic tradition: in his *Commentary on the "Timaeus"* (3,97) as in his *Elements of Theology* (propositions 67–69) Proclus distinguishes between three kinds of wholeness: (1) anterior to the parts; (2) composed of the parts; and (3) knitting into one stuff the parts and the whole (as translated in Inge 1918, 34). Cf. proposition 67, "Every whole is either a whole-before-the-parts, a whole-of-parts, or a whole-in-the part" (Proclus 1963, 65); and: "Wholeness [...] being triple, and originating supernally from intelligibles, it is necessary that this world being the image of the most beautiful of intelligibles, should subsist according to each of these wholenesses; according to the first indeed, which is prior to parts, according to the second also, which is from parts; and through this according to the remaining wholeness [which is in a part]" (Proclus 1998b, 811). For further discussion of the three kinds of wholeness in relation to Eustratius of Nicaea (c. 1050/1060-c. 1120) and his response to Proclus, see Stephen Gersh's account of universals, wholes, and *logoi* (Gersh 2021, 35–40).
32. On the "image of God" (*imago dei*), see the paper published by the International Theologian Commission entitled "Communion and Stewardship: Human Persons Created in the Image of God" (2004). Available at http://www.vatican.va/roman_curia/congregations/cfaith/cti_documents/rc_con_cfaith_doc_20040723_communion-stewardship_en.html. Accessed 14.01.2022.
33. Angelus *Silesius, Aus dem Cherubinischen Wandersmann (book 1, §10)* (Angelus Silesius 1966, 23).
34. For further discussion of the *chôra* and the significance in recent thought, see Verity Harte, "The Receptacle and the Primary Bodies: Something from Nothing", and Zina Giannopoulou, "Derrida's *Khôra*, or Unnaming the Timaean Receptacle", in Mohr and Sattler (eds) 2010, 131–140 and 165–178.
35. See Plutarch, "On the E at Delphi" (in Plutarch 1936, vol. 5, 229).

Bibliography

Altman, William H.F. 2013. The Missing Speech of the Absent Fourth: Reader Response and Plato's *Timaeus-Critias*. *Plato Journal* 13: 7–26.

Aristotle. 1984. *The Complete Works of Aristotle*. Ed. by Jonathan Barnes, 2 vols. Princeton, NJ: Princeton University Press.

Bloom, Allan, ed. 1991. *The Republic of Plato: Translated, with Notes and an Interpretive Essay*. New York: Basic Books.
Brown, Robert F., ed. 1974. *Schelling's Treatise on "The Deities of Samothrace": A Translation and an Interpretation*. Missoula, MT: Scholars Press.
Burkert, Walter. 1972. *Lore and Science in Ancient Pythagoreanism*. Trans. by Edwin L. Minar, Jr. Cambridge, MA: Harvard University Press.
Caldwell, C.K., and Y. Xiong. 2002. What Is the Smallest Prime?. *Journal of Integer Sequences* 15: article 12.9.7.
Cherniss, H.F. 1957. The Relation of the *Timaeus* to Plato's Later Dialogues. *The American Journal of Philology* 78 (3): 225–266.
Cornford, Francis MacDonald. 1997. *Plato's Cosmology: The "Timaeus" of Plato* [1935]. Indianapolis, IN: Hackett.
Driver, Christine. 2020. *The Self and the Quintessence: A Jungian Perspective*. Abingdon: Routledge.
Edelstein, Ludwig. 1966. *Plato's Seventh Letter*. Leiden: Brill.
Freud, Sigmund. 1993. *Historical and Expository Works on Psychoanalysis* [*Penguin Freud Library*, Vol. 15]. Trans. under James Strachey, ed. by Albert Dickson. Harmondsworth: Penguin.
Gersh, Stephen. 2021. Universals, Wholes, *Logoi*: Eustratios of Nicaea's Response to Proclus' *Elements of Theology*. In *Reading Proclus and the "Book of Causes" Volume 2: Translations and Acculturations*, ed. Dragos Calma, 32–55. Leiden and Boston: Brill.
Giegerich, Wolfgang. 2020. "Dreaming the Myth Onwards": C.G. Jung on Christianity and on Hegel: Part 2 of "The Flight into the Unconscious" [*Collected English Papers*, Vol. 6] [2013]. London and New York: Routledge.
Goethe, Johann Wolfgang. 1987. *Faust: Part One*. Trans. by David Luke. Oxford and New York: Oxford University Press.
———. 2001. *Faust: A Tragedy*. Ed. by Cyrus Hamlin, trans. by Walter Arndt. 2nd ed. New York and London: Norton.
Gomperz, Theodor. 1901–1912. *Greek Thinkers*. Trans. by L. Magnus and G.G. Berry, 4 vols. London: Murray.
———. 1909. *Griechische Denker: Eine Geschichte der antiken Philosophie*, 2nd ed., Vol. 2. Leipzig: Veit.
Grant, Edward, ed. 1974. *A Source Book in Medieval Science*. Cambridge, MA: Harvard University Press.
Griffith, F.L. 1898. *A Collection of Hieroglyphs* [Archaeological Survey of Egypt, 6th Memoir]. London: Egypt Exploration Fund.
Harnack, Adolf von. 1909. *Lehrbuch der Dogmengeschichte, vol. 2, Die Entwickelung des kirchlichen Dogmas I*, 4th and Revised ed. Tübingen: Mohr (Siebeck).
Heath, Thomas, ed. and trans. 1908. *The Thirteen Books of Euclid's Elements*, 3 vols. Cambridge: Cambridge University Press.
———. 1921. *A History of Greek Mathematics*, 2 vols. Oxford: Clarendon Press.

Henderson, David. 2021. [Review of] *The Self and the Quintessence: A Jungian Perspective* by Christian Driver. *British Journal of Psychotherapy* 37 (4): 725–727.
Inge, William. 1918. *Christian Mysticism: Considered in Eight Lectures Delivered before the University of Oxford* [The Bampton Lectures, 1899], 4th ed. London: Methuen.
Jung, C.G. 1953. *Two Essays on Analytical Psychology*. Trans. by R.F.C. Hull = *CW*, Vol. 7. London: Routledge & Kegan Paul.
———. 1966. *The Spirit in Man, Art, and Literature*. Trans. by R.F.C. Hull = *Collected Works*, Vol. 15. London: Routledge & Kegan Paul.
———. 1968. *Psychology and Alchemy*. Trans. by R.F.C. Hull = *Collected Works*, Vol. 12, 2nd ed. London: Routledge.
———. 1969. *Psychology and Religion*: West and East. Trans. by R.F.C. Hull = *Collected Works*, Vol. 11, 2nd ed. London: Routledge & Kegan Paul.
———. 1970. *Mysterium coniunctionis: An Inquiry into the Separation and Synthesis of Psychic Opposites in Alchemy*. Trans. by R.F.C. Hull = *Collected Works*, Vol. 14, 2nd ed.. Princeton, NJ: Princeton University Press.
———. 1971. *Psychological Types*. Trans. by H.G. Baynes, rev. by R.F.C. Hull = *Collected Works*, Vol. 6. Princeton, NJ: Princeton University Press.
———. 1976. *The Symbolic Life: Miscellaneous Writings*. Trans. by R.F.C. Hull = *Collected Works*, Vol. 18. Princeton, NJ: Princeton University Press.
———. 2012. *The Red Book: Liber Novus* [Reader's Edition]. Ed. by Sonu Shamdasani, trans. by Mark Kyburz, John Peck, and Sonu Shamdasani. New York and London: Norton.
———. 2020. *The Black Books, 1813–1932: Notebooks of Transformation*. Ed. by Sonu Shamdasani, trans. by Martin Liebscher, John Peck, Sonu Shamdasani, 7 vols. New York and London: Norton.
Jung, C.G., and Carl Kerényi. 1969. *Essays on a Science of Mythology: The Myth of the Divine Child and the Mysteries of Eleusis*. Trans. by R.F.C. Hull. Princeton, NJ: Princeton University Press.
Kerényi, Karl. 1978. *Humanistische Seelenforschung*. Wiesbaden: VMA-Verlag.
Klosko, George. 1981. Implementing the Ideal State. *The Journal of Politics* 43 (2): 365–389.
———. 2012. *History of Political Theory: An Introduction, Vol. 1, Ancient and Medieval*. Oxford: Oxford University Press.
Lampert, Laurence, and Christopher Planeaux. 1998. Who's Who in Plato's *Timaeus-Critias* and Why. *The Review of Metaphysics* 52 (1): 87–125.
Lao Tzu. 1963. *Tao Te Ching*. Trans. by D.C. Lau. Harmondsworth: Penguin.
Leibrand, Werner. 1951. C.G. Jungs Versuch einer psychologischen Deutung des Trinitätsdogmas. *Zeitschrift für Religions- und Geistesgeschichte* 3: 122–134.
Macrobius. 1990. *Commentary on the Dream of Scipio*. Ed. and trans. by William Harris Stahl. New York: Columbia University Press.
Marcuse, Ludwig. 1947. *Plato and Dionysius: A Double Biography*. Trans. by Joel Ames. New York: Knopf.

Mohr, Richard D., and Barbara M. Sattler, eds. 2010. *One Book, The Whole Universe: Plato's "Timaeus" Today*. Las Vegas, Zurich, Athens: Parmenides Publishing.
Noll, Richard. 1994. Mysteria: Jung and the Ancient Mysteries (Unpublished Page Proofs, 1994). https://www.researchgate.net/268034481/Mysteria_Jung_ and_the_Ancient_Mysteries_unpublished_page_proofs.
Owen, G.E.L. 1953. The Place of the *Timaeus* in Plato's Dialogues. *The Classical Quarterly* [NS] 3 (1–2): 79–95.
Patai, Raphael. 1995. *The Jewish Alchemists: A History and Source Book*. Princeton, NJ: Princeton University Press.
Plato. 1929. *Plato with an English Translation, Vol. 7, Timaeus; Critias; Cleitophon; Menexenus; Epistles*. Trans. by R.G. Bury. London; New York: Heinemann; Putnam.
———. 1989. *Collected Dialogues of Plato*. Ed. by Edith Hamilton and Huntington Cairns. Princeton, NJ: Princeton University Press.
———. 1996. *Works of Plato in Five Volumes*, Vol. 2. Trans. by Thomas Taylor and Floyer Sydenham [TTS, Vol. 10]. Sturminster Newton: Prometheus Trust.
Plutarch. 1936. Moralia, Vol. 5. Trans. by F.C. Babbitt. London; Cambridge, MA: Heinemann; Harvard University Press.
Proclus. 1963. *The Elements of Theology: A Revised Text with Translation, Introduction and Commentary*. Ed. by E.R. Dodds, 2nd ed. Oxford: Clarendon Press.
———. 1998a. *Commentary on the "Timaeus" of Plato*, Vol. 1. Trans. by Thomas Taylor [TTS, Vol. 15]. Sturminster Newton: Prometheus Trust.
———. 1998b. *Commentary on the "Timaeus" of Plato*, Vol. 2. Trans. by Thomas Taylor [TTS, Vol. 16]. Sturminster Newton: Prometheus Trust.
Rieff, Philip. 1966. *The Triumph of the Therapeutic*. London: Chatto & Windus.
Schelling, Friedrich Wilhelm Joseph. 1815. *Ueber die Gottheiten von Samothrace*. Stuttgart and Tübingen: Cotta.
Schöne, Albrecht. 2005. *Goethe—"Faust": Kommentare*. Frankfurt am Main: Deutscher Klassiker Verlag.
Silesius, Angelus. 1966. *Aus dem "Cherubinischen Wandersmann"*. Stuttgart: Reclam.
Taylor, A.E. 1928. *A Commentary on Plato's "Timaeus"*. Oxford: Clarendon Press (Reprinted New York: Garland, 1967).
Taylor, Thomas, ed. and trans. 2006. *The Theoretic Arithmetic of the Pythagoreans* [TTS, Vol. 30]. Sturminster Newton: Prometheus Trust.
Zeller, Eduard. 1876. *Die Philosophie der Griechen in ihrer geschichtlichen Entwicklung dargestellt*, 4th ed., Part 1, *Allgemeine Einleitung; Vorsokratische Philosophie*. Leipzig: Fues (Reisland).
———. 1881. *A History of Greek Philosophy from the Earliest Period to the Time of Socrates*. Trans. by S.F. Alleyn, 2 vols. London: Longmans, Green.

CHAPTER 4

The *Timaeus* and Cosmology; The Third and the Fourth in Alchemy and Synchronicity

Abstract This chapter considers Jung's account in the *Black Books* of "an unforgettable night in the desert" when he "saw the X for the first time" and "understood the Platonic myth", an experience he later also recounted on his seminar on Nietzsche's *Thus Spoke Zarathustra*. It examines Jung's further discussions of the motif of the Third and the Fourth (as well as the Seventh and the Eighth) in various alchemical texts, as well as a passage in his paper on "Synchronicity" in which he synthesizes his earlier accounts of Plato, Dorn, Goethe, and Maria Prophetissa, and relates them to this "a-causal connecting principle". Finally, it investigates how the parallel between the problem of the Third and the Fourth, as stated in the opening of Plato's *Timaeus* and as explored in the Cabiri scene in Goethe's *Faust*, first set up in 1942 in "A Psychological Approach to the Dogma of the Trinity", recurs (and, in fact, the two interpretative lines converge) in Jung's late great work of 1955–1956, *Mysterium coniunctionis*.

Keywords *Black Books* • Plato • Gerhard Dorn • Goethe • Maria Prophetissa • Synchronicity • *Mysterium coniunctionis*

Here we reach the point in our analysis where it seems we might have to make a decision. In regard to the depiction in Jung's *Red Book* of his "confrontation with the unconscious" (or, in German, *die Auseinandersetzung mit dem Unbewussten*, which places a much stronger emphasis on the interactive, processual nature of this "confrontation"), Peter Kingsley draws on the work of the Swiss classicist, Maria Laura Gemelli Marciano, to ask: are we dealing with "literary concepts" or "attitudes" as opposed to "hard inner experience"?[1] But could this itself be a false binary? After all, Sonu Shamdasani has argued that Jung derived his ideas about the collective unconscious from his library, going so far as to describe the collective unconscious as "the library within" (Shamdasani 2012, 49). As examples, Shamdasani points to Jung's reference to Cicero in "Nox secunda" or to the episode in "First Day", where Jung encounters the figure of Izdubar (or Gilgamesh) which draws on the *Ausführliches Lexikon der griechischen und römischen Mythologie* (1884–1937) compiled by Wilhelm Roscher (1817–1894) (Jung 2012, 336 and 277–283). Shamdasani argues that, "while Jung's self-investigation marked a turn away from scholarship, his fantasies and his reflections were marked by and indebted to his extensive scholarly readings" and "[his] self-experimentation was largely undertaken while seated in his library" (Shamdasani 2012, 90). (Does Shamdasani's thesis about the collective unconscious as "the library within" in itself refute Jung's ideas about the collective unconscious? Or could it rather be said to modify our understanding of the transmission of those ideas, perhaps helping us change our idea of the collective unconscious from something *metaphysical* to something *cultural*, albeit (for that very reason) no less *real*?)

It is Jung's reliance on the dream which maintains the characteristic tension in his thought between the experiential and the visionary. In the seventh of his *Black Books*, Jung tells us how he used a dream to solve a philosophical problem. In 1920, he had accompanied a close friend and neighbour, the businessman Hermann Sigg (1875–1927), on a business trip to North Africa. Now Jung's response to Africa is often read as evidence of the need to "decolonize" analytical psychology, and it is true that there are passages in Jung's writings that smack of "white privilege".[2] Yet over and above the problematic aspects of his response, there is one that relates to the problem of the Three and the Four as well. In a letter to Emilii Medtner (1872–1936) of March 1920, Jung described his impression of Africa as follows: "The most mysterious here are the nights of the waxing moon that wanders in indescribably silver clarity across the dark clear sky of Africa. The symbol of the Punic tombs of Carthage, [☪], Astarte herself, came close to me, when I saw the moon slowly descend over the tops of the palm trees for the first time. I came here according to inner necessity, already prepared by the unconscious, a symbolic act of the grandest style, nevertheless the meaning is still dark" (Ljunggren 1994, 215; cited in Jung 2020, vol. 1, 76).

In Tunis in 1920, Jung had a dream that revealed the "overwhelming force" with which he had been struck in his encounter with Arab culture—a dream that involved the fantasy or dream figure of an Arab youth, who emerged from a mandala-like citadel or casbah with four (!) gates and wrestled Jung, much as Jacob wrestled with the angel of Yahweh (Jung 1963, 270–272; cf. Genesis 32: 23–33). This figure returns to Jung in a fantasy of 6 January 1922, where he is described to Jung by his soul in Angelus-Silesius-like terms as "a god, who can't exist with you and without whom you can't either" (*ein Gott, der ohne dich nicht sein kann und ohne den auch du nicht sein kannst*) and who "must be reached again" (*muss wieder erreicht werden*) (Jung 2020, vol. 7, 213). The figure of the Arab youth is in turn closely related to another, the figure of Wotan, who visits Jung a year later on 2–3 January 1923 in Castagnola (ibid., vol. 7, 224–226). What links these figures is a philosophical question which is resolved for Jung in a dream. The question, which first arises in the case of the figure of the Arab youth, is how he can "seem rather to appear than to be" (*jedoch scheine ich mehr zu sein, als dass ich wirklich wäre*) or how he can "veil [him]self in either being or non-being" (*mich auch in's Sein hüllen, so gut wie ins Nichtsein*) (ibid., vol. 7, 225). Subsequently on 3 January 1923, Jung's soul says of "the foreign guest […] the dark one" (*den fremden Gast … den Dunklen*) that it is "as if he were above being being and non-being" (*jenseits von Sein und Nichtsein*): "It seems that he can be and not be" (*Es scheint, als ob er sein und nicht sein könnte*), which gives rise to the question, "What is beyond being and non-being?" (*Was ist jenseits von Sein und Nichtsein?*) (ibid., vol. 7, 226).

The problem of being and non-being is arguably the core philosophical question that characterizes ancient Greek philosophy from the end of the sixth century to the second half of the fourth century BCE. Neither Parmenides' understanding of being and not-being as two completely opposed, irreconcilable notions, nor Plato's attempt to demonstrate how being and not-being are not exclusive and can be combined, nor Aristotle's rejection of the notion of not-being and proposal of a broader, richer notion of being solved the problem. In modern times, G.W. Leibniz (1646–1716) reformulated the question as, "Why is there something rather than nothing?"[3] which Martin Heidegger (1889–1976) described as "the fundamental question of metaphysics" (Heidegger 1959, 7–8).

For Jung, the question acquires urgency, not as a metaphysical or ontological matter, but as a psychological one: how can the fantasy figure of the Arab youth who turns into the figure of Wotan both be and not be? Responding directly to his soul's question, "what is beyond being and not-being", Jung describes this question as "essential" (*ein wesentlicher Eindruck*) (Jung 2020, vol. 7, 227). Here Jung has recourse to the notion of the Demiurge, found both in the *Timaeus* and in Gnostic writings (where it refers to the creator of the material world), and which he associates with another notion, common to early Christianity and Gnosticism alike, the Pleroma (πλήρωμα, i.e. the "fullness"): "The demiurge is being and non-being, since he is the fulness and the emptiness. But beyond being and non-being is the inconceivable Pleroma, without qualities" (ibid., p. 227). Thus the question arises—could the figure of Wotan be "something pleromatic"?

At this point Jung recalls another dream that he had during his trip to North Africa in 1920, a dream which is said to have "revealed the 'existence'" (*enthüllte die "Existenz"*) to Jung of this enigmatic, demiurgic, Pleromatic figure, which he linked to an insight gained from an experience in Africa. In turn, Jung goes on to link this insight to the myth of the creation in Plato's *Timaeus* and specifically to the passage where the Demiurge takes this compound of three ingredients (i.e. Sameness, Difference, and Existence) as if it were a long strip of soul-stuff, splits it lengthwise into two strips, binds them at their middles, and bends round into two circles or rings (36b–c; Plato 1929, 71–73). As we have seen, this myth had already long interested Jung, and the allusion in *Black Book* 7 to this passage from the *Timaeus* forms part of a larger reception of this Platonic dialogue in Jung's work to which his lecture "A Psychological Approach to the Dogma of the Trinity" also belongs. Here in this memory of Africa in the *Black Books*, however, the emphasis is not so much on the scholarly interpretation of Plato as on the *experiential* dimension: in that "unforgettable night in the desert", we read, Jung "saw the X for the first time" and "understood the Platonic myth" (*das X sah und den Platonischen Mythus verstand*) (Jung 2020, vol. 7, 227). Yet this understanding is conveyed not conceptually, but *imagistically*: "In the zenith there was a large radiant planet exactly at the intersection", a sight that is interpreted as an image (*Bild*) that constitutes "an expression of the mystery of individuation" (*ein Ausdruck des Geheimnisses der Individuation*) (ibid., 227).

Many years later, in his seminar on Nietzsche's *Thus Spoke Zarathustra* held between 1934 and 1939, Jung returned on two occasions to this experience in the desert. In his lecture of 27 February 1935, Jung responded to a discussion about the nature and structure of the self by commenting as follows on the symbol of the cross: "The cross was a very important time symbol already in antiquity; it has always been explained as the position of the spring equinox, the intersection of the equator with the so-called ecliptic", that is, the great circle that is the plane of Earth's orbit around the Sun and its apparent path among the constellations in the course of a year (Jung 1989, vol. 1, 422). Rejecting the claim that "the Greek letter X [i.e., *chi*] in Platonism represents that spring equinox" (i.e. the time when the plane of the Earth's equator passes through the geometrical centre of the sun's disc and the subsolar point as seen from Earth appears to leave the southern hemisphere and cross the celestial equator, heading north), Jung says instead that it is "the visible cross in the sky which one sees in certain latitudes, not the constellation of the Southern Cross" (i.e. a constellation centred on four bright stars in a cross-shaped group of stars (or asterism) also known as Crux), but "the intersection of the Milky Way with the zodiacal line" (ibid., vol. 1, 422). Jung remembers that he had seen it in the desert in North Africa, but speculates it can also be seen in Greece because it is the same latitude (as one of the seminar members, Hans Fierz, confirms). The memory prompts Jung further to recall two Platonic myths: the myth in the *Timaeus*, where "the demiurge created a round universe which he cut into four parts and then stuck together again", and the myth in the *Symposium*, where "man was made as a perfect form, a globe with double sex, which had to be cut asunder" (i.e. cut into two parts) (ibid., vol. 1, 422).

Subsequently, in his lecture of 13 November 1935 Jung explained how he understood Plato's *Timaeus* as preserving an account of "the primordial experience of the dawn of consciousness, that division of the world-soul" (Jung 1989, vol. 1, 679). Here he discussed the Platonic concepts of *tauton* (ταὐτὸν) and *thateron* (θάτερον), introduced by Plato in *The Sophist* as part of his argument that the antinomy of *on* (being) and *mē-on* (non-being) does not really exist, but that the antinomy of *tauton* (i.e. the same) and *thateron* (i.e. the other, something different) does.[4] (This pair of concepts recurs in such later dialogues as the *Parmenides* [139sq.] and the *Theaetetus* [186a], as well as in the account in the *Timaeus* of how the Demiurge blends a third form of Being out of the Same and the Other [35a].) What, for Plato, is a metaphysical or ontological category becomes, for Jung, a psychological one: *tauton*, "the same", or that which is identical with itself, is identified by Jung as consciousness, while *thateron*, "the other" or "different", is what is "not 'I,' not my consciousness" (ibid., 678). In addition, Jung sees this distinction between *tauton* and *thateron*, between consciousness and non-consciousness, as a discrimination that is the source of significance and values: so "the origin of consciousness means the origin of values and significance", the precision with which these concepts are defined in early Greek philosophy illustrating Plato's proximity to the origin of philosophical consciousness (ibid., 678).[5]

This epochal move on Plato's part (i.e. the connection of discrimination with consciousness) had immense repercussions: "when consciousness developed out of the general unconsciousness", Jung argued, "a split went through the whole world" and suddenly "the whole world was divided" (Jung 1989, vol. 1, 679). For Jung, this is the meaning of the myth of the Demiurge in the *Timaeus*, which he reprises as follows: "In the beginning, when the Demiurgos had made the world-soul, he separated it crosswise [...]. There were three staffs, with the world-soul as a sort of axis. He cut the thing in the middle and bent two staffs back into the form of wheels, and then pushed them into each other obliquely, and when you look at those circles in the prolongation of their plane, you see it like this" (ibid., p. 679) (see Fig. 2.2 above and Fig. 4.1).

Fig. 4.1 The "chi"

And this is how Jung explains this figure of "the Platonic *chi*, the fourfold division of the world":

> You can see it in the sky in the division of the zodiacal light [i.e., the band of light in the night sky that appears to extend from the direction of the sun and along the ecliptic, especially visible in the tropics where the ecliptic is approximately vertical, caused by sunlight reflected from interplanetary dust] and the Milky Way. This peculiar symbolism is the mythological remnant of that primordial experience of becoming conscious; in the moment when consciousness appeared, there was division. Of course the creator is

always creating a new understanding, a new level of consciousness; he expands or extends consciousness, conquers a new world perhaps or a new continent, adding it to the existing image of the world; and so he has created new significances and new values. (Jung 1989, vol. 1, 679–680)

A decade and a half after his experience in Africa, the impression of this "unforgettable night in the desert" had evidently *not* been forgotten, and Jung was still having recourse to Plato's *Timaeus* to explain in philosophical terms some of the key tenets of his own system of psychology.

In the wake of this experience in the desert and this insight into the Platonic myth of the *Timaeus*, in his entry in his *Black Books* for 3 January 1923, Jung recalls that, four days after this experience in 1920, he had the dream of the Arab youth, "the dream that was one of the greatest experiences of my life" (Jung 2020, vol. 7, 227). (The persistence of the impact of this dream is suggested by the fact that, on 6 January 1922, Jung had another version of it [ibid., 212].) Now Jung connects the dream of the Arab youth and his unease about the being and non-being of Wotan by proposing a definition of the self that translates the metaphysical notion of the Pleroma into psychological terms: "Should it be the self, that inconceivable essence [*das Selbst, jenes unvorstellbare Wesen*], which is greater than I and of which we do not even know if it is human, humanlike, or finally not at all comparable to humankind?", he asks (ibid., 227). At this point Jung recalls the words of the fantasy figure of ΦΙΛΗΜΩΝ (or Philemon), spoken on 30 January 1916 in a text that would, in the *Red Book*, become the first of the *Septem Sermones ad mortuos* (i.e. *Seven Sermons to the Dead*) (Jung 2020, vol. 5, 284–285 and vol. 6, 207–210; cf. Jung 2012, 509–514).[6] Now Jung understands what Philemon's teaching means: namely that "the self is the Pleroma, a part and yet the whole [*ein Theil und doch das Ganze*]", adding that the figure of Wotan "calls himself appearance, that can be everything or nothing [*Schein, der Alles sein oder nicht sein kann*]" (Jung 2020, vol. 7, 277). As a "pleromatic" figure, Wotan stands in contrast to Abraxas—the "supreme deity" of the Gnostics, a "time god", and "identical" with the Demiurge,[7] whom Jung introduces into the cosmology he proposes in his entry for 16 January 1916 (Jung 2020, vol. 5, 269–277) and incorporates into his painting *Systema Mundi Totius* (see vol. 1, 130–161; and Jung 2012, 560–561). In an exchange that will become the second of the *Septem Sermones*, Abraxas is defined as "effect" (*Wirkung*), as "force, duration, change" (*Kraft, Dauer, Wandel*), and as distinct from God as *HELIOS* or sun (Jung 2020, vol. 6, 212; 2012, 517).

The identification of the self with the Pleroma gives rise to a key question, which one could with good reason describe as *the* central question of analytical psychology: as Jung's soul puts it, "But how is it conceivable that the Pleroma manifests?" (*Aber, wie ist es denkbar, dass das Pleroma erscheint?*) (Jung 2020, vol. 7, p. 227). Or as Jung himself reformulates the question: "What does it mean that the Pleroma would like to become something determinate?" (*Was heisst das, dass das Pleroma etwas Bestimmtes werden möchte?*) (ibid., 277). To this question, Jung's soul has no reply, and the entry comes to an abrupt end. (This problematic is taken up again by Jung in his *Answer to Job* [1952].)

The Third and the Fourth in Jung's Writings on Alchemy

In 1928, Jung ceased work on the *Red Book* after he had received from Richard Wilhelm (1873–1930) a copy of his translation into German of the Chinese Taoist classic about neidan (or internal alchemical) meditation called *The Secret of the Golden Flower* (太乙金華宗旨, i.e. *Tàiyĭ Jīnhuá Zōngzhĭ*). Thereafter Jung turned his attention to alchemy, building over time a significant collection of alchemical texts (currently in the process of being digitized) (see Fischer 2011). The significance of alchemy for Jung is reflected in the fact that, of the twenty volumes of his *Collected Works*, three of them are entirely dedicated to alchemy: *Psychology and Alchemy* (vol. 12), *Alchemical Studies* (vol. 13), and *Mysterium coniunctionis* (vol. 14). Thus it is in the context of his interpretation of alchemy that Jung returns on numerous occasions in the papers collected in these volumes to his reading of Plato, of the *Timaeus*, and the problem of the Third and the Fourth. In these works on alchemy Jung repeatedly points to links between alchemy and Platonic philosophy, not just in the form of the *Liber Platonis quartorum* (which can only loosely be said to be Platonic) but also the *Timaeus*.

In "Individual Dream Symbolism in Relation to Alchemy" (1936), in which Jung analysed a sequence of dreams by a client, a dream in which his dreamer-client wishes but is unable to kick away a death's-head skull, which gradually changes into a red ball and then into a woman's head which emits light, prompts Jung to reflect on how in Neoplatonic philosophy the soul has "definite affinities" with the sphere (Jung 1968, §107). These affinities are exemplified by the way in which, in *Hermes Trismegistus an die menschliche Seele* (1870) by Heinrich Leberecht Fleischer (1801–1888), the soul substance is "laid round the concentric spheres of the four elements above the fiery heaven" (ibid., §109), as well as by the spherical form of Plato's Original Man (as related by Aristophanes in the *Symposium*)[8] and the *sphairos* (σφαῖρος) or the blissful god of Empedocles (Jung 1989, vol. 2, 781–782),[9] while the alchemical *anima mundi* (or World Soul) is—like the *anima mundi* of the *Timaeus*—spherical, as reflected in the depiction of the winged sphere (*aurum aurae*) as the end-product of the alchemical *opus* and its reflection in the fountain of life in *Aurum hermeticum* (1765) by the German alchemist Christian Adolf Balduin (1632–1682) (Jung 1968, §109, fn. 38; cf. fig. 209). (The connection between the *rotundum* and the skull or head is discussed further in "Transformation Symbolism in the Mass" (cf. Jung 1969a, §363–§373), where Jung suggests there is a link between skull worship and the severed head of Osiris, whose crossing of the sea symbolizes the idea of resurrection [ibid., §366 and §372].)

In "Religious Ideas in Alchemy" (1937), Jung cites in a footnote view of the Byzantine commentator John the Lydian or John Lydus (ca. 490–ca. 565) in his account of the various pagan festivals of the year. According to his *Liber de mensibus* (*On the Months*) (IV, 53), what is described in the *Timaeus* as "that which is Existent always and has no Becoming" (27d; Plato 1929, 49) was identified by the Egyptians and Hermes with Osiris (Jung 1968, §456, fn. 35). And in "The Visions of Zosimos" (1938; 1954), Jung suggests that the notion of a "round white stone" (*lapis albus rotundus*) which "has within itself the three colours and the four natures and is born of a living thing", the *rotundum* which "changes the metal into four", and the *aqua permanens* in Julius Ruska's edition of the *Turbas philosophorum*,[10] as well as Johann Christoph Steeb's account of the origin of the idea of the "divine water" of the alchemists (and how, "when the celestial waters were animated by the spirit, they immediately fell into a circular motion, from which arose the perfect spherical form of the *anima mundi*"),[11] were all ideas that "refer expressly" to Plato's *Timaeus* (Jung 1967b, §102).

In "Paracelsus as a Spiritual Phenomenon" (1942), Jung clarifies the "psychic factor" at work in alchemy by explaining that "the artifex accompanies his chemical work with a simultaneous mental operation"—that is, *imaginatio* (or "meditating")—"which is performed by means of the imagination"; and he defines the Paracelsian notion of the Iliaster as "a spiritual, invisible principle, although it is also something like the *prima materia*, which [...] in alchemical usage by no means corresponds to what we understand by matter" (Jung 1967b, §173). In addition, he notes that "the symbolical names of the *prima materia* all point to the *anima mundi*, Plato's Primordial Man, the Anthropos and mystic Adam", that is, a figure described as "a sphere (= wholeness), consisting of four parts (uniting different aspects in itself), hermaphroditic (beyond division by sex), and damp (i.e., psychic)"—all details which are said to paint "a picture of the self, the indescribable totality of the human individual" (ibid., §173).

In "The Spirit Mercurius" (1943; 1948) he cites from Happelius's *Aphorismi Basilian*, the *Veruis Hermes* (1620), Siebmacher's *The Sophic Hydrolith*, and J.C. Steeb's *Coelum Sephiroticum Hebraeorum* (1679), as supporting the claim that "it is clear from a number of texts that the alchemists related their concept of the *anima mundi* on the one hand to the world soul in Plato's *Timaeus* and on the other to the Holy Spirit [...]" (Jung 1967b, §263). And in "The Philosophical Tree" (1945; 1954), in the context of a discission of the medieval notion of the human being as an inverted tree, Jung suggests that a link with Indian conceptions (as found in the Bhagavadgītā, chapter 15, and in the Chāndogya Upanishad [VIII, 5, 3]) is provided by a remark by Plato in the *Timaeus* (ibid., §412). Here Timaeus explains that "we are not an earthly but a heavenly plant" and that consequently God "has given to each of us, as his daemon, that kind of soul which is housed in the top of our body and which raises us [...] up from earth toward our kindred in the heaven" (90a; Plato 1929, 245); an idea also found in an Orphic fragment (no. 228a), according to which "the soul of the human individual is rooted in the aether [αἰθέρος]" (Kern 1972, 244).

(In passing, one might note that there could be no greater contrast than that between the Orphic-cum-Platonic explanation of the fact that human beings stand upright in terms of a "divine part" within us, expressing our "celestial affinity" (Cornford 1997, 353), and the one proposed by Freud. In his *Notes upon a Case of Obsessional Neurosis* (or the "Rat Man") (1909), where he wondered whether "the atrophy of the sense of smell (which was an inevitable result of man's assumption of an erect posture) and the consequent organic repression of his pleasure in smell may not have had a considerable share in the origin of his susceptibility to nervous disease" (Freud 1979, 127), and then again in *Civilization and its Discontents* (1930 [1929]), where he suggested that "the diminution of the olfactory stimuli seems itself to be a consequence of man's raising himself from the ground, of his assumption of an upright gait; this made his genitals, which were previously concealed, visible and in need of protection, and so provoked feelings of shame in him" (Freud 1991, 288–289, fn. 1), Freud was insistent on an evolutionary account of the relation between sexuality, neurosis, and erect posture. In contrast to the Orphic, Platonist, and Christian view (as expressed by the author of the First Letter of St Peter and by Macarius of Egypt in his *Spiritual Homilies*) of the human being as an inheritor of divine royalty,[12] Freud traced the "fateful process of civilization" back to humankind's adoption of an erect posture: "From that point the chain of events would have proceeded through the devaluation of olfactory stimuli and the isolation of the menstrual period to the time when visual stimuli were paramount and the genitals become visible, and thence to the continuity of sexual excitation, the founding of the family and so to the threshold of human civilization" [ibid., 289, f. 1].)[13]

At the same time, Jung also recurs in these writings on alchemy to the problem of the Third and the Fourth (or the Seventh and the Eighth) in Goethe's *Faust*. In "Individual Dream Symbolism in Relation to Alchemy", the thirteenth dream involves Jung's client going on a dangerous walk up and down many ladders with his father and mother, until the father calls out anxiously, "That is the seventh!" (Jung 1968, §82). According to Jung, "seven" stands in the language of initiation for the "highest stage of illumination" (i.e. *illumination* or enlightenment), corresponding to the alchemical stage of *solificatio* (ibid., §83 and §68). (To the "rational attitude of the conscious mind, which recognizes only intellectual enlightenment as the highest form of understanding and insight", any other form of illumination sounds "mystical", even "chimerical"; nevertheless, Jung insists, playing furiously with the metaphor of light, *solificatio* inaugurates "a *lighting up of the unconscious* [*eine Erhellung des Unbewußten*] [...] which has far more the character of *illuminatio* than of rational 'elucidation' [*»Erklärung«*]" [ibid., §68].)[14]

In psychological terms, the sun is "a symbol of the source of life and the ultimate wholeness of the individual": despite St Augustine's argument in his *In Joannis Evangelium Tractatus* (*Tractates on the Gospel According to St John*) that Christ is not the sun that was made, but He by whom the sun was made (Tractate XXXIV, §2), early Christians had, Jung claims, some difficulty distinguishing the rising sun from Christ, and he suggests that any allusion to alchemy "wafts one back to the ancient world and makes one suspect regression to pagan levels" (ibid., §112); indeed, he refers to *solificatio* as a "blasphemous pagan idea" (ibid., §101). At the same time,

Jung recognizes that the seventh can also mean "something rather more ominous", reflected in the fact that Tom Thumb is the youngest of seven brothers and it is he who leads them to the ogre's lair: in a sense, he is the ogre himself (ibid., §84). Since ancient times, "the seven" have represented the seven gods of the planets (i.e. the moon, Mercury, Venus, the sun, Mars, Jupiter, and Saturn); the Pyramid inscriptions refer to a *paut neteru* (a "company of gods"), described sometimes as nine, but sometimes ten—or more! Yet it is not the precise number that matters, but the status of one of the gods in particular, that is, Hermes or Mercury, whose "double nature" is reflected in his representation as a chthonic god of revelation *or* the spirit of quicksilver, as the *prima materia* (and hence the lowest) *or* the *lapis philosophorum* (i.e. the highest)—for the alchemist, good luck, and/or ruin (ibid., §84).

At this point we find ourselves back at the Cabiri scene in *Faust II*—and a possible identification of Mercurius as the Seventh and/or the Eighth, that is, the eighth on Olympus "whom nobody thought of" (Jung 1968, §84). Here Jung makes the claim that *Faust* is "an alchemical drama from beginning to end",[15] which works on the level of the unconscious: while our consciousness is "far from understanding everything", the unconscious "keeps an eye on the 'age-old, sacred things,' however strange they may be, and reminds us of them at a suitable opportunity" (ibid., §85). The expression "age-old, sacred" (*uralt heil'gen*) is, as likely as not, taken from a poem by the Austrian poet Robert Hamerling (1830–1889) who, as Rudolf Steiner (1861–1925) put it, links "grey primordial time with the immediate present" (*graue Vorzeit an unmittelbare Gegenwart an[knüpft]*).[16] Indeed, the unconscious mind is said to have affected Goethe himself, during whose studies as a young man during his Leipzig days of Paracelsus under the tutelage of Fräulein von Klettenberg, Jung suggests, "the mysterious equivalence of seven and eight sank deep into his soul, without his conscious mind ever unravelling the mystery" (ibid., §85).[17]

In the twenty-second dream of the sequence of 59 discussed (the first third of a series of some four hundred dreams and visions), the dreamer-client has a dream of being in an American hotel and going in its lift (or elevator) to the third or fourth floor, then to the seventh or eighth floor: a detail which Jung interprets as expression of the "tendency to re-establish a state of wholeness" and as an engagement with the "problem of the fourth function' (Jung 1968, §201 and §202). In Jungian terms, wholeness involves the use of all four functions—thinking, feeling, sensation, and intuition—but this dream, Jung suggests, expresses a certain hesitation "before the last step to wholeness" (ibid., §203)—at which point Jung broadens his discussion by returning to *Faust II* and its numerological motifs in its Cabiri scene. Here as later in his Eranos lecture on the Trinity, the focus is fairly (and squarely) on the numerological aspects of this scene: what he calls "the problem of three and four, seven and eight" (Jung 1968, §209).

Whereas, in his lecture on the Trinity, Jung anchors his discussion of the Cabiri scene in his approach to the opening of the *Timaeus*, here in "Individual Dream Symbolism in Alchemy" he anchors it in his account of the alchemical tradition. According to Jung, "the problem of three and four, seven and eight" was "a great puzzle to alchemy", which can be traced back historically to texts ascribed to an anonymous seventh-century author called Christianos (Jung 1968, §209). (Jung relies on Marcelin Berthelot's *Origines de l'alchimie* (1885) for the dating of Christianos as a contemporary of the Byzantine philosopher and teacher Stephanos of Alexandria who was active from c. 580 to c. 640.)[18] In a treatise in Berthelot's *Alchimistes grecs* (vol. 3, 388–390) entitled "The Production of the 'Mysterious Water'", we read how "the Hebrew prophetess cried without restraint, 'One becomes two, two becomes three, and out of the third comes the One as the fourth'" (*De là vient que la prophétesse hébraïque s'est écriée sans réticence: «Un devient deux, et deux deviennent trois, et au moyen du troisième, le quatrième accomplit l'unité; ainsi deux ne font plus qu'un»*)—a saying identified by Berthelot in a footnote as the axiom of Maria Prophetissa (or Mary the Jewess) and interpreted as meaning that "the transmutation is achieved by the successive combination of 3 or 4 metal bodies, initially distinct, but identical at the end of the operation". In a footnote of his own, Jung notes how "the almost bestial κραυγάξειν [*kraugazein*] (shriek)" points most likely to an "ecstatic condition" (Jung 1968, §209, fn. 75).[19]

In another text, "Consilium coniugii" in the *Ars chemica* (1566), the "philosophical man" is said to consist of "the four natures of the stone", three of which are earthy or in the earth, but "the fourth nature is the water of the stone, namely the viscous gold which is called red gum and with which the three earthy natures are tinted" (cited in Jung 1968, §209). This critical fourth nature is duplex (i.e. masculine and feminine), and "at the same time the one and only *aqua mercurialis*" (ibid., §209). On Jung's reading, this fourth nature leads straight to "the Anthropos idea" or the notion of human wholeness—the conception of a single being who existed before humankind and at the same time represents its goal (ibid., §210). As Jung puts it (thinking of an illustration in the "Ripley Scrowle" of the three manifestations—body, soul, and spirit—of the Anthropos during his transformation), "the one joins the three as the fourth and thus produces the synthesis of the four in a unity" (ibid., §210). (In a footnote, he cites a different formulation from the "Allegoriae sapientum" in *Theatrum chemicum*, vol. 5, representing both the quartering (*tetrameria*) of the One and the synthesis of the Four in One: "One, and it is two; two, and it is three; and three, and it is four; and four, and it is three; and three, and it is two; and two, and it is one" [Distinction XIV; cited in ibid., §210, fn. 86].)

So much for the solution for the problem of Three and Four in alchemy. The structure of the problem of Seven and Eight is said to be similar, even if this motif occurs less frequently. In Paracelsus's *Ein ander Erklärung der gantzen Astronomey* (apparently known to Goethe),[20] we read, "One is powerful, Six are subjects, the Eighth is also powerful" (*Eins ist gewaltig / Sechs seind Subiecten /das Achtet ist auch gewaltig*),[21] and Jung adds that this Eighth is somewhat more powerful than the first (cited in Jung 1968, §210). Exactly this situation of the "one" as the king and the "six" as his servants is depicted in the *Pretiosa margarita novella* (or *Precious New Pearl*) of the late mediaeval alchemist Petrus Bonus of Ferrara as King Sol and the six planets or metallic homunculi. In *this* text the Eighth does not appear, and Jung surmises that it is Paracelsus's invention. Because the Eighth is "[more] powerful" than the first, surely the crown is bestowed on him? On Jung's account, the motif of the Eighth recurs in *Faust II* in the figure of the eighth who dwells on Olympus—a "direct reference", Jung says, to the Paracelsian text, insofar as this work describes the "astrology of Olympus" (i.e. the structure of the *corpus astrale*).[22]

Next Jung quotes the exchange between the Nereids and Tritons and the Sirens, focusing on the problem of the Three and the Four (ll. 8186–8189; Goethe 2001, 232). According to Jung, it is typical of Goethe's "feeling-toned" nature that the fourth function is thinking, that is, the fourth Cabir is the thinker (Jung 1968, §204). Recalling the line, "Feeling is all" (*Gefühl ist alles*), from the scene in "Martha's Garden" in *Faust*, Part One, where Faust and Gretchen discuss religion (l. 3456), Jung argues that, if feeling is the supreme principle, then thinking has to play a less favourable role, become submerged, and disappear. On his account, this development is portrayed in *Faust I*; a development for which Goethe is said to have served as his own model. In such cases, thinking becomes the fourth (or "taboo") function, and through its contamination with the unconscious it acquires the grotesque form of the Cabiri; for, as chthonic gods, the Cabiri are correspondingly misshapen. ("I call them pot-bellied freaks of common clay", says Homunculus [ll. 8219–8220].) Thus the Cabiri stand "in grotesque contrast" to the heavenly gods, poking fun at them (much as "the devil is the ape of God" [*der Teufel ist der Affe Gottes*], as Luther once said).

This structure of the Three/Four returns in the form of the problem of Seven and Eight, as reflected in the song of the Nereids and the Tritons (ll. 8194–8205; Goethe 2001, 232). Here the problem of the Fourth repeats itself with the Eighth: we are told there are "really" (*eigentlich*) seven Cabiri, but although the Sirens confusedly (and confusingly) ask about the other three, the Nereids and Tritons insist on the eighth. Whereas the initial emphasis in the song of the Nereids and Tritons was on the "lowly origin in the dark" of the Cabiri as "unseen, creative dwarf gods, hooded and cloaked manikins [...] kept hidden in the dark *cista*" (Jung 1968, §203), now the Cabiri are relocated to Olympus, the home of the twelve gods in Greek mythology. Because they are "eternally striving from the depths to the heights", the Cabiri are always to be found "both below *and* above" (ibid., §205). In an analogous way, the "severe image" (*strenges Gebilde*) (l. 8171) on the huge shell of Chelone, a nymph transformed by Hermes into a sea tortoise (and the *testudo* or tortoise was an alchemical instrument, as Jung reminds us), represents "an unconscious content that struggles towards the light" (§205), and for this reason Jung identifies it with what elsewhere he calls the "treasure hard to attain".[23]

Jung finds confirmation of this reading in the following lines of the Sirens:

> The heroes of legend.
> Of theirs we grow weary,
> Wherever, however extolled,
> They carried off the fleece of gold,
> You, the Cabiri. (ll. 8212–8216; Goethe 2001, 232)

In Greek mythology, the Golden Fleece is a symbol of divine authority, the coveted goal of the adventure on which Jason and his crew of Argonauts embark at the behest of King Pelias or, as Jung puts it, "the perilous quest that is one of the synonyms for attaining the unattainable" (Jung 1968, §206). A few lines on, the philosopher Thales declares, "That is indeed what men most seek on earth; / 'Tis rust alone that gives the coin its worth!" (ll. 8223–8224). Jung interprets this paradoxical remark as a kind of "alchemical quip", expressing the insight that "there is no light without shadow and no psychic wholeness without imperfection" (ibid., §208). In order to achieve its rounding itself out (*Vollendung*), Jung says, life calls not for "perfection" (*Vollkommenheit*) but for "completeness" (*Vollständigkeit*), and hence there is always a need for the "thorn in the flesh": without "the suffering of defects" there can be no "progress" and no "ascent" (§208). Between them, the Cabiri and the Golden Fleece thus represent the transformative powers of the unconscious.

In a beautiful riff on a passage from the *Rosarium philosophorum* (see *Artis Auriferae*, vol. 2, 220), Jung describes the unconscious as "the fly in the ointment, the skeleton in the cupboard, the painful lie given to all idealistic pronouncements, the earthliness that clings to our human nature and sadly clouds the crystal clarity we long for" (Jung 1968, §207). In the alchemical view, however, rust is, like verdigris, "the metal's sickness", but at the same time "this leprosy is the *vera prima materia*, the basis for the preparation of the philosophical gold" (ibid., §207). Linking this excursus on *Faust II* back to the clinical material of his client's dream, Jung identifies the red-haired man in the twenty-second dream with the man with the pointed beard of the fourteenth, and both with "the shrewd Mephisto, who magically changes the scene because he is concerned with something that Faust himself never saw: namely, the 'severe image' [*"strenges Gebilde"*], which means the supreme treasure, something 'immortal' [*das "Unsterbliche"*]" (ibid., §211). There is a specifically Goethean resonance here for, in the concluding scene of *Faust II*, the angels bear Faust's "immortal part" (*"Unsterbliches"*) to heaven. (In the words of the original draft, Faust's immortal part is called his "entelechy" [*Entelechie*].) In "Paracelsus as a Spiritual Phenomenon", Jung even makes a fascinating claim for a parallel between Goethe's *Faust II* and the *Metamorphoses* or *Golden Ass* of Apuleius; in a footnote, he notes the analogies between the prayer to the Mater Gloriosa at the end of *Faust* and the prayer to Isis at the end of the *Golden Ass* (Jung 1967b, §228, fn. 19).[24] (As far as I know, the possibility of this parallel has never been pursued further.)[25]

Synchronicity

Aside from his work on alchemy, in the 1950s Jung—inspired by his friendships with Richard Wilhelm (who introduced him to ancient Chinese thought, in particular Taoism, and to the *I Ching*) and with the physicist Wolfgang Pauli (1900–1958) (thanks to whom Jung sought a connection between analytical psychology and quantum mechanics)—developed the notion of an "a-causal connecting principle" he dubbed "synchronicity".[26] Although Jung had first used the term "synchronicity" in 1930 in his memorial address for Richard Wilhelm (Jung 1966, §81–§85), a remarkable passage in his contribution to the monograph co-authored with Pauli, *Naturerklärung und Psyche* (1952), embeds his exposition of synchronicity in his discussion elsewhere of the "recalcitrant 'Fourth'" (*das widerstrebende Vierte*) and his reading of Goethe, Dorn, and Plato.

In "Synchronicity: An A-Causal Connecting Principle" Jung adds to the triad of classical physics (i.e. space, time, and causality) a fourth or supplementary factor, that is, synchronicity, turning the triad into a tetrad or *quaternio* of principles which "makes possible a whole judgment" (Jung 1969b, §961). Cross-referencing his discussion of the *Timaeus* in his essay on the dogma of the Trinity, Jung claims that synchronicity is "to the three other principles as the one-dimensionality of time is to the three-dimensionality of space", a gnomic remark which becomes no less gnomic when he compares synchronicity to "the recalcitrant 'Fourth' in the *Timaeus*, which, Plato says, can only be added 'by force' to the other three" (ibid., §962).

(The expression "by force" is used by Plato in *Timaeus* [35a] in the context of how the Demiurge takes the Same, the Other, and a mixture of them, and blends them together into one form "by forcing the Other into union with the Same", that is, τὴν θατέρου [*thateron*] φύσιν δύσμεικτον οὖσαν εἰς ταὐτὸν [*tauton*] συναρμόττων βίᾳ [Plato 1929, 65–67]. On Wolfgang Giegerich's account, Jung is so fascinated with this one minor phrase "by force" (βίᾳ = *bia*, i.e. "bodily strength", "force", "act of violence") in Plato that he gives it "a totally exaggerated significance, blowing it up to almost mythic relevance beyond the really only pragmatic, almost technical meaning it has in the doings of the demiurge" [Giegerich 2020, 117].)

"Just as", Jung continues, using his favourite device of argumentation by parallel, the introduction of time "as the fourth dimension in modern physics postulates an irrepresentable [*unanschaulichen*] space-time continuum", so the idea of synchronicity as an a-causal factor "with its inherent quality of meaning produces a picture of the world so irrepresentable as to be completely baffling [*einer zunächst beinahe verwirrenden Unanschaulichkeit*]" (Jung 1969b, §962). But by adding this factor, he concludes, a view is made possible which "includes the psychoid[27] factor in our description and knowledge of nature—that is, an *a priori*[28] meaning or 'equivalence' [*eine »Gleichartigkeit«*]" (ibid., §962).

At this point Jung explicitly links synchronicity to his discussion of Plato, Dorn, and Goethe, beginning with Maria Prophetissa. For synchronicity is held to be the answer to the "problem"—a problem which here "repeats and resolves itself" (*wiederholt und löst sich*)—that runs "like a red thread through the speculations of alchemists for fifteen hundred years [...] the so-called axiom of Maria the Jewess (or Copt)", that is, "Out of the Third comes the One as the Fourth" (ibid., §962; cf. Jung 1968, §26) (see third chapter above). "The old dream of the alchemists", Jung continues, or the "much derided idea" of "the transmutation of chemical elements", has "become a reality in our own day", and the symbolism of alchemy has acquired a fresh significance in the context of the psychology of the unconscious (Jung 1969b, §962). Now Jung recapitulates his historical gallery of examples of "the dilemma of three and four": beginning with the scenario that serves as the setting for the *Timaeus*, via Gerhard Dorn's constellation of the Christian Trinity and the *serpens quadricornutus* (or the four-horned serpent, i.e. the Devil), to the Cabiri scene in *Faust*, Part Two (ibid., §962).

But he also extends and nuances this overview: in his *De tenebris contra naturam*, Dorn protests—on the grounds that it arises from the binarius (i.e. the number 2) and is therefore "something material, feminine, and devilish"—against the "pagan" quaternary otherwise beloved of the alchemists, and this protest is read by Jung as if it were "[an] anticipation of things to come" (*in Vorahnung kommender Dinge*) and as a revival of trinitarian thinking of the kind that can also be found (as Jung believed Marie-Louise von Franz had demonstrated) in "The Parable of the Fountain" by the fifteenth-century Italian alchemist (now believed to be fictional) Bernard of Treviso; in the *Amphitheatrum sapientiae aeternae* (*Ampitheatre of Eternal Wisdom*) (Hamburg, 1595; [2]1609) of the German physician, Hermeticist, and alchemist, Heinrich Khunrath (c. 1560–1605); in the works of the German physician and alchemist who was associated with the court of Rudolf II Habsburg, Michael Maier (see below); and in the *Hydrolithus Sophicus seu Aquarium Sapientium* (*The Water Stone of*

Wisdom or the Aquarium of the Wise), sometimes attributed to Johann Ambrosius Siebmacher (1561–1611) (ibid., §962). And indeed Pauli, in his contribution to *The Interpretation of Nature and the Psyche* entitled "The Influence of Archetypal Ideas on the Scientific Theories of Kepler", examined the contrast between the doctrine of three principles and the doctrine of correspondence as reflected in the polemical exchange between the German astronomer and mathematician Johannes Kepler (1571–1630) and the English Paracelsian physician and astrologer Robert Fludd (1574–1637) (ibid., §962).

In fact, there is an important numerological aspect to Jung's theory of synchronicity, reflected in his and Pauli's attempt to discover whether, at the root of the universe, there is a number—a kind of primal number, on which the entire world hinges. For Jung and Pauli, the number 137 seemed to fulfil this function, describing the atom's fine-structure constant while also having great significance as the sum of the Hebrew letters of the word "Kabbalah".[29] Around the number 137, it seemed, medieval alchemy, the *I Ching*, dream interpretation, the occult, and modern science all circle: but there was an important historical dimension as well, which links in more directly with our concerns here.[30] For Pauli, Kepler and Fludd represented a kind of study in psychological opposing types. As a scientist, Pauli felt drawn to Kepler, whose perfect number was three, while he increasingly came to realize the legitimacy of the world-view proposed by Fludd, for whom four was "the eternal fountainhead of nature" (Pauli 1994, 271). Writing to Markus Fierz on 3 October 1951, Pauli described Kepler as a trinitarian and Fludd as a quaternarian, the "polemic" between whom "resonated" within Pauli himself as an "inner conflict" (Pauli 1996, 375). As Arthur Miller interprets this conflict, to move from three to four quantum numbers was a "momentous step", one that represented not only a break with Niels Bohr's conception of the atom as a tiny solar system, but also a step into the unknown as evoked in the following lines from Friedrich Schiller's poem, *Spruch des Konfucius* ("Saying of Confucius"), "Only fullness leads to clarity / And truth lies in the abyss" (*Nur die Fülle führt zur Klarheit / Und im Abgrund wohnt die Wahrheit*) (Miller 2009, 88; cf. Schiller 2004, 51). On this account, Kepler was able to assimilate the three-dimensionality of space to the triplicate nature of the Holy Trinity, but found himself "overwhelmed" by the quaternary nature of the mystical profundities of alchemy and its contrasting insistence on the number four (op. cit., 88; cf. Thiel 2006).

For his part, in his essay on synchronicity Jung agreed with Pauli's historical analysis, arguing that "the decision in favour of the triad, which in certain respects ran counter to the alchemical tradition, was followed by a scientific epoch that knew nothing of the *correspondentia* and clung with passionate insistence to a triadic view of the world, which continued the type of the Trinity, i.e., the world as described and explained in terms of space, time, and causality" (Jung 1969b, §962). But now, he maintained, the discovery of radioactivity had led in turn to a revolution in physics that had considerably modified its classical views. Correspondingly, he and Pauli proposed a fourfold schema to replace the classical view, consisting of a *quaternio* of (1) indestructible energy; (2) constant connection through effect (causality); (3) inconstant connection through contingene, or equivalence or "meaning" (synchronicity); and (4) space-time continuum (ibid., §963).

On this account, the so-called recalcitrant fourth can be identified with the a-causal connecting principle of synchronicity as an addition to the classical triad of space, time, and causality; in place of the Newtonian world-view, there is a quantum perspective on the world that somehow integrates uncertainty, yet also significance, into its world-view. We have, in other words, entered a view of the world described by Fritjof Capra (b. 1939) in his *The Tao of Physics: An Exploration of the Parallels Between Modern Physics and Eastern Mysticism* (1975) and applied (using holism and systems theory) to the West's scientific and economic crises in *The Turning Point: Science, Society, and the Rising Culture* (1982)—and it may seem, as a result, as if we have long left Plato way behind. Yet there is still a deep connection between synchronicity and Jung's abiding concerns regarding Plato, the *Timaeus*, and the problem of the Third and the Fourth. For, as a kind of prolegomenon to our discussion of *Mysterium coniunctionis* in the next section (see below), we might note that, in this work, Jung examined in chapter 6 (entitled "The Conjunction") the three stages of the alchemical *coniunctio* as described by Gerhard Dorn in his *De Philosophia meditativa* (*On the Meditative Philosophy*).[31]

The first stage, the *unio mentalis*, in fact begins with a "separation" or *distractio*, a kind of "voluntary death", in which the mind (*mens*) is separated from the body as a prerequisite for their subsequent reunion, because "only separated things can unite" (Jung 1970, §671). The *unio mentalis*, or the uniting of the soul and the spirit, involves "the difficult act of self-knowledge", or "the attainment of full knowledge of the heights and depths of one's own character" (ibid., §674; cf. §711). For "just as the soul is animated by the spirit", so "the soul animates the body" and "tends to favour the body and everything bodily, sensuous, and emotional"—thus "caught 'in the chains' of Physis" and "desir[ing] 'beyond physical necessity'", the soul must be "called back by the 'counsel of the spirit' from her lostness in matter and the world" (ibid., §673). The second stage, the *unio corporalis*, involves the conjoining of the *unio mentalis*, that is, the unity of spirit and soul, with the body, expressed by the striving of the adepts to "realise their speculative ideas in the form of a chemical substance which they thought was endowed with all kinds of magical powers" (ibid., §664, §677, §679; cf. §738–§758).[32]

And the third stage is the *unio mystica*, when "the unity of spirit, soul, and body is made one with the original *unus mundus*", that is to say, with "the potential world of the first day of creation, when nothing was yet *in actu*, i.e., divided into two and many, but was still one" (because "one is not a number; the first number is two, and with it multiplicity and reality begin")—a union "not with the world of multiplicity as we see it but with a potential world, the eternal Ground of all empirical being, just as the self is the ground and origin of the individual personality past, present, and future" (ibid., §664, §659, §760; cf. §759–§789). Thus, on Jung's reading of Dorn, the consummation of the *mysterium coniunctionis* resides in "the union of the alchemically produced *coelum* [i.e., heaven] with the *unus mundus*"—which is emphatically *not* "a fusion of the individual with their environment, or even their adaptation to it", but rather "a *unio mystica* with the potential world" (§767). In other words, these three stages of conjunction involve:

- the separation of the soul from the body and its union with the spirit, thus realizing an inner psychic integration;
- the union of a psyche thus integrated with the body and the world of physical reality;
- and the union of the integrated spirit, mind, and body with the world of potential as a source of all actualization. (Main 2019; cf. Main 2022)

If, as Roderick Main has argued, synchronicity relates to the second of these stages (cf. Jung 1970, §758), inasmuch as it makes psychic events "more embodied" and physical events "more ensouled" (Main 2001), it highlights why, for Jung, the second stage of conjunction, that is, the "reuniting of the *unio mentalis* with the body", should be "particularly important" (Jung 1970, §679). After all, the "reuniting of the spiritual position with the body obviously means that the insights gained should be *made real*", and this second stage therefore involves "*making a reality* of the individual who has acquired some knowledge of their paradoxical wholeness" (ibid., §679; my emphases). In other words, synchronicity touches on precisely the issue which Wolfgang Giegerich in his paper finds so problematic about Jung's treatment of Plato—the question of how to realize something that is "merely thought" (Giegerich 2020, 94–95), or the question of how to realize one's intellectual insights in the actual world, as exemplified for Jung by Plato's several (failed) attempts at intervention in the world of politics.

MYSTERIUM CONIUNCTIONIS (1955–1956)

The parallel between the problem of the Third and the Fourth as stated in the opening of Plato's *Timaeus* and as explored in the Cabiri scene in Goethe's *Faust*, which is first set up in 1940 in "On the Psychology of the Idea of the Trinity" (later "A Psychological Approach to the Dogma of the Trinity"), recurs (and in fact the two interpretative lines converge) in Jung's late, great work of 1955–1956, *Mysterium coniunctionis*. If we are to believe Jung's foreword, Jung got the idea of writing this, his last, book in 1941 when he read Kerényi's essay on the Aegean Sea Festival in *Faust* (Jung 1970, xiii). (Let us recall that, in that work, Kerényi had argued that, whatever the mysteries of the Cabiri might have been, they centred— like the mysteries at Eleusis (associated with the cult of Demeter) or those at Lycosura (said by Pausanias to be the oldest city in the world and the site of the sanctuary of the goddess Despoina, the daughter of Demeter and Poseidon)—on the mystery of birth, expressed in the Aegean Sea Festival through the marriage of Homunculus and Galatea.)

On Jung's account, the "literary prototype" of Goethe's Aegean festival was *The Chymical Wedding of Christian Rosenkreutz* (*Chymische Hochzeit Christiani Rosencreutz Anno 1459*) (1616), a work attributed to Johann Valentin Andreae (1586–1654) and often regarded as one of the great manifestos of the Fraternity of the Rose Cross (i.e. the Rosicrucians). In its turn, *The Chymical Wedding* drew on the traditional "hierogamos symbolism of alchemy" (Jung 1970, xiii). Understanding this symbolism was bound up with Jung's project (underway since 1928 and his reading of Richard Wilhelm's translation of *The Secret of the Golden Flower*) of demonstrating that the world of alchemical symbols "does not belong to the rubbish heap of the past" but rather "stands in a very real and living relationship to [...] the psychology of the unconscious" (ibid., xiii). Building on the work of the Austrian psychoanalyst Herbert Silberer (1882–1923) in his *Problems of Mysticism and its Symbolism* (1914) (ibid., xiv; cf. §792), Jung explored how the so-called spagyric art, whose method was captured in the slogan *solve et coagula* (i.e. "dissolve and coagulate"), involved a dual process of separation (or analysis) and consolidation (or synthesis). This process, Jung argued, did not simply offer a parallel to the dissociation of the personality arising from the conflict of the opposites and the subsequent search to resolve this conflict, *it was one and the same process in both cases* (ibid., xv).

The compositional structure of *Mysterium coniunctionis*, which might be thought of as analogous to a late Romantic symphony or to a string quartet, is based on a theme—the components of the alchemical transformation—and its variations (example piled upon example of how these ideas are expressed in the form of symbols, emblems, and motifs). Thus Jung considers the components of the coniunctio (the opposites, Mercurius, the significance of such symbols as the orphan, the widow, and the moon); the "paradoxa" of the arcane substance, the point, and the scintilla; the personification of the opposites in the figures of Sol, sulphur, Luna, and salt); the alchemical King and Queen (Rex and Regina); Adam and Eve (particularly the "old Adam" versus the "new"); and finally the conjunction itself (its various stages, the production of the quintessence, the psychological significance of the procedure, and the constellation of the self). In the course of chapter 3, called "The Personification of the Opposites", Jung highlights the "mystic peregrination" undertaken by Michael Maier (1568–1622) in his *Symbola aureae mensae duodecim nationum* (or *The Symbols of the Golden Table of the Twelve Nations*) (1617),[33] in which he reaches the Red (or "Erythraean") Sea by journeying in four directions: to the north (Europe), to the west (America), to the east (Asia), and finally to the south (Africa), corresponding to the elements of earth, water, air, and fire, respectively (Jung 1970, §276).

Taking these four directions and their corresponding four elements as "symbolic equivalents" of the four basic functions of consciousness (i.e. thinking, feeling, sensation, intuition), Africa functions both as the fourth and last or the "inferior" function (i.e. the darkest and the most unconscious function), and—precisely because it *is* the "inferior" function—as crucial for the attainment of "Paradise [...] the primordial image of wholeness" and "the goal of his journey" as lying in "the attainment of this wholeness" (Jung 1970, §276). (In the light of Jung's own experience in

Africa and his "unforgettable night in the desert", where he "saw the X for the first time and understood the Platonic myth" [Jung 2020, vol. 7, 227], this choice of location in Maier's work acquires a fresh significance.) On the one hand, Africa is described as "uncultivated, torrid, parched, sterile and empty"; on the other, Maier reaches Africa at a time when the astrological signs are at their most propitious: the sun is in its house, Leo, and the moon is in Cancer, the proximity of these two houses indicating "a *coniunctio Solis et Lunae*, the union of supreme opposites, and [...] the crowning of the opus and the goal of the peregrination" (Jung 1970, §276).

In other words, Maier's *Symbola aureae mensae* is a kind of alchemical journey in its own right, but for Jung the most noteworthy detail is the fact that Maier reaches the "Erythraean Sea" at precisely the moment when he has completed his journey through the three other continents and is on the point of entering the fourth, and critical, region (given that Africa is both a kind of "hell" and Paradise itself). Not surprisingly, this numerical symbolism recalls the motif of the transition from Three to Four that Jung sees thematized in the opening of Plato's *Timaeus* (17a) and in the axiom of Maria, as well as in the Cabiri scene in Goethe's *Faust II*—works which Jung here brings together in one and the same paragraph (Jung 1970, §278), thus cementing his fusion of *Psychology and Alchemy* and "A Psychological Approach to the Dogma of the Trinity".

Indeed, Jung now adds yet *another* version of the problem of the transition from Three to Four, citing an Armenian legend about Alexander the Great, according to which, after he had been born, he ran about the room, but when he came to the fourth corner an angel struck him down to show him he would conquer only three-quarters of the world; while, in a second legend, Alexander goes on to conquer three-quarters of the world, but not the fourth—which belongs to the "righteous poor" (ibid., §279, fn. 514). (This reference to Alexander, one of history's most successful military commanders, acknowledges the political dimension of the problem of the Three and the Four as reflected in Jung's discussion of Plato's political career.)

Thus Jung's claim that we come across the dilemma of Three and Four "in any number of guises" may be considered to have been amply confirmed, but the actual significance of the step from Three to Four as "an important development" is shown in Maier's *Symbola aureae mensae* where it is presaged by the vision of Paradise (Jung 1970, §279). When Maier leaves Asia and turns south to Africa, he discovers a statue of Mercury, made of silver and with a golden head. The statue is pointing to

Paradise, which Maier espies far off in the distance; as the abode of the originally androgynous Primordial Man (i.e. Adam) and because of its four rivers (i.e. Pishon, Gihon, Chidekel [the Tigris], and Phirat [the Euphrates]), Paradise or the Garden of Eden is "a symbol of totality and—from the psychological point of view—the self" (ibid., §276). Maier's reaction to reaching the region of the Red Sea, which is proverbially hot, at the end of July and hence "in the intense heat of summe", by himself becoming extremely hot, is explained by the fact he is said to be approaching a region said to be inhabited by "Pans, Satyrs, dog-headed baboons, and half men"—or in other words, what Jung calls "the animal soul in man" (ibid., §279).

This reading is substantiated for Jung by Maier's encounter with the fabulous, four-footed Ortus, a creature which combines the four alchemical colours of black, white, red, and yellow. Maier identifies the Ortus with the phoenix, the mythical bird which, "after consuming itself in the land of Egypt, each time rose renewed, like the reborn sun in Heliopolis" (ibid., §282). As well as the Ortus (or his "animal soul"), Maier discovers in the vicinity of the Red Sea a virgin or a kind of feminine soul—the (Cumaean) Sibyl, said (in Virgil's Fourth Eclogue) to have foretold the coming of Christ. Thus by the Red Sea Maier meets both his animal soul—"a monstrous quaternity, symbolizing [...] the *prima materia* of the self and, as the phoenix, rebirth", *and* the anima—"a feminine psychopomp who showed him the way to Mercurius and also how to find the phoenix" (ibid., §282).

For Jung, confirmation of this thesis is provided by its compatibility with other examples: in the case of Maier's Erythraean quadruped, the Ortus, its similarity to the four-wheeled chariot of Pseudo-Aristotle,[34] and to the tetramorph of early mediaeval iconography that combined the four winged creatures of Ezekiel's vision into a four-footed monster (Jung 1970, §285)—and across Jung's writings, innumerable other examples could be found.[35] And the same applies to a symbol closely related to the quaternity: the sphere. In his chapter in *Mysterium coniunctionis* on the alchemical King and Queen ("Rex and Regina"), Jung turned to a work by the English Augustinian canon and alchemist, George Ripley (c. 1415–1490)—his *Cantilena* (sometimes called *George Ripley's Song*), which Jung hails as "one of the most perfect parables of the renewal of the king" (ibid., §463).

The reference in stanza 9 of Ripley's *Cantilena*, which contains the line, "My Mother in a Sphaere gave birth to mee", prompts Jung to identify the "house of the sphere" with the *vas rotundum*, the alchemical vessel "whose roundness represents the cosmos and, at the same time, the world-soul" (ibid., §373). The "secret content" of this Hermetic vessel is said to be "the original chaos from which the world was created", but it is also the site of the *opus*, the place where, as "the filius Macrocosmi and the first man", the alchemical King is destined for "rotundity", that is, *wholeness*—a wholeness which he is prevented from achieving by his "original defect" (§373). In this respect, alchemy introduces a notion of imperfection which is absent from its Platonic analogue, where "the world-soul [...] surrounds the physical from outside" (§373). Yet Jung would doubtless regard the affinities between Platonic thought and the alchemical tradition as outweighing these differences.

Notes

1. Kingsley (2018, vol. 2, 493–494); citing Gemelli Marciano (2013, 231–233 and 280).
2. See, for example, Jung's account of swinging his rhinoceros whip and shouting loudly in Swiss German to bring a dance to an end during his visit to Kenya and Uganda in 1925 (Jung 1963, 300–301). For further discussion, see Burleson (2005); and Brooke (2019).
3. Leibniz, *Principles of Nature and Grace* (1714), article 7 (in Leibnitz 1890, 213).
4. See Jordan, "Plato's Task in *The Sophist*" (1984).
5. In a fascinating excursus at this point, Jung explains the difference between Presocratic and Platonic philosophy in terms of their *psychological* difference: one could say, he concludes, that "the pre-Socratic philosophy was on the objective plane", that is, it could not think of sameness, consciousness, or self-identity, but put it into the object as two opposing principles, seeing it *outside* rather than *inside* human consciousness, whereas "the Platonic philosophy [had] already arrived at the subjective plane", that is, the use of the old nature philosophy persisted in Plato *but as a myth* (Jung 1989, vol. 1, 678–679).
6. For further discussion and analysis of the *Septem Sermones*, a collection of "Gnostic" texts published privately by Jung in 1916 under the title *VII Sermones ad mortuous: Die sieben Belehrungen der Toten: Geschrieben von Basilides in Alexandria, der Stadt, wo der Osten den Westen berührt* (i.e. *Seven Sermons to the Dead, written by Basilides of Alexandria, the city where East and West meet*), see Fodor (1964), Heisig (1972), Hoeller (1982), Hubback (1986), Brenner (1990), Maillard (1993, 2017), Ribi (2013), and Greene (2018a). And for further discussion of Jung's relation to

Gnosticism, see Altizer (1959), Quispel (1968), Lesmeister (1991), Segal (1992), and Greene (2018b).
7. For further discussion of Abraxas, see Jung's comments in his *Visions* seminar on 7 June 1933 (Jung 1997, vol. 2, 1041–1042; cited in Jung 2020, vol. 5, p. 274).
8. See also Jung (1989, vol. 1, 678; 1967b, §39; 1970, §587; and so on).
9. Cf. Jung's later alignment of the *Übermensch* with the Upanishads and Tantric philosophy; with the Christian conception of the "kingdom of heaven" within oneself, and its concomitant symbolism of the self as a fortified city, as the precious pearl, as a stone, or as gold; as well as Empedocles' conception of "the all-rounded being, the *sphairos*" as "the *eudaimonéstatos theós*, the most blissful god" (Jung 1989, vol. 2, 905). Cf. Empedocles, fragment 27, "In this way it is held fast in the close covering of Harmony, a rounded Sphere, rejoicing in its pleasant rest" (Barnes 1987, 177); and fragment 28, "But he [i.e., the divine and homogeneous Sphere], from all directions equal to himself and completely boundless, rejoicing in his pleasant rest" (DK fragment B 28) (ibid., 179). For further discussion, see Hladký (2017).
10. See the note on the Codex Vadiensis 390 in St Gallen as well as *Liber, in quo discipulorum suorum prudentiores Arisleus congregavit, Pitagoram sc. Philosophum et sapientium vera*, sermon 41 and sermon 10, in Ruska's *Turba Philosophorum* (Ruska 1931, 903, 148 and 118). For further discussion of this work and its significance, see Plessner (1954).
11. See Steeb, *Coelum Sephiroticum, Hebraeorum*, chapter 1, §2 (in Steeb 1679, p. 33).
12. See 1 Peter 2: 9; St Macarius of Egypt (1921, 27, §1 and §4, 200 and 202); and Vergely (2004, 46–47).
13. Freud admitted that this was "only a theoretical speculation", albeit one that deserved "careful checking with reference to the conditions of life which obtain among animals closely related to man" (Freud 1991, 289, fn. 1); but he saw *prima facie* evidence for it in the claim that, while "'beauty' and 'attraction' are originally attributes of the sexual object [...] the genitals themselves, the sight of which is always exciting, are nevertheless hardly ever judged to be beautiful; the quality of beauty seems, instead, to attach to certain secondary sexual characters" (ibid., 271).
14. Compare with the metaphor of illumination in Plotinus and his description of an experience of pure brilliance or sheer luminosity, notably in *Enneads*, IV.9, §9 (Plotinus 1966–1988, vol. 7, 339). For further discussion, see Ahbel-Rappe 2014 (esp. 168–172 on "Plotinus' Metaphysics of Light").
15. This claim might strike one as exaggerated; perhaps Jung is closer to the mark when, in "Paracelsus as a Spiritual Phenomenon" (1942) he invites the reader to concede that the second part of *Faust* "presents only inciden-

tally and in doubtful degree an aesthetic problem, but primarily and in far greater degree a human one" (Jung 1967b, §210).
16. Rudolf Steiner, "Ein vergessenes Streben nach Geisteswissenschaft innerhalb der deutschen Gedankenentwickelung" (Berlin, 25 February 1916); in Steiner (2000, 407–457 [here: 455–456]).
17. For further discussion, see the standard work on Goethe's interest in alchemy (Gray 1952) and, more recent, Wilkerson (2019). In his lecture "Paracelsus as a Spiritual Phenomenon", Jung repeats this view that "the arcane teaching of alchemy" constitutes "an essential part of the Paracelsan spirit" and had exerted "a profound influence on Goethe"—"so much so that the impressions he gained in his Leipzig days continued to engross him even in old age: indeed, they formed the matrix for *Faust*" (Jung 1967b, §159).
18. See Berthelot (1885, 99–100).
19. Is there, Jung wonders, a link between this Maria, variously known as Maria Prophetissa, Mary the Jewess, sister of Moses, or Mary the Copt, and the Maria of Gnostic tradition, that is, Mariamne and the Mary Magdalene of the *Pistis Sophia* (Jung 1968, §209)? For the text about the "bestial shriek" uttered by Maria, see Berthelot (1888, 404; translated in Berthelot 1888, 389).
20. See Bartscherer (1911, 206). The original German of Jung's text refers in a footnote to Goethe's *Dichtung und Wahrheit*, but *Dichtung und Wahrheit* does not specifically mention this work by Paracelsus; for a general reference to Paracelsus, see Part Two, book 8 (Goethe 1955, p. 342). As Gero von Wilpert notes, Goethe's engagement with Paracelsus during a period of convalescence in 1769 followed his reading—at the instigation of Susanne von Klettenberg (1723–1774)—of the *Opus mago-cabbalisticum* by Georg von Welling (1655–1727), and one should add that it accompanied his reading of writings by the fifteenth-century alchemist Basilius Valentinus, Jan Baptist van Helmont (1580–1644), the founder of "pneumatic chemistry", and George Starkey (1628–1665), who wrote under the pseudonym Eirenaeus Philalethes. Certain Paracelsian motifs, such as the doctrine of microcosm and macrocosm, the four elementary spirits, the Earth Spirit (*Erdgeist*), and the figure of the homunculus in the retort, not to mention the father's medical campaign against the plague, seem to have influenced—not without a certain irony in their usage—Goethe's *Faust* (von Wilpert 1998, 807). For further discussion, see Sudhoff (1932), Murase (2020), Domandl (1976), and Binswanger and Smith (2000). Not surprisingly, the constellation of Paracelsus and Goethe caught the attention of the anthroposophist Rudolf Steiner, reflected in his lectures entitled "Von Paracelsus zu Goethe", given in Munich on 19 November 1911 and in Winterthur on 13 January 1912 (Steiner 2017, 491–510 and 511–539).

21. Cited by Jung from Paracelsus, *Sämtliche Werke*, ed. Karl Sudhoff and Wilhelm Matthiesen, vol. 12; here from Paracelsus (1589–1591), vol. 10, p. 451. This text continues: "And is the same as the first / And is more than the first in numerous points" (*und ist gleich dem ersten / und ist mehr dann das erst in ettlichen Puncten*).
22. Cited by Jung from Paracelsus (1589–1591), vol. 1, 530. For further discussion of Paracelsus, see Paracelsus (1979, 1999, 2008). Two of Jung's three major essays on Paracelsus, "Paracelsus" (1934) (a paper delivered under the auspices of the Literarisches Club Zürich in the house in which Paracelsus was born at Einsiedeln, Canton Schwyz), "Paracelsus the Physician" (1942) (a lecture delivered to the Schweizerische Gesellschaft für Geschichte der Medizin und der Naturwissenschaften at the annual meeting of the Naturforschende Gesellschaft in Basel), and "Paracelsus as a Spiritual Phenomenon" (1942) (a lecture delivered on the occasion of the Paracelsus celebrations in Einsiedeln) (see Jung 1966, §1–§17 and §18–43; Jung 1967b, §145–§238) are usefully collected (in German) in Jung 1942 (the "Foreword" to which is translated in Jung 1967b, 110). On the compromised political context in which Paracelsus was sometimes seen in the Thirties and Forties, see Johnson (1991) and Rudolph (2013).
23. See Jung (1968) (= *CW* 12), §155, §205, §222, §438, §442–§446 and §448; cf. Jung (1967a) (= *Symbols of Transformation*, *CW* 5), §393, §450, §510, §569 and §659.
24. For further discussion of Lucius's prayer in book 11 of *Metamorphoses*, see Keulen et al. (2015); especially Friedemann Drews, "A Platonic Reading of the Isis Book" (517–528).
25. It has been suggested that the ass's head of the figure of the Empusa in the Classical Walpurgis Night of *Faust*, Part Two (ll. 7744–7747) and the verses, "The roses on their cheeks may please, / But warn of metamorphoses" (ll. 7758–7759; Goethe 2001, 220), represent a recollection of Apuleius's *Metamorphoses* (Rüdiger 1963, 81). According to Hans Ruppert's guide to the *Goethe Bibliothek* (nos. 1359 and 1427), Goethe did not own a copy of the *Metamorphoses*, but his library did contain the *Apologia* (see Sandy 1972, 181), and Horst Rüdiger suggests that Goethe may well have known the *Metamorphoses* in translation.
26. For discussion of synchronicity in the context of Jung's engagement with Kant, see Bishop (2000); and for a discussion of how the notion of synchronicity is central to Jung's work as a critic of Western culture, see Main (2004).
27. The notion of the psychoid refers to a level in the unconscious which is entirely inaccessible to consciousness, which is neither wholly psychological nor wholly physiological, and which describes the archetype's embrace of the physiological-instinctual and the spiritual-imagistic poles (Samuels et al. 1986, 122).

28. In its Kantian sense, the term *a priori* refers to something that is prior to all experience (i.e. is transcendental) (as opposed to *a posteriori*, or based on experience, i.e. empirical).
29. In physics, the fine-structure constant (or Sommerfeld's constant), denoted by α, refers to the strength of electromagnetic interaction between elementary charged particles, expressed by this formula: $\alpha = e2/4\pi\varepsilon 0\hbar c = 0.0072973525693$.
30. For further discussion, see Pauli and Jung (2001), Gieser (2005), and Miller (2009).
31. In his letter to Wolfgang Pauli of 24 October 1853, Jung linked Dorn's work to his own and Pauli's synchronistic concerns as follows: "[GERARDUS DORNEUS] is a remarkable man in many ways. For him, the objective of the alchemical opus is, on the one hand, self-knowledge, which is at the same time knowledge of God, and on the other it is the union of the physical body with the so-called *unio mentalis*, consisting of soul and spirit, which comes about through self-knowledge. From this (third) stage of the opus there emerges, as he states, the *Unus Mundus*, the *one* world, a Platonic prior or primeval world that is also the future of the *eternal world*. [...] Oddly enough, the problem is still the same 2000-year-old one: How does one get from Three to Four?" (Pauli/Jung, 128–129). For further discussion of these stages, see Power (2017, 44–49), Stein (2019), Le Mouël (2021), and Main (2022).
32. Although Jung does not use the term *unio corporalis*, it is used by Marie-Louise von Franz in her commentary on the *Aurora consurgens* (an alchemical work attributed to Thomas Aquinas), published as the third part of *Mysterium coniunctionis* in the *Gesammelte Werke* (14/iii); see von Franz (1978, §505). For clarification of Jung's use of these terms, I am grateful to Roderick Maine.
33. The title page of the *Symbola Aureae Mensae duodecim nationum* shows a golden table (Aurea Mensa), around which alchemists from twelve nations are seated: Hermes Trismegistos and Maria the Egyptian preside over Democritus, Morienus, Avicenna, Albertus Magnus, Arnaldus de Villa Nova, Thomas Aquinas, Ramon Llull, Roger Bacon, Melchior Cibinensis, and an anonymous Sarmatian (an inhabitant of a region north of the Black Sea, now part of Poland and southern Russia).
34. "Take the serpent, and place it on the chariot with four heels, and let it be turned about on the earth until it is immersed in the depths of the sea, and nothing more is visible but the blackest dead sea" (*Tractatus Aristotelis*, in *Theatrum chemicum*, vol. 5, p. 885; cited in Jung 1968, §469).
35. In his seminar on Nietzsche's *Zarathustra*, Jung remarks that "it is an archaic truth that the essential thing consists of four", tracing the notion that "the living unit consisted of four" back to "the dawn of time": he

refers to Pythagoras, and to the notion in medieval philosophy that the self consists of four elements, that is, earth, water, fire, and air, or the four kinds of temperament, which he links to his own notion of the four psychological functions (Jung 1989, vol. 1, 422).

BIBLIOGRAPHY

Ahbel-Rappe, Sara. 2014. Metaphysics: The Origin of Becoming and the Resolution of Ignorance. In *The Routledge Handbook of Neoplatonism*, ed. Pauliina Remes and Svetla Slaveva-Griffin, 166–181. London and New York: Routledge.
Altizer, Thomas J.J. 1959. Science and Gnosis in Jung's Psychology. *The Centennial Review of Arts and Science* 3 (3): 304–320.
Barnes, Jonathan. 1987. *Early Greek Philosophy*. Harmondsworth: Penguin.
Bartscherer, Agnes. 1911. *Paracelsus, Paracelsisten und Goethes "Faust": Eine Quellenstudie*. Dortmund: F.W. Ruhfus.
Berthelot, Marcellin. 1885. *Origines de l'alchimie*. Paris: G. Steinheil.
———. 1888. *Collection des anciens alchemistes grecs, Vol. 3*. Paris: Steintheil.
Binswanger, H.C., and K.R. Smith. 2000. Paracelsus and Goethe: Founding Fathers of Environmental Health. *Bulletin of the World Health Organization* 78 (9): 1162–1164.
Bishop, Paul. 2000. *Synchronicity and Intellectual Intuition in Kant, Swedenborg, and Jung* [Problems in Contemporary Philosophy, Vol. 46]. Lewiston: E. Mellen.
Brenner, E.M. 1990. Gnosticism and Psychology: Jung's *Septem Sermones ad Mortuos*. *Journal of Analytical Psychology* 35: 397–419.
Brooke, Roger. 2019. Jung's Fantasies of Africa and Africa's Healing of Analytical Psychology. *International Journal of Jungian Studies* 11: 140–159.
Burleson, Blake W. 2005. *Jung in Africa*. London: Continuum.
Cornford, Francis MacDonald. 1997. *Plato's Cosmology: The "Timaeus" of Plato* [1935]. Indianapolis, IN: Hackett.
Domandl, Sepp. 1976. Goethe als Paracelsuskenner: Zwei neue Belege. *Jahrbuch des Wiener Goethe-Vereins* 80: 41–48.
Fischer, Thomas. 2011. The Alchemical Rare Book Collection of C.G. Jung. *International Journal of Jungian Studies* 3 (2): 169–180.
Fodor, Nandor. 1964. Jung's Sermons to the Dead. *The Psychoanalytic Review* 51: 74–78.
Franz, Marie-Louise von. 1978. *Mysterium Coniunctionis: Untersuchung über die Trennung und Zusammensetzung der seelischen Gegensätze in der Alchmie: Ergänzungsband «Aurora Consurgens»: Ein dem Thomas von Aquin zugeschriebenes Dokument der alchemistichen Gegensatzproblematik*. Olten and Freiburg im Breisgau: Walter-Verlag.

Freud, Sigmund. 1979. *Case Histories II* [*Pelican Freud Library*, Vol. 9]. Trans. under James Strachey, ed. by Angela Richards. Harmondsworth: Penguin.
———. 1991. *Civilization, Society and Religion* [*Penguin Freud Library*, Vol. 12]. Ed. under James Strachey, ed. by Albert Dickson. Harmondsworth: Penguin.
Gemelli Marciano, M. Laura et al. 2013. *Parmenide: Suoni, Immagini, Esperienza.* Sankt Augustin: Academia Verlag.
Giegerich, Wolfgang. 2020. *"Dreaming the Myth Onwards": C.G. Jung on Christianity and on Hegel: Part 2 of "The Flight into the Unconscious"* [*Collected English Papers*, Vol. 6] [2013]. London and New York: Routledge.
Gieser, Suzanne. 2005. *The Innermost Kernel: Depth Psychology and Quantum Physics: Wolfgang Pauli's Dialogue with C.G. Jung.* Berlin and Heidelberg: Springer Verlag.
Goethe, Johann Wolfgang. 1955. *Werke.* Ed. Erich Trunz, Vol. 9, *Autobiographische Schriften: Erster Band.* Hamburg: Wegner.
———. 2001. *Faust: A Tragedy.* Ed. by Cyrus Hamlin, trans. by Walter Arndt. 2nd ed. New York and London: Norton.
Gray, Ronald D. 1952. *Goethe the Alchemist: A Study of Alchemical Symbolism in Goethe's Literary and Scientific Works.* Cambridge: Cambridge University Press.
Greene, Liz. 2018a. *Jung's Studies in Astrology: Prophecy. Magic, and the Qualities of Time.* London and New York: Routledge.
———. 2018b. *The Astrological World of Jung's "Liber Novus": Daimons, Gods, and the Planetary Journey.* London and New York: Routledge.
Heidegger, Martin. 1959. *Introduction to Metaphysics.* Trans. by Ralph Manheim. New Haven and London: Yale University Press.
Heisig, James W. 1972. The VII Sermones: Play and Theory. *Spring*: 206–218.
Hladký, Vojtěch. 2017. Empedocles' Sphairos. *Rhizomata: A Journal for Ancient Philosophy and Science* 5 (1): 1–24.
Hoeller, Stephan A. 1982. *The Gnostic Jung and the Seven Sermons to the Dead.* Wheaton, IL: Theosophical Publishing House.
Hubback, Judith. 1986. VII Sermones ad mortuos. *Journal of Analytical Psychology* 11 (2): 95–112.
Johnson, Sheila. 1991. Ideological Ambiguity in G.W. Pabst's 'Paracelsus' (1943). *Monatshefte* 83 (2): 104–126.
Jordan, R.W. 1984. Plato's Task in the Sophist. *The Classical Quarterly* 34 (1): 113–129.
Jung, C.G. 1928. *Contributions to Analytical Psychology.* Trans. by H.G. and Cary F. Baynes. London: Kegan Paul, Trench, Trubner.
———. 1948. Versuch zu einer psychologischen Deutung des Trinitätsdogmas. In *Symbolik des Geistes: Studien über psychische Phänomenologie*, 321–446. Zurich: Rascher.
———. 1952. Religion and Psychology: A Reply to Martin Buber. *CW* 18, §663–§670.

———. 1954. *The Development of Personality*. Trans. by R.F.C. Hull = *Collected Works*, Vol. 17. London and Henley: Routledge & Kegan Paul.
———. 1963. *Memories, Dreams, Reflections*. Ed. by Aniela Jaffé. Trans. by Richard and Clara Winston. London: Collins; Routledge & Kegan Paul.
———. 1966. *The Spirit in Man, Art, and Literature*. Trans. by R.F.C. Hull = *Collected Works*, Vol. 15. London: Routledge & Kegan Paul.
———. 1967a. *Symbols of Transformation: An Analysis of the Prelude to a Case of Schizophrenia*. Trans. by R.F.C. Hull = *Collected Works*, Vol. 5, 2nd ed. Princeton, NJ: Princeton University Press.
———. 1967b. *Alchemical Studies*. Trans. by R.F.C. Hull = *Collected Works*, Vol. 13. Princeton, NJ: Princeton University Press.
———. 1968. *Psychology and Alchemy*. Trans. by R.F.C. Hull = *Collected Works*, Vol. 12, 2nd ed. London: Routledge.
———. 1969a. *Psychology and Religion: West and East*. Trans. by R.F.C. Hull = *Collected Works*, Vol. 11, 2nd ed. London: Routledge & Kegan Paul.
———. 1969b. *The Structure and Dynamics of the Psyche*. Trans. by R.F.C. Hull. *Collected Works*, Vol. 8, 2nd ed. Princeton, NJ: Princeton University Press.
———. 1970. *Mysterium coniunctionis: An Inquiry into the Separation and Synthesis of Psychic Opposites in Alchemy*. Trans. by R.F.C. Hull = *Collected Works*, Vol. 14, 2nd ed.. Princeton, NJ: Princeton University Press.
———. 1989. *Nietzsche's "Zarathustra": Notes of the Seminar Given in 1934–1939*. Ed. by James L. Jarrett, 2 vols. London: Routledge.
———. 1997. *Visions: Notes of the Seminar Given in 1930–1934*. Ed. by Claire Douglas, 2 vols. Princeton, NJ: Princeton University Press.
———. 2012. *The Red Book: Liber Novus* [Reader's Edition]. Ed. by Sonu Shamdasani, trans. by Mark Kyburz, John Peck, and Sonu Shamdasani. New York and London: Norton.
———. 2020. *The Black Books, 1813–1932: Notebooks of Transformation*. Ed. by Sonu Shamdasani, trans. by Martin Liebscher, John Peck, Sonu Shamdasani, 7 vols. New York and London: Norton.
Kern, Otto, ed. 1972. *Orphicorum fragmenta* [1922]. Berlin: Weidmann.
Keulen, W.H., S. Tilg, L. Nicolini, L. Graverini, S.J. Harrison, S. Panayotakis, and D. van Mal-Maeder. 2015. *Apuleius Madaurensis Metamorphoses, Book XI, The Isis Book: Text, Introduction and Commentary*. Leiden: Brill.
Kingsley, Peter. 2018. *Catafalque: Carl Jung and the End of Humanity*, 2 vols. London: Catafalque Press.
Le Mouël, Christophe. 2021. Experiencing the Unus Mundus. *Psychological Perspectives* 64 (4): 437–442.
Leibniz, Gottfried Wilhelm. 1890. *The Philosophical Works of Leibnitz*. Trans. by George Martin Duncan. New Haven: Tuttle, Morehouse & Taylor.
Lesmeister, Roman. 1991. Die Gnosis als unbewältigte esoterische Erbe der Analytischen Psychologie C.G. Jungs. *Analytische Psychologie* 22: 191–208.

Ljunggren, Magnus. 1994. *The Russian Mephisto: A Study of the Life and Work of Emilii Medtner*. Stockholm: Almqvist & Wiksell.

Macarius of Egypt, St. 1921. *Fifty Spiritual Homilies of Saint Macarius the Egyptian*. Trans. by A.J. Mason. London: SPCK.

Maillard, Christine. 1993. *Les sept sermons aux morts de Carl Gustav Jung: du Plérome à l'Étoile*. Nancy: Presses universitaires de Nancy.

———. 2017. *Au cœur du Livre Rouge: Les Sept Sermons aux morts: Aux sources de la pensée de C. G. Jung*. Paris: Éditions Imago.

Main, Roderick. 2001. *Putting the Sinn Back into Synchronicity: Some Spiritual Implications of Synchronistic Experiences*. RERC Second Series Occasional Papers, no. 28. https://repository.uwtsd.ac.uk/id/eprint/423/

———. 2004. *The Rupture of Time: Synchronicity and Jung's Critique of Modern Western Culture*. Hover and New York: Brunner-Routledge.

———. 2019. *Synchronicity and Holism*, 59–74. Hors série: *Revue de Psychologie Analytique*.

Main, Roderick. 2022. *Breaking the Spell of Disenchantment: Mystery, Meaning, and Metaphysics in the Work of C.G. Jung* [The Zürich Lecture Series, vol. 8]. Asheville, NC: Chiron.

Miller, Arthur I. 2009. *Deciphering the Cosmic Number: The Strange Friendship of Wolfgang Pauli and Carl Jung*. New York and London: Norton.

Murase, Amadeo. 2020. The Homunculus and the Paracelsian *Liber de imaginibus*. *Ambix* 67 (1): 47–61.

Paracelsus. 1589–1591. *Bücher und Schrifften, des Edlen, Hochgelehrten und Bewehrten Philosophi und Medici, Philippi Theophrasti Bombast von Hohenheim, Paracelsi genannt*. Ed. by Johannes Huser, 10 vols. Basel: Waldkirch.

———. 1979. *Selected Writings*. Ed. by Jolande Jacobi [1951]. Princeton, NJ: Princeton University Press.

———. 1999. *Essential Readings*. Ed. and trans. by Nicholas Goodrick-Clarke. Berkeley, CA: North Atlantic Books.

Paracelsus (Theophrastus Bombastus von Hohenheim, 1493–1541). 2008. *Essential Theoretical Writings*. Ed. and trans. by Andrew Weeks. Leiden and Boston: Brill.

Pauli, Wolfgang. 1994. *Writings on Physics and Philosophy*. Ed. by Charles P. Enz and Karl von Meyenn, trans. by Robert Schlapp. Berlin: Springer-Verlag.

———. 1996. *Wissenschaftlicher Briefwechsel mit Bohr, Einstein, Heisenberg u.a., Vol. 4, Part 1, 1950–1952*. Ed. by Karl von Meyenn. Berlin, Heidelberg, New York: Springer-Verlag.

Pauli, Wolfgang, and C.G. Jung. 2001. *Atom and Archetype: The Pauli/Jung Letters, 1932–1958*. Ed. by C.A. Meier, trans. by David Roscoe. Princeton, NJ: Princeton University Press.

Plato. 1929. *Plato with an English Translation, Vol. 7, Timaeus; Critias; Cleitophon; Menexenus; Epistles.* Trans. by R.G. Bury. London; New York: Heinemann; Putnam.

Plessner, M. 1954. The Place of the *Turba Philosophorum* in the Development of Alchemy. *Isis* 45 (4): 331–338.

Plotinus. 1966–1988. *Works.* Trans. by A.H. Armstrong. 7 vols. Cambridge, MA, and London: Harvard University Press; Heinemann.

Power, Pamela. 2017. 'The Psychological Difference' in Jung's Mysterium Coniunctionis. In *Psychology as the Discipline of Interiority: 'The Psychological Difference' in the Work of Wolfgang Giegerich*, ed. Jennifer M. Sandoval and John C. Knapp, 43–54. London and New York: Routledge.

Quispel, Gilles. 1968. C.G. Jung und die Gnosis. *Eranos-Jahrbuch* 37: 277–298.

Ribi, Alfred. 2013. *The Search for Roots: C.G. Jung and the Tradition of Gnosis.* Los Angeles and Salt Lake City: Gnosis Archive Books.

Rüdiger, Horst. 1963. Curiositas und Magie: Apuleius und Lucius als literarische Archetypen der Faust-Gestalt. In *Wort und Text: Festschrift für Fritz Schalk*, ed. Harri Maier and Hans Sckommodau, 57–82. Frankfurt am Main: Klostermann.

Rudolph, Hartmut. 2013. Zum Paracelsusbild im Nationalsozialismus, vornehmlich bei Erwin Metzke. In *Die Wiederkehr der Renaissance im 19. und 20. Jahrhundert / The Revival of the Renaissance in the Nineteenth and Twentieth Centuries*, ed. Helmut Koopmann and Frank Baron, 115–136. Münster: Mentis.

Ruska, Julius. 1931. *Turba Philosophorum: Ein Beitrag zur Geschichte der Alchemie* [Quellen und Studien zur Geschichte der Naturwissenschaften und der Medizin, Vol. 1] (Berlin and Heidelberg: Springer-Verlag).

Samuels, Andrew, Bani Shorter, and Fred Plaut. 1986. *A Critical Dictionary of Jungian Analysis.* London and New York: Routledge.

Sandy, G. 1972. Knowledge and Curiosity in Apuleius' *Metamorphoses. Latomus* 31 (1): 179–183.

Schiller, Friedrich. 2004. *Sämtliche Gedichte und Balladen.* Ed. by Georg Kurscheidt. Frankfurt am Main and Leipzig: Insel.

Segal, Robert A., ed. 1992. *The Gnostic Jung*, 1992. Princeton, NJ: Princeton University Press.

Shamdasani, Sonu. 2012. *C.G. Jung: A Biography in Books.* New York and London: Norton.

Steeb, Johann Christoph. 1679. *Coelum Sephiroticum, Hebraeorum.* Mainz: Sumptibus Ludovicii Bourgeat, typis Christophori Küchleri.

Stein, Murray. 2019. Psychological Individuation and Spiritual Enlightenment: Some Comparisons and Points of Contact. *Journal of Analytical Psychology* 64 (1): 6–22.

Steiner, Rudolf. 2000. *Aus dem mitteleuropäischen Geistesleben: Fünfzehn öffentliche Vorträge gehalten zwischen dem 2. Dezember und dem 15. April 1916 im Architektenhaus zu Berlin.* Dornach: Rudolf Steiner Verlag.

———. 2017. *Goethe und die Gegenwart: Fünfunddreißig Vorträge in verschiedenen Städten 1889–1912*. Ed. by Monika Philippi. Basel: Rudolf Steiner Verlag.
Sudhoff, Karl. 1932. Paracelsus und Goethe. *Die medizinische Welt* 6: 1409–1412.
Thiel, Bernward. 2006. Von der Drei zur Vier: Individuationsprozeß und Naturerkenntnis bei Wolfgang Pauli. In *Wegmarken der Individuation*, ed. Thomas Arzt and Axel Holm, 51–82. Würzburg: Königshausen & Neumann.
Vergely, Bertrand. 2004. *La Foi, ou la nostalgie de l'admirable*. Paris: Albin Michel.
Wilkerson, Stephen Y. 2019. *A Most Mysterious Union: The Role of Alchemy in Goethe's "Faust"*. Asheville, NC: Chiron Publications.
Wilpert, Gero von. 1998. *Goethe-Lexikon*. Stuttgart: Kröner.

CHAPTER 5

Conclusion

Abstract This brief concluding chapter argues that the reason why the Third must become the Fourth is because, within the terms of Jung's Platonic-cum-alchemical discourse, in this way it can achieve the quaternity, and thereby a geometrical approximation to the circle which is, in turn, the symbol of wholeness or perfection. For Jung, the significance of the so-called Platonic Riddles lay in their paradoxical combination of humour and seriousness; since "only the paradox comes anywhere near to comprehending the fulness of life". In the end, Jung's Platonism is equally paradoxical: characterized by a tension between shying away from metaphysical assumptions and restating them in terms of psychology. Thus the insistence that the Third become the Fourth exemplifies his translation of Plato's cosmology in the *Timaeus* into the terms of his *own* psychology, and it is in the clinical or therapeutic justification for this move that Jung is perhaps most eminently a disciple of Plato.

Keywords Platonic Riddles • Enigma of Bologna • Sir James Jeans • Allegory of the cave • Martin Buber

Within the terms of Jung's Platonic-cum-alchemical discourse, the Third must become the Fourth, because in this way it achieves the quaternity, a geometrical approximation to the circle which is, in turn, the symbol of wholeness or perfection. The sheer range of cultural references in Jung's

© The Author(s), under exclusive license to Springer Nature Switzerland AG 2022
P. Bishop, *Reading Plato through Jung*,
https://doi.org/10.1007/978-3-031-16812-3_5

prosecution of this case remains astonishing: if the collective unconscious is, as Shamdasani has suggested, "the library within" (Shamdasani 2012, 49), then Jung's *Collected Works* must surely be the "library without"! Yet aside from Jung's repeated references to the *Timaeus*, there is another side to his engagement with Plato.

In the second chapter of *Mysterium coniunctionis*, called "The Paradoxa", Jung cites one of the "Platonic riddles" which is mentioned in Maier's *Symbola aureae mensae duodecim nationum* (or *The Symbols of the Golden Table of the Twelve Nations*) (1617). In the scholium to Plato's *Republic*, this riddle runs as follows: "A man that was not a man, seeing yet not seeing, in a tree that was not a tree, smote but did not smite with a stone that was not a stone a bird that was not a bird, sitting yet not sitting" (cited Jung 1970, §90). The solution, alluded to by Glaucon in book 5 of the *Republic* (479b–c), is: a one-eyed eunuch grazed with a pumice stone a bat hanging from a bush! (In Greek, the word *bolē* can mean both "throwing" and "hitting the mark" [Bloom ed., 461].) Like the so-called Epigram of the Hermaphrodite attributed to Mathieu de Vendôme, or the Aelia-Laelia-Crispis Inscription known as the Enigma of Bologna (see Jung 1970, §51–§88),[1] this text is a joke—but it is, to borrow the expression employed by Goethe about his *Faust*, a "serious joke" (*diese sehr ernsten Scherze*). Yet if the alchemists took the Enigma of Bologna (although probably not the Epigram of the Hermaphrodite or the Platonic Riddle) seriously, they were (Jung believed) right to do so: first, because there is "something serious in every joke"; and second, because "paradox is the natural medium for expressing transconscious facts" (ibid., §90).

For Jung, paradox remained a valuable tool: because "non-ambiguity and non-contradiction are one-sided and thus unsuited to express the incomprehensible", whereas "only the paradox comes anywhere near to comprehending the fulness of life" (Jung 1968, §18). This fulness is reflected in the fact that "empirical reality has a transcendental background"—an insight expressed by the physicist and popularizer of science, Sir James Jeans (1877–1946), in *The Mysterious Universe* (1930), with reference to Plato's parable of the cave—[2] the allegory told by Socrates at the beginning of book 7 in the *Republic* (514a–519d), and related to the preceding analogies in book 6 of the sun (507b–509c) and of the divided line (509d–511e).[3] Seen in this light, Jung regards microphysics and analytical psychology alike as a means of finding a way out of the cave—and into a way of understanding that the universe is something "as much physical as psychic and therefore neither"—"a third thing, a neutral nature which can at most be grasped in hints since in essence it is transcendental" (Jung 1970, §768).

In a lecture originally given in Zurich to the Gesellschaft für deutsche Sprache und Literatur in May 1922 entitled "On the Relation of Analytical Psychology to Poetic Art", Jung drew a distinction between Freud's understanding of the symbol—which, Jung argued, was more akin to a *sign* or a *symptom*—and his own, according to which the symbol should be understood as "the expression of an intuitive perception which can as yet, neither be apprehended better, nor expressed differently" (Jung 1928, 232). On this account, Plato's expression of the whole problem of the theory of cognition in the allegory of the cave was akin to Christ's parables about the Kingdom of Heaven: both were "genuine and true symbols; namely, attempts to express a thing, for which there exists as yet no adequate verbal concept" (ibid., 232).

When Freud or rather those who followed him—such as Norman O. Brown (1913–2002) who, in acknowledgement of Melanie Klein's notion of the mother's womb as a cave to which the child and the regressing adult wish to return, wrote in *Love's Body* (1966) that "we are still unborn; we are still in a cave; Plato's cave" (Brown 1990, 37)—are tempted to read the allegory of the cave in a typically Freudian way, they fall short in Jung's view of understanding what the cave parable really means: "If we were to interpret Plato's metaphor in the manner of Freud we should naturally come to the uterus, and we should have proved that even the mind of Plato was deeply stuck in the primeval levels of 'infantile sexuality.' But in doing so", he continued, "we should also remain in total ignorance of what Plato actually created from the primitive antecedents of his philosophical intuition; we should, in fact, carelessly have overlooked his most essential product, merely to discover that he had 'infantile' phantasies like every other mortal" (Jung 1928, 232). "Such a conclusion could possess value only for the man who regards Plato as a super-human being, and who is therefore able to find a certain satisfaction in the fact that even Plato was also a man", he added, asking: "But who would want to regard Plato as a god? Surely only a man who is afflicted by the tyranny of infantile phantasies, in other words, a neurotic mentality. For such an one the reduction to universal human truths is profitable on medical grounds. *But this would have nothing whatever to do with the meaning of the Platonic parable*" (ibid., 232; my emphasis).

Yet in his later years Jung seems less interested in this *symbolic* dimension and insists instead on reading the allegory of the cave in an almost entirely non-metaphysical way! In his two letters to Bernhard Lang in 1957, responding to his correspondent's questions about the controversy between Jung and the Austrian-Israeli philosopher Martin Buber (1878–1965) over Jung's alleged Gnosticism,[4] Jung firmly aligned himself in the first letter with Kant—"It is a thoroughly outmoded standpoint, and has been so ever since the time of Kant, to think that it lies within the power of man to assert a metaphysical truth", for "this is and remains the prerogative of belief", which "in turn is a psychological fact, though it is far from being a proof" (Jung 1973–1975, vol. 2, 368)—and in the second doubled down on this position by aligning himself with Plato: "What I assert is not belief but knowledge, not of God himself but of the facts of the psyche. Apparently they are totally unknown to Buber, even though Plato has expounded this whole problem with unsurpassable clarity in his parable of the cave" (ibid., vol. 2, 372).

As we have seen, however, in the course of this study, Jung's Platonism is itself paradoxical: characterized by a tension between, on the hand, apparently shying away from metaphysical assumptions and, on the other, restating them in terms of psychology. Thus the insistence that the Third become the Fourth exemplifies his translation of Plato's cosmology in the *Timaeus* into the terms of his *own* system of analytical psychology, and the justification for this move is said to be clinical or therapeutic. In this respect, however, Jung is eminently a disciple of Plato: for just as the ascent of the soul from lower to higher levels of Being is enabled through its ascent from lower to higher levels of Knowing (i.e. *eikasia, pistis, dianoia*, and finally *noesis*), and hence is essentially experiential, so the constellation within the individual undergoing analysis of the archetype of the self—including the change of the Third into the Fourth—is something not simply intellectually *known*, but existentially *lived out*. Hence Diotima tells Socrates (as he recalls in the *Symposium*), "the right way to approach the things of love, or to be led there by another, is [....] to mount for that beauty's sake ever upwards, as if by a flight of steps" and "come at last to that perfect learning which is the learning solely of that beauty itself, and [...] know at last that which is the perfection of beauty"—"there in life and there alone, my dear Socrates, is life worth living" (211c–d; Plato 1956, 105–106).

Notes

1. For a juxtaposition of Jung's use of the Enigma of Bologna with Jacques Lacan's reading of Edgar Allan Poe's short story, "The Purloined Letter" (1845), see Gardner 2008; and with Jung's essays on "Flying Saucers" and "Synchronicity", see Gardner 2013, 75–87. Jung himself described the epitaph as "sheer nonsense, a joke" (*ein völliger Unsinn, eine scherzhafte Erfindung*), but as one that had "for centuries brilliantly fulfilled its function as a flypaper [*als Mausefalle*] for every conceivable projection", and hence served as "a paradigm for that peculiar attitude of mind which made uit possible for individuals of the Middle Ages to write hundreds of treatises about something that did not exist and was therefore completely unknowable" (Jung 1970, §52)!
2. In the final chapter entitled "Into the Deep Waters", Jeans wrote: "To speak in terms of Plato's well-known simile, we are still imprisoned in our cave, with our backs to the light, and can only watch the shadows on the wall. At present the only task immediately before science is to study these shadows, to classify them and explain them in the simplest possible way. And what we are finding, in a whole torrent of surprising new knowledge, is that the way which explains them more clearly, more fully and more naturally than any other is the mathematical way, the explanation in terms of mathematical concepts" (Jeans 1931, 111). In his major theoretical statement "On the Nature of the Psyche" (1947; 1954), Jung had earlier included a reference to this passage, in effect rewriting Plato's allegory when he interprets Sir Jeans as saying that "the shadows on the wall of Plato's cave are just as real as the invisible figures that cast them and whose existence can only be inferred mathematically" (Jung 1969, §416).
3. The perennial nature of the problems involved in the allegory of the cave is discussed in Herman (2013) and Bishop (2019), while the persistence (or indeed increase) of interest in the twentieth century is exemplified by the study, *Höhlenausgänge* (or *Exits from the Cave*), published in 1989 by Hans Blumenberg (1920–1996), which includes a brief discussion of Jung (Blumenberg 1996, 692–696).
4. For this controversy, see *Eclipse of God* (1952), republished as Buber (2016); and Jung's "Religion and Psychology: A Reply to Martin Buber" (1952; 1976, §1499–§1513). For discussion of the continuing resonance of this controversy within the analytical psychological community, see Stephens (2001); and Dourley et al. (2002).

Bibliography

Bishop, Paul. 2019. *German Political Thought and the Discourse of Platonism: Finding the Way Out of the Cave*. Cham: Palgrave Macmillan.

Blumenberg, Hans. 1996. *Höhlenausgänge*. Frankfurt am Main: Suhrkamp.

Brown, Norman O. 1990. *Love's Body* [1966]. Berkeley, Los Angeles, and London: University of California Press.

Buber, Martin. 2016. *Eclipse of God: Studies in the Relation between Religion and Philosophy*. Princeton, NJ, and Oxford: Princeton University Press.

Dourley, John, Warren Colman, David Tresan, and Barbara Stephens. 2002. Responses. *Journal of Analytical Psychology* 47 (3): 479–502.

Gardner, Leslie. 2008. Writing about Nothing. In *Psyche and the Arts: Jungian Approaches to Music, Architecture, Literature, Painting and Film*, ed. Susan Rowland, 139–147. London and New York: Routledge.

———. 2013. *Rhetorical Investigations: G.B. Vico and C.G. Jung*. London and New York: Routledge.

Herman, Arthur. 2013. *The Cave and the Light: Plato Versus Aristotle, and the Struggle for the Soul of Western Civilization*. New York: Random House.

Jeans, Sir James. 1931. *The Mysterious Universe*. Cambridge: Cambridge University Press.

Jung, C.G. 1928. *Contributions to Analytical Psychology*. Trans. by H.G. and Cary F. Baynes. London: Kegan Paul, Trench, Trubner.

———. 1952. Religion and Psychology: A Reply to Martin Buber. *CW* 18, §663–§670.

———. 1954. *The Development of Personality*. Trans. by R.F.C. Hull = *Collected Works*, Vol. 17. London and Henley: Routledge & Kegan Paul.

———. 1968. *Psychology and Alchemy*. Trans. by R.F.C. Hull = *Collected Works*, Vol. 12, 2nd ed. London: Routledge.

———. 1969. *The Structure and Dynamics of the Psyche*. Trans. by R.F.C. Hull. *Collected Works*, Vol. 8, 2nd ed. Princeton, NJ: Princeton University Press.

———. 1970. *Mysterium coniunctionis: An Inquiry into the Separation and Synthesis of Psychic Opposites in Alchemy*. Trans. by R.F.C. Hull = *Collected Works*, Vol. 14, 2nd ed.. Princeton, NJ: Princeton University Press.

———. 1973–1975. *Letters*. Ed. by Gerhard Adler and Aniela Jaffé, trans. by R.F.C. Hull, 2 vols. Princeton, NJ: Princeton University Press.

———. 1976. *The Symbolic Life: Miscellaneous Writings*. Trans. by R.F.C. Hull = *Collected Works*, Vol. 18. Princeton, NJ: Princeton University Press.

Plato. 1956. *Great Dialogues of Plato*. Trans. by W.H.D. Rouse, ed. by Eric H. Warmington and Philip G. Rouse. New York and Toronto: New American Library.

Shamdasani, Sonu. 2012. *C.G. Jung: A Biography in Books*. New York and London: Norton.
Stephens, Barbara D. 2001. The Martin Buber-Carl Jung Disputations: Protecting the Sacred in the Battle for the Boundaries of Analytical Psychology. *Journal of Analytical Psychology* 46 (3): 455–491.

BIBLIOGRAPHY

Adler, Gerhard. 1961. *The Living Symbol: A Case Study in the Process of Individuation*. New York: Pantheon.
Adler, Donna M. Altimari. 2019. *Plato's "Timaeus" and the Missing Fourth Guest: Finding the Harmony of the Spheres*. Leiden and Boston: Brill.
Ahbel-Rappe, Sara. 2014. Metaphysics: The Origin of Becoming and the Resolution of Ignorance. In *The Routledge Handbook of Neoplatonism*, ed. Pauliina Remes and Svetla Slaveva-Griffin, 166–181. London and New York: Routledge.
Altizer, Thomas J.J. 1959. Science and Gnosis in Jung's Psychology. *The Centennial Review of Arts and Science* 3 (3): 304–320.
Altman, William H.F. 2010. The Reading Order of Plato's Dialogues. *Phoenix* 64 (1/2): 18–51.
———. 2013. The Missing Speech of the Absent Fourth: Reader Response and Plato's *Timaeus-Critias*. *Plato Journal* 13: 7–26.
———. 2016. *The Guardians in Action: Plato the Teacher and the Post-"Republic" Dialogues from "Timaeus" to "Theatetus"*. Lanham, ML: Lexington Books.
Anderson, Warren. 1980. Plato. In *The New Grove Dictionary of Music and Musicians*, ed. Stanley Sadie, vol. 14, 853–857. London, New York, Hong Kong: Macmillan.
Aristotle. 1984. *The Complete Works of Aristotle*. Ed. by Jonathan Barnes, 2 vols. Princeton, NJ: Princeton University Press.
Ballew, Lynne. 1974. Straight and Circular in Parmenides and the 'Timaeus'. *Phronesis* 19 (3): 189–209.
Barnes, Jonathan. 1987. *Early Greek Philosophy*. Harmondsworth: Penguin.

Bartscherer, Agnes. 1911. *Paracelsus, Paracelsisten und Goethes "Faust": Eine Quellenstudie*. Dortmund: F.W. Ruhfus.
Baynes, H.G. 1969. *Mythology of the Soul; A Research into the Unconscious from Schizophrenic Dreams and Drawings*. London: Ryder.
Benjamin, Jessica. 2004. Beyond Doer and Done To: An Intersubjective View of Thirdness. *The Psychoanalytic Quarterly* 73 (1): 5–46.
———. 2005. From Many into One: Attention, Energy, and the Containing of Multitudes. *Psychoanalytic Dialogues* 15 (2): 185–201.
Bernadete, Seth. 1993. *The Tragedy and Comedy of Life: Plato's "Philebus"*. Chicago and London: University of Chicago Press.
Bernardini, Riccardo. 2011. *Jung a Eranos: Il progetto della psicologia complessa*. Milan: FrancoAngeli.
Berthelot, Marcellin. 1885. *Origines de l'alchimie*. Paris: G. Steinheil.
———. 1888. *Collection des anciens alchemistes grecs, Vol. 3*. Paris: Steintheil.
Bertine, Eleanor, John M. Billinsky, Edward F. Edinger, M. Esther Harding, Fowler McCormick, Paul Mellon, Henry A. Murray, F.S.C. Northrop, Paul Johannes Tillich, and Arnold J. Toynbee. 1962. *Carl Gustav Jung, 1875–1961: A Memorial Meeting, New York, December 1, 1961*. New York: Analytical Psychology Club of New York.
Bertozzi, Alberto. 2021. *Plotinus on Love: An Introduction to His Metaphysics through the Concept of "Eros"*. Leiden and Boston: Brill.
Binswanger, H.C., and K.R. Smith. 2000. Paracelsus and Goethe: Founding Fathers of Environmental Health. *Bulletin of the World Health Organization* 78 (9): 1162–1164.
Bishop, Paul. 2000. *Synchronicity and Intellectual Intuition in Kant, Swedenborg, and Jung* [Problems in Contemporary Philosophy, Vol. 46]. Lewiston: E. Mellen.
———. 2019. *German Political Thought and the Discourse of Platonism: Finding the Way Out of the Cave*. Cham: Palgrave Macmillan.
Bloom, Allan, ed. 1991. *The Republic of Plato: Translated, with Notes and an Interpretive Essay*. New York: Basic Books.
Blumenberg, Hans. 1996. *Höhlenausgänge*. Frankfurt am Main: Suhrkamp.
Brenner, E.M. 1990. Gnosticism and Psychology: Jung's *Septem Sermones ad Mortuos*. *Journal of Analytical Psychology* 35: 397–419.
Brisson, Luc. 1974. *Le même et l'autre dans la structure ontologique du "Timée" de Platon: Un commentaire systématique du "Timée" de Platon*. [Publications de l'Université de Paris X Nanterre, Lettres et Sciences Humaines, Série A : Thèses et Travaux, No 23]. Paris: Klincksieck.
———. 1998. *Plato the Myth Maker* [*Platon, les mots et les mythes: Comment et pourquoi Platon nomma le mythe?*]. Ed. and trans. by Gerard Naddaf. Chicago and London: University of Chicago Press.

———. 2004. *How Philosophers Saved Myths: Allegorical Interpretation and Classical Mythology* [*Introduction à la philosophie du mythe*, vol. 1, *Sauver les mythes*]. Trans. by Catherine Tihanyi. Chicago and London: University of Chicago Press.
Brisson, Luc, and Walter Meyerstein. 1995. *Inventing the Universe: Plato's "Timaeus", the Big Bang, and the Problem of Scientific Knowledge*. Albany, NY: State University of New York Press.
Brooke, Roger. 2019. Jung's Fantasies of Africa and Africa's Healing of Analytical Psychology. *International Journal of Jungian Studies* 11: 140–159.
Brown, Robert F., ed. 1974. *Schelling's Treatise on "The Deities of Samothrace": A Translation and an Interpretation*. Missoula, MT: Scholars Press.
Brown, Norman O. 1990. *Love's Body* [1966]. Berkeley, Los Angeles, and London: University of California Press.
Buber, Martin. 2016. *Eclipse of God: Studies in the Relation between Religion and Philosophy*. Princeton, NJ, and Oxford: Princeton University Press.
Bullock, Percy, trans. 1983. *The Dream of Scipio (Somnium Scipionis)* [1894]. Wellingborough: The Aquarian Press.
Burkert, Walter. 1972. *Lore and Science in Ancient Pythagoreanism*. Trans. by Edwin L. Minar, Jr. Cambridge, MA: Harvard University Press.
Burleson, Blake W. 2005. *Jung in Africa*. London: Continuum.
Burnet, John. 1916. *The Socratic Doctrine of the Soul*. [British Academy: Second Annual Philosophical Lecture, Henriette Hertz Trust]. London: Published for the British Academy by H. Milford, Oxford University Press.
C.G. Jung-Bibliothek. 1967. *Katalog*. Küsnacht-Zürich: [Privately Printed].
Caldwell, C.K., and Y. Xiong. 2002. What Is the Smallest Prime?. *Journal of Integer Sequences* 15: article 12.9.7.
Cherniss, H.F. 1957. The Relation of the *Timaeus* to Plato's Later Dialogues. *The American Journal of Philology* 78 (3): 225–266.
Cicero. 1923. *Works, Vol. 20, On Old Age; On Friendship; On Divination*. Trans. by W.A. Falconer. Cambridge, MA: Harvard University Press.
Collobert, Catherine, Pierre Destrée, and Francisco J. Gonzalez, eds. 2012. *Plato and Myth: Studies on the Use and Status of Platonic Myths*. Leiden and Boston: Brill.
Cooper, Diana, and Shaaron Hutton. 2005. *Discover Atlantis: A Guide to Reclaiming the Wisdom of the Ancients*. London: Hodder & Stoughton.
Cornford, Francis MacDonald. 1960. *Plato's Theory of Knowledge: The "Theaetetus" and the "Sophist" of Plato Translated with a Running Commentary* [1935]. London: Routledge & Kegan Paul.
———. 1997. *Plato's Cosmology: The "Timaeus" of Plato* [1935]. Indianapolis, IN: Hackett.
Domandl, Sepp. 1976. Goethe als Paracelsuskenner: Zwei neue Belege. *Jahrbuch des Wiener Goethe-Vereins* 80: 41–48.

Dominey, Charles Kent. 1977. *Archetype and Idea: Some Points of Correspondence between Jung's Theory of Archetypes and Plato's Theory of Forms.* Diploma Thesis, C.G. Jung Institute, Zurich.
Dourley, John P. 2008. *Paul Tillich, Carl Jung and the Recovery of Religion.* London and New York: Routledge.
Dourley, John, Warren Colman, David Tresan, and Barbara Stephens. 2002. Responses. *Journal of Analytical Psychology* 47 (3): 479–502.
Drews, Arthur. 1907. *Plotin und der Untergang der antiken Weltanschauung.* Jena: Diederichs.
Driver, Christine. 2020. *The Self and the Quintessence: A Jungian Perspective.* Abingdon: Routledge.
Dušanic, Slobodan. 1982. Plato's Atlantis. *L'Antiquité Classique* 51: 25–52.
Edelstein, Ludwig. 1966. *Plato's Seventh Letter.* Leiden: Brill.
Edinger, Edward F. 1973. *Ego and Archetype: Individuation and the Religious Function of the Psyche.* Baltimore, ML: Penguin Books.
Evans, Dylan. 1996. *Dictionary of Lacanian Psychoanalysis.* London and New York: Routledge.
Finamore, John F., and Emilie Kutash. 2017. Proclus on the *Psychê*: World Soul and the Individual Soul. In *All From One: A Guide to Proclus*, ed. Pieter d'Hoine and Marije Martijn, 122–137. New York: Oxford University Press.
Fischer, Thomas. 2011. The Alchemical Rare Book Collection of C.G. Jung. *International Journal of Jungian Studies* 3 (2): 169–180.
Fodor, Nandor. 1964. Jung's Sermons to the Dead. *The Psychoanalytic Review* 51: 74–78.
Franz, Marie-Louise von. 1978. *Mysterium Coniunctionis: Untersuchung über die Trennung und Zusammensetzung der seelischen Gegensätze in der Alchmie: Ergänzungsband «Aurora Consurgens»: Ein dem Thomas von Aquin zugeschriebenes Dokument der alchemistichen Gegensatzproblematik.* Olten and Freiburg im Breisgau: Walter-Verlag.
———. 2000. *The Problem of the Puer Aeternus.* 3rd ed. Toronto: Inner City Books.
Freud, Sigmund. 1977. *On Sexuality* [*Pelican Freud Library*, Vol. 7]. Trans. under James Strachey, ed. by Angela Richards. Harmondsworth: Penguin.
———. 1979. *Case Histories II* [*Pelican Freud Library*, Vol. 9]. Trans. under James Strachey, ed. by Angela Richards. Harmondsworth: Penguin.
———. 1991. *Civilization, Society and Religion* [*Penguin Freud Library*, Vol. 12]. Ed. under James Strachey, ed. by Albert Dickson. Harmondsworth: Penguin.
———. 1993. *Historical and Expository Works on Psychoanalysis* [*Penguin Freud Library*, Vol. 15]. Trans. under James Strachey, ed. by Albert Dickson. Harmondsworth: Penguin.
———. 1999. *Gesammelte Werke: Chronologisch geordnet.* Ed. by Anna Freud, Edward Bibring, and Ernst Kris. 18 vols. Frankfurt am Main: Fischer.

Frobenius, Leo, ed. 1926. *Die Atlantische Götterlehre* [*Atlantis: Volksmärchen und Volksdichtungen Afrikas*, Vol. 10]. Jena: Diederichs.
Gardner, Leslie. 2008. Writing about Nothing. In *Psyche and the Arts: Jungian Approaches to Music, Architecture, Literature, Painting and Film*, ed. Susan Rowland, 139–147. London and New York: Routledge.
———. 2013. *Rhetorical Investigations: G.B. Vico and C.G. Jung*. London and New York: Routledge.
Gemelli Marciano, M. Laura, et al. 2013. *Parmenide: Suoni, Immagini, Esperienza*. Sankt Augustin: Academia Verlag.
Gersh, Stephen. 2021. Universals, Wholes, *Logoi*: Eustratios of Nicaea's Response to Proclus' *Elements of Theology*. In *Reading Proclus and the "Book of Causes" Volume 2: Translations and Acculturations*, ed. Dragos Calma, 32–55. Leiden and Boston: Brill.
Giegerich, Wolfgang. 2020. *"Dreaming the Myth Onwards": C.G. Jung on Christianity and on Hegel: Part 2 of "The Flight into the Unconscious"* [*Collected English Papers*, Vol. 6] [2013]. London and New York: Routledge.
Gieser, Suzanne. 2005. *The Innermost Kernel: Depth Psychology and Quantum Physics: Wolfgang Pauli's Dialogue with C.G. Jung*. Berlin and Heidelberg: Springer Verlag.
Goethe, Johann Wolfgang. 1955. *Werke*. Ed. Erich Trunz, Vol. 9, *Autobiographische Schriften: Erster Band*. Hamburg: Wegner.
———. 1987. *Faust: Part One*. Trans. by David Luke. Oxford and New York: Oxford University Press.
———. 2001. *Faust: A Tragedy*. Ed. by Cyrus Hamlin, trans. by Walter Arndt. 2nd ed. New York and London: Norton.
Gomperz, Theodor. 1901–1912. *Greek Thinkers*. Trans. by L. Magnus and G.G. Berry, 4 vols. London: Murray.
———. 1909. *Griechische Denker: Eine Geschichte der antiken Philosophie*, 2nd ed., Vol. 2. Leipzig: Veit.
Grant, Edward, ed. 1974. *A Source Book in Medieval Science*. Cambridge, MA: Harvard University Press.
Gray, Ronald D. 1952. *Goethe the Alchemist: A Study of Alchemical Symbolism in Goethe's Literary and Scientific Works*. Cambridge: Cambridge University Press.
Green, André. 2000. *André Green at the Squiggle Foundation*. Ed. Jan Abram. London: Karnac Books.
Greene, Liz. 2018a. *Jung's Studies in Astrology: Prophecy. Magic, and the Qualities of Time*. London and New York: Routledge.
———. 2018b. *The Astrological World of Jung's "Liber Novus": Daimons, Gods, and the Planetary Journey*. London and New York: Routledge.
Griffith, F.L. 1898. *A Collection of Hieroglyphs* [Archaeological Survey of Egypt, 6th Memoir]. London: Egypt Exploration Fund.

Grimes, Pierre. 1997a. Jung: The Dialectic and Plato's Divided Line. *Wisdom Literature and the Platonic Tradition*. NSPRS 075 and 076, 2 DVDs. Los Angeles, CA: Opening Mind Academy.
———. 1997b. 1997-06-23 NSPRS 063—Plato's *Timaeus*. https://archive.org/details/19970623NSPRS063.
Grimes, Pierre, and Regina L. Uliana. 1998. *Philosophical Midwifery: A New Paradigm for Understanding Human Problems*. Costa Mesa, CA: Hyparxis Press.
Guthrie, W.K.C. 1978. *A History of Greek Philosophy, Vol. 5, The Later Plato and the Academy*. Cambridge: Cambridge University Press.
Haar, James. 1980. Music of the Spheres. In *The New Grove Dictionary of Music and Musicians*, ed. Stanley Sadie, vol. 12, 835–836. London, New York, Hong Kong: Macmillan.
Hakl, Hans Thomas. 2013. *Eranos: An Alternative Intellectual History of the Twentieth Century* [2001]. Trans. Christopher McIntosh. Montréal, QC: McGill-Queen's University Press.
Halliwell, Stephen. 2007. The Life-and-Death Journey of the Soul: Interpreting the Myth of Er. In *The Cambridge Companion to Plato's "Republic"*, ed. G.R.F. Ferrari, 445–473. New York: Cambridge University Press.
Harding, M. Esther. 1963. *Psychic Energy: Its Source and its Transformation*. Princeton, NJ: Princeton University Press.
Harnack, Adolf von. 1909. *Lehrbuch der Dogmengeschichte, vol. 2, Die Entwickelung des kirchlichen Dogmas I*, 4th and Revised ed. Tübingen: Mohr (Siebeck).
Hasse, Dag Nikolaus. 2002. Plato Arabico-Latinus: Philosophy—Wisdom Literature—Occult Sciences. In *The Platonic Tradition in the Middle Ages: A Doxographic Approach*, ed. Stephen Gersh and Maarten J.F.M. Hoenen, 31–65. Berlin and New York: de Gruyter.
Heath, Thomas, ed. and trans. 1908. *The Thirteen Books of Euclid's Elements*, 3 vols. Cambridge: Cambridge University Press.
———. 1921. *A History of Greek Mathematics*, 2 vols. Oxford: Clarendon Press.
Heidegger, Martin. 1959. *Introduction to Metaphysics*. Trans. by Ralph Manheim. New Haven and London: Yale University Press.
Heisig, James W. 1972. The *VII Sermones*: Play and Theory. *Spring*: 206–218.
Henderson, David. 2021. [Review of] *The Self and the Quintessence: A Jungian Perspective* by Christian Driver. *British Journal of Psychotherapy* 37 (4): 725–727.
Herman, Arthur. 2013. *The Cave and the Light: Plato Versus Aristotle, and the Struggle for the Soul of Western Civilization*. New York: Random House.
Hladký, Vojtěch. 2017. Empedocles' Sphairos. *Rhizomata: A Journal for Ancient Philosophy and Science* 5 (1): 1–24.
Hoeller, Stephan A. 1982. *The Gnostic Jung and the Seven Sermons to the Dead*. Wheaton, IL: Theosophical Publishing House.
Hoenig, Christina. 2018. *Plato's "Timaeus" and the Latin Tradition*. Cambridge: Cambridge University Press.

Hubback, Judith. 1986. VII Sermones ad mortuos. *Journal of Analytical Psychology* 11 (2): 95–112.
Inge, William. 1918. *Christian Mysticism: Considered in Eight Lectures Delivered before the University of Oxford* [The Bampton Lectures, 1899], 4th ed. London: Methuen.
Jeans, Sir James. 1931. *The Mysterious Universe*. Cambridge: Cambridge University Press.
Johansen, Thomas K. 2011. The *Timaeus* on the Principles of Cosmology. In *The Oxford Handbook of Plato*, ed. Gail Fine, 463–483. New York: Oxford University Press.
———. 2015. *Timaeus* and *Critias*. In *The Bloomsbury Companion to Plato*, ed. Gerald A. Press, 99–100. London: Bloomsbury.
Johnson, Sheila. 1991. Ideological Ambiguity in G.W. Pabst's 'Paracelsus' (1943). *Monatshefte* 83 (2): 104–126.
Jones, E. Michael. 1994. *Dionysos Rising: The Birth of Cultural Revolution Out of the Spirit of Music*. San Francisco: Ignatius Press.
Jordan, R.W. 1984. Plato's Task in the Sophist. *The Classical Quarterly* 34 (1): 113–129.
Jung, C.G. 1928. *Contributions to Analytical Psychology*. Trans. by H.G. and Cary F. Baynes. London: Kegan Paul, Trench, Trubner.
———. 1942a. *Paracelsica: Zwei Vorlesungen über den Arzt und Philosophen Theophratus*. Zurich and Leipzig: Rascher.
———. 1942b. Zur Psychologie der Trinitätsidee. In *Eranos Jahrbuch 1940–41*, 31–64. Zurich: Rhein-Verlag.
———. 1948. Versuch zu einer psychologischen Deutung des Trinitätsdogmas. In *Symbolik des Geistes: Studien über psychische Phänomenologie*, 321–446. Zurich: Rascher.
———. 1952. Religion and Psychology: A Reply to Martin Buber. *CW* 18, §663–§670.
———. 1953. *Two Essays on Analytical Psychology*. Trans. by R.F.C. Hull = *CW*, Vol. 7. London: Routledge & Kegan Paul.
———. 1954. *The Development of Personality*. Trans. by R.F.C. Hull = *Collected Works*, Vol. 17. London and Henley: Routledge & Kegan Paul.
———. 1959. *Aion: Researches into the Phenomenology of the Self*. Trans. by R.F.C. Hull. *Collected Works*, Vol. 9/ii. Princeton, NJ: Princeton University Press.
———. 1963. *Memories, Dreams, Reflections*. Ed. by Aniela Jaffé. Trans. by Richard and Clara Winston. London: Collins; Routledge & Kegan Paul.
———. 1964. *Civilization in Transition*. Trans. by R.F.C. Hull = *Collected Works*, Vol. 10. London and New York: Routledge.
———. 1966. *The Spirit in Man, Art, and Literature*. Trans. by R.F.C. Hull = *Collected Works*, Vol. 15. London: Routledge & Kegan Paul.

———. 1967a. *Symbols of Transformation: An Analysis of the Prelude to a Case of Schizophrenia*. Trans. by R.F.C. Hull = *Collected Works*, Vol. 5, 2nd ed. Princeton, NJ: Princeton University Press.

———. 1967b. *Alchemical Studies*. Trans. by R.F.C. Hull = *Collected Works*, Vol. 13. Princeton, NJ: Princeton University Press.

———. 1968. *Psychology and Alchemy*. Trans. by R.F.C. Hull = *Collected Works*, Vol. 12, 2nd ed. London: Routledge.

———. 1969a. *The Archetypes and the Collective Unconscious*. Trans. by R.F.C. Hull = *Collected Works*, Vol. 9/i. Princeton, NJ: Princeton University Press,

———. 1969b. *Psychology and Religion: West and East*. Trans. by R.F.C. Hull = *Collected Works*, Vol. 11, 2nd ed. London: Routledge & Kegan Paul.

———. 1969c. *The Structure and Dynamics of the Psyche*. Trans. by R.F.C. Hull. *Collected Works*, Vol. 8, 2nd ed. Princeton, NJ: Princeton University Press.

———. 1970. *Mysterium coniunctionis: An Inquiry into the Separation and Synthesis of Psychic Opposites in Alchemy*. Trans. by R.F.C. Hull = *Collected Works*, Vol. 14, 2nd ed.. Princeton, NJ: Princeton University Press.

———. 1971. *Psychological Types*. Trans. by H.G. Baynes, rev. by R.F.C. Hull = *Collected Works*, Vol. 6. Princeton, NJ: Princeton University Press.

———. 1973–1975. *Letters*. Ed. by Gerhard Adler and Aniela Jaffé, trans. by R.F.C. Hull, 2 vols. Princeton, NJ: Princeton University Press.

———. 1976. *The Symbolic Life: Miscellaneous Writings*. Trans. by R.F.C. Hull = *Collected Works*, Vol. 18. Princeton, NJ: Princeton University Press.

———. 1989. *Nietzsche's "Zarathustra": Notes of the Seminar Given in 1934–1939*. Ed. by James L. Jarrett, 2 vols. London: Routledge.

———. 1991. *Psychology of the Unconscious: A Study of the Transformations and Symbolisms of the Libido: A Contribution to the History of the Evolution of Thought* [1916]. Trans. by Beatrice M. Hinkle. London: Routledge.

———. 1997. *Visions: Notes of the Seminar Given in 1930–1934*. Ed. by Claire Douglas, 2 vols. Princeton, NJ: Princeton University Press.

———. 2012. *The Red Book: Liber Novus* [Reader's Edition]. Ed. by Sonu Shamdasani, trans. by Mark Kyburz, John Peck, and Sonu Shamdasani. New York and London: Norton.

———. 2015. *On Psychological and Visionary Art: Notes from C.G. Jung's Lecture on Gérard de Nerval's "Aurélia"*. Ed. by Craig Stephenson. Princeton and Oxford: Princeton University Press.

———. 2020. *The Black Books, 1813–1932: Notebooks of Transformation*. Ed. by Sonu Shamdasani, trans. by Martin Liebscher, John Peck, Sonu Shamdasani, 7 vols. New York and London: Norton.

Jung, C.G., and Carl Kerényi. 1969. *Essays on a Science of Mythology: The Myth of the Divine Child and the Mysteries of Eleusis*. Trans. by R.F.C. Hull. Princeton, NJ: Princeton University Press.

Kant, Immanuel. 1997. *Critique of Pure Reason*. Ed. and trans. by Paul Guyer and Allen W. Wood. Cambridge: Cambridge University Press.
Kaufmann, Walter. 1978. *Hegel: A Reinterpretation*. Notre Dame, IN: University of Notre Dame Press.
Kerényi, Karl. 1978. *Humanistische Seelenforschung*. Wiesbaden: VMA-Verlag.
Kern, Otto, ed. 1972. *Orphicorum fragmenta* [1922]. Berlin: Weidmann.
Keulen, W.H., S. Tilg, L. Nicolini, L. Graverini, S.J. Harrison, S. Panayotakis, and D. van Mal-Maeder. 2015. *Apuleius Madaurensis Metamorphoses, Book XI, The Isis Book: Text, Introduction and Commentary*. Leiden: Brill.
Kiefer, Otto. 1905. *Plotin: Enneaden in Auswahl*. 2 vols. Jena and Leipzig: Diederichs.
Kingsley, Peter. 2018. *Catafalque: Carl Jung and the End of Humanity*, 2 vols. London: Catafalque Press.
Klosko, George. 1981. Implementing the Ideal State. *The Journal of Politics* 43 (2): 365–389.
———. 2012. *History of Political Theory: An Introduction, Vol. 1, Ancient and Medieval*. Oxford: Oxford University Press.
Kojève, Alexandre. 1980. *Introduction to the Reading of Hegel* [²1947], Assembled by Raymond Queneau, ed. by Allan Bloom, trans. by James H. Nichols, Jr. Ithaca and London: Cornell University Press.
Kreeft, Peter. 2018. *The Platonic Tradition*. South Bend, IN: St. Augustine's Press.
Lacan, Jacques. 1991. *The Seminar of Jacques Lacan, Book I: Freud's Papers on Technique, 1953–1964* [1975]. Ed. by Jacques-Alain Miller, trans. by John Forrester. New York and London: Norton.
———. 2011. La Troisième. Ed. by Jacques-Alain Miller, *La Cause freudienne*, no. 79: 11–33.
———. 2019. The Third. Trans. by Philip Dravers, *The Lacanian Review*, no. 7, *Get Real*. Spring, 83–109.
Lamborn, Amy Bentley. 2011. Revisiting Jung's 'A Psychological Approach to the Dogma of the Trinity': Some Implications for Psychoanalysis and Religion. *Journal of Religion and Health* 50: 108–119.
Lampert, Laurence, and Christopher Planeaux. 1998. Who's Who in Plato's *Timaeus-Critias* and Why. *The Review of Metaphysics* 52 (1): 87–125.
Lao Tzu. 1963. *Tao Te Ching*. Trans. by D.C. Lau. Harmondsworth: Penguin.
Latura, George. 2012. Plato's Visible God: The Cosmic Soul Reflected in the Heavens. *Religions* 3: 880–886.
Le Mouël, Christophe. 2011/2012. Four: A Reflection on the Wholeness of Nature. Parts 1 and 2. *Psychological Perspectives* 54 (2) and (June and December): 54–79 and 175–196; Part 3. *Psychological Perspectives*, Vol. 55, Vol. 2 (June): 219–245.
———. 2021. Experiencing the Unus Mundus. *Psychological Perspectives* 64 (4): 437–442.

Leibnitz, Gottfried Wilhelm. 1890. *The Philosophical Works of Leibnitz*. Trans. by George Martin Duncan. New Haven: Tuttle, Morehouse & Taylor.
———. 1896. *New Essays Concerning Human Understanding*. Trans. by Alfred Gideon Langley. New York: Macmillan.
Leibrand, Werner. 1951. C.G. Jungs Versuch einer psychologischen Deutung des Trinitätsdogmas. *Zeitschrift für Religions- und Geistesgeschichte* 3: 122–134.
Lesmeister, Roman. 1991. Die Gnosis als unbewältigte esoterische Erbe der Analytischen Psychologie C.G. Jungs. *Analytische Psychologie* 22: 191–208.
Lisi, Francisco. 2007. Individual Soul, World Soul and the Form of the Good in Plato's *Republic* and *Timaeus*. *Études platoniciennes* 4: 105–118.
Ljunggren, Magnus. 1994. *The Russian Mephisto: A Study of the Life and Work of Emilii Medtner*. Stockholm: Almqvist & Wiksell.
Loewald, Hans W. 1988. *Sublimation: Inquiries into Theoretical Psychoanalysis*. New Haven: Yale University Press.
Lorenz, Hendrik. 2011. Plato on the Soul. In *The Oxford Handbook of Plato*, ed. Gail Fine, 243–266. New York: Oxford University Press.
Macarius of Egypt, St. 1921. *Fifty Spiritual Homilies of Saint Macarius the Egyptian*. Trans. by A.J. Mason. London: SPCK.
Macrobius. 1990. *Commentary on the Dream of Scipio*. Ed. and trans. by William Harris Stahl. New York: Columbia University Press.
Maillard, Christine. 1993. *Les sept sermons aux morts de Carl Gustav Jung: du Plérome à l'Étoile*. Nancy: Presses universitaires de Nancy.
———. 2017. *Au cœur du Livre Rouge: Les Sept Sermons aux morts: Aux sources de la pensée de C. G. Jung*. Paris: Éditions Imago.
Main, Roderick. 2001. *Putting the Sinn Back into Synchronicity: Some Spiritual Implications of Synchronistic Experiences*. RERC Second Series Occasional Papers, no. 28. https://repository.uwtsd.ac.uk/id/eprint/423/
———. 2004. *The Rupture of Time: Synchronicity and Jung's Critique of Modern Western Culture*. Hover and New York: Brunner-Routledge.
———. 2019. Synchronicity and Holism, 59–74. Hors série: *Revue de Psychologie Analytique*.
———. 2022. *Breaking the Spell of Disenchantment: Mystery, Meaning, and Metaphysics in the Work of C.G. Jung* [The Zürich Lecture Series, vol. 8]. Asheville, NC: Chiron.
Marcuse, Ludwig. 1947. *Plato and Dionysius: A Double Biography*. Trans. by Joel Ames. New York: Knopf.
Miller, Jeffrey C. 2004. *The Transcendent Function: Jung's Model of Psychological Growth through Dialogue with the Unconscious*. Albany, NY: State University of New York Press.
Miller, Arthur I. 2009. *Deciphering the Cosmic Number: The Strange Friendship of Wolfgang Pauli and Carl Jung*. New York and London: Norton.

Mohr, Richard D., and Barbara M. Sattler, eds. 2010. *One Book, The Whole Universe: Plato's "Timaeus" Today*. Las Vegas, Zurich, Athens: Parmenides Publishing.
Morgan, Kathryn A. 1998. Designer History: Plato's Atlantis Story and Fourth-Century Ideology. *The Journal of Hellenic Studies* 118: 101–118.
Mueller, Gustav E. 1958. The Hegel Legend of 'Thesis-Antithesis-Synthesis.' *Journal of the History of Ideas* 19 (3): 411–414; reprinted *The Hegel Myths and Legends*, ed. by Jon Stewart, pp. 301–305. Evanston, IL: Northwestern University Press, 1996.
Müller, Hermann Friedrich. 1878–1880. *Die Enneaden des Plotin*. 2 vols. Berlin: Weidmann.
Murase, Amadeo. 2020. The Homunculus and the Paracelsian *Liber de imaginibus*. *Ambix* 67 (1): 47–61.
Nerval, Gérard de. 1966. *Œuvres*. Ed. by Henri Lemaitre. Paris: Garnier.
Neuhouser, Frederick. 2000. *Foundations of Hegel's Social Theory*. Cambridge, MA: Harvard University Press.
Noll, Richard. 1994. Mysteria: Jung and the Ancient Mysteries (Unpublished Page Proofs, 1994). https://www.researchgate.net/268034481/Mysteria_Jung_and_the_Ancient_Mysteries_unpublished_page_proofs.
Ogden, Thomas E. 1997. *Reverie and Interpretation: Sensing Something Human*. Northvale, NJ, and London: Jason Aronson.
———. 2004. The Analytic Third: Implications for Psychoanalytic Theory and Technique. *The Psychoanalytic Quarterly* 73 (1): 167–195.
Onfray, Michel. 2006. *Les Sagesses antiques* [*Contre-histoire de la philosophie*, Vol. 1]. Paris: Grasset.
Ovid. 1987. *Metamorphoses*. Trans. by A.D. Melville. Oxford and New York: Oxford University Press.
Owen, G.E.L. 1953. The Place of the *Timaeus* in Plato's Dialogues. *The Classical Quarterly* [NS] 3 (1–2): 79–95.
Paracelsus. 1589–1591. *Bücher und Schrifften, des Edlen, Hochgelehrten und Bewehrten Philosophi und Medici, Philippi Theophrasti Bombast von Hohenheim, Paracelsi genannt*. Ed. by Johannes Huser, 10 vols. Basel: Waldkirch.
———. 1967. *The Hermetic and Alchemical Writings of Paracelsus*. Trans. by A.R. Waite, Vol. 1. New Hyde Park, NY: University Books.
———. 1979. *Selected Writings*. Ed. by Jolande Jacobi [1951]. Princeton, NJ: Princeton University Press.
———. 1999. *Essential Readings*. Ed. and trans. by Nicholas Goodrick-Clarke. Berkeley, CA: North Atlantic Books.
Paracelsus (Theophrastus Bombastus von Hohenheim, 1493–1541). 2008. *Essential Theoretical Writings*. Ed. and trans. by Andrew Weeks. Leiden and Boston: Brill.

Patai, Raphael. 1995. *The Jewish Alchemists: A History and Source Book*. Princeton, NJ: Princeton University Press.
Pauck, Wilhelm, and Marjon Pauck (1978). *Paul Tillich: Sein Leben und Denken*, 2 vols. Stuttgart; Frankfurt am Main: Evangelisches Verlagswerk; Lembeck.
Pauli, Wolfgang. 1994. *Writings on Physics and Philosophy*. Ed. by Charles P. Enz and Karl von Meyenn, trans. by Robert Schlapp. Berlin: Springer-Verlag.
———. 1996. *Wissenschaftlicher Briefwechsel mit Bohr, Einstein, Heisenberg u.a.*, *Vol. 4, Part 1, 1950–1952*. Ed. by Karl von Meyenn. Berlin, Heidelberg, New York: Springer-Verlag.
Pauli, Wolfgang, and C.G. Jung. 2001. *Atom and Archetype: The Pauli/Jung Letters, 1932–1958*. Ed. by C.A. Meier, trans. by David Roscoe. Princeton, NJ: Princeton University Press.
Pius XII. 1950. *Apostolic Constitution of Pope Pius XII Munificentissimus Deus defining the dogma of the Assumption*. Available https://www.vatican.va/content/pius-xii/en/apost_constitutions/documents/hf_p-xii_apc_19501101_munificentissimus-deus-html.
Plato. 1854–1859. *Platons ausgewählte Schriften in deutscher Übersetzung*. Trans. by Ludwig von Georgii, Franz Susemihl, Julius Deuschle, W.S. Teuffel, and Wilhelm Wiegand, 3 vols (Vol. 1: *Platon's Leben, Gastmahl, Apologie, Kriton, Phaidon*; Vol. 2, *Phaidros, Protagoras, Gorgias*; Vol. 3, *Die Staatsverfassung*). Stuttgart: Metzler.
———. 1906. *Platons Gastmahl ins Deutsche übertragen*. Trans. by Rudolf Kassner, 2nd ed. Leipzig: Diederichs.
———. 1909. *Timaeus, Kritias, Gesetze X*. Trans. by Otto Kiefer. Jena: Diederichs.
———. 1922. *Platons Dialoge "Timaeus" und "Kritias"*. Trans. by Otto Apelt [Philosophische Bibliothek, Vol. 179]. Leipzig: Meiner.
———. 1925. *Parmenides; Philebos*. Trans. by Otto Kiefer. Jena: Diederichs.
———. 1929. *Plato with an English Translation, Vol. 7, Timaeus; Critias; Cleitophon; Menexenus; Epistles*. Trans. by R.G. Bury. London; New York: Heinemann; Putnam.
———. 1942. *Von Mensch und Staat: Sokrates und Platon: Die antike Botschaft der Gerechtigkeit*. Ed. and trans. by Edgar Salin [Sammlung Klosterberg Europäische Reihe]. Basel: Schwabe.
———. 1945. *Apologie, Kriton, Phaidon*. Trans. by Edgar Salin. Basel: Schwabe.
———. 1956. *Great Dialogues of Plato*. Trans. by W.H.D. Rouse, ed. by Eric H. Warmington and Philip G. Rouse. New York and Toronto: New American Library.
———. 1984. *The Being of the Beautiful: Plato's "Theaetetus", "Sophist", and "Statesman"*. Trans. by Seth Bernadete. Chicago and London: Chicago University Press.
———. 1988. *The Laws of Plato*. Ed. and trans. by Thomas L. Pangle. Chicago and London: University of Chicago Press.

———. 1989. *Collected Dialogues of Plato*. Ed. by Edith Hamilton and Huntington Cairns. Princeton, NJ: Princeton University Press.
———. 1909. *Timaios, Kritias, Gesetze X*. Trans. Otto Kiefer. Jena: Diederichs.
———. 1996. *Works of Plato in Five Volumes*, Vol. 2. Trans. by Thomas Taylor and Floyer Sydenham [TTS, Vol. 10]. Sturminster Newton: Prometheus Trust.
———. 2004. *Selected Myths*. Ed. by Catalin Partenie. New York: Oxford University Press.
Plessner, M. 1954. The Place of the *Turba Philosophorum* in the Development of Alchemy. *Isis* 45 (4): 331–338.
Plotinus. 1905. *Enneaden in Auswahl übersetzt*. Trans. by Otto Kiefer, 2 vols. Jena: Diederichs.
———. 1924. *On the Nature of the Soul, Being the Fourth Ennead*. Trans. by Stephen MacKenna. London and Boston: The Medici Society.
———. 1951/1959. *Opera*, Vol. 1, *Porphyrii vita Plotini; Enneades I–III*; Vol. 2, *Enneades IV–V*, ed. by Paul Henry and Hans-Rudolf Schwyzer. Paris; Brussels: Desclée de Brouwer; L'Édition universelle.
———. 1966–1988. *Works*. Trans. by A.H. Armstrong. 7 vols. Cambridge, MA, and London: Harvard University Press; Heinemann.
Plutarch. 1936. *Moralia*, Vol. 5. Trans. by F.C. Babbitt. London; Cambridge, MA: Heinemann; Harvard University Press.
Power, Pamela. 2017. 'The Psychological Difference' in Jung's Mysterium Coniunctionis. In *Psychology as the Discipline of Interiority: 'The Psychological Difference' in the Work of Wolfgang Giegerich*, ed. Jennifer M. Sandoval and John C. Knapp, 43–54. London and New York: Routledge.
Proclus. 1963. *The Elements of Theology: A Revised Text with Translation, Introduction and Commentary*. Ed. by E.R. Dodds, 2nd ed. Oxford: Clarendon Press.
———. 1987. *Commentary on Plato's "Parmenides"*. Trans. by Glenn R. Morrow and John M. Dillon. Princeton, NJ: Princeton University Press.
———. 1998a. *Commentary on the "Timaeus" of Plato*, Vol. 1. Trans. by Thomas Taylor [TTS, Vol. 15]. Sturminster Newton: Prometheus Trust.
———. 1998b. *Commentary on the "Timaeus" of Plato*, Vol. 2. Trans. by Thomas Taylor [TTS, Vol. 16]. Sturminster Newton: Prometheus Trust.
———. 2006. *Commentary on Plato's "Timaeus", Vol. 1, Book 1: Proclus on the Socratic State and Atlantis*. Trans. by Harold Tarrant, ed. by Dirk Baltzly and Harold Tarrant. New York: Cambridge University Press.
Quispel, Gilles. 1968. C.G. Jung und die Gnosis. *Eranos-Jahrbuch* 37: 277–298.
Ribi, Alfred. 2013. *The Search for Roots: C.G. Jung and the Tradition of Gnosis*. Los Angeles and Salt Lake City: Gnosis Archive Books.
Rieff, Philip. 1966. *The Triumph of the Therapeutic*. London: Chatto & Windus.

Riel, Gerd Van. 2017. The One, the Henads, and the Principles. In *All From One: A Guide to Proclus*, ed. Pieter d'Hoine and Marije Martijn, 73–97. New York: Oxford University Press.
Robinson, T.M. 1970. *Plato's Psychology*. Toronto: University of Toronto Press.
———. 2015. Soul (*psychê*). In *The Bloomsbury Companion to Plato*, ed. Gerald A. Press, 247–249. London: Bloomsbury.
Rosenmeyer, T.G. 1956. Plato's Atlantis Myth: 'Timaeus' or 'Critias'? *Phoenix* 10 (4): 163–172.
Rüdiger, Horst. 1963. Curiositas und Magie: Apuleius und Lucius als literarische Archetypen der Faust-Gestalt. In *Wort und Text: Festschrift für Fritz Schalk*, ed. Harri Maier and Hans Sckommodau, 57–82. Frankfurt am Main: Klostermann.
Rudolph, Hartmut. 2013. Zum Paracelsusbild im Nationalsozialismus, vornehmlich bei Erwin Metzke. In *Die Wiederkehr der Renaissance im 19. und 20. Jahrhundert / The Revival of the Renaissance in the Nineteenth and Twentieth Centuries*, ed. Helmut Koopmann and Frank Baron, 115–136. Münster: Mentis.
Ruska, Julius. 1931. *Turba Philosophorum: Ein Beitrag zur Gechichte der Alchemie* [Quellen und Studien zur Geschichte der Naturwissenschaften und der Medizin, Vol. 1] (Berlin and Heidelberg: Springer-Verlag).
Samuels, Andrew, Bani Shorter, and Fred Plaut. 1986. *A Critical Dictionary of Jungian Analysis*. London and New York: Routledge.
Sandy, G. 1972. Knowledge and Curiosity in Apuleius' *Metamorphoses*. *Latomus* 31 (1): 179–183.
Schelling, Friedrich Wilhelm Joseph. 1815. *Ueber die Gottheiten von Samothrace*. Stuttgart and Tübingen: Cotta.
Schiller, Friedrich. 2004. *Sämtliche Gedichte und Balladen*. Ed. by Georg Kurscheidt. Frankfurt am Main and Leipzig: Insel.
Schöne, Albrecht. 2005. *Goethe—"Faust": Kommentare*. Frankfurt am Main: Deutscher Klassiker Verlag.
Segal, Robert A., ed. 1992. *The Gnostic Jung*, 1992. Princeton, NJ: Princeton University Press.
Shamdasani, Sonu. 2003. *Jung and the Making of Modern Psychology: The Dream of a Science*. Cambridge: Cambridge University Press.
———. 2012. *C.G. Jung: A Biography in Books*. New York and London: Norton.
Shiffman, Mark. 2021. Hermeneutical Platonism in Plutarch's *Isis and Osiris*. In *Proceedings of the Boston Area Colloquium in Ancient Philosophy, Vol. 36*, ed. M. Gary, S.J. Gurtler, and Daniel P. Maher, 99–122. Leiden and Boston: Brill.
Shoemaker, Stephen J. 2004. *The Ancient Traditions of the Virgin Mary's Dormition and Assumption*. New York: Oxford University Press.
Silesius, Angelus. 1966. *Aus dem "Cherubinischen Wandersmann"*. Stuttgart: Reclam.
Singer, Dorothea Whaley. 1946. Alchemical Texts Bearing the Name of Plato. *Ambix* 2 (3–4): 115–128.

Steeb, Johann Christoph. 1679. *Coelum Sephiroticum, Hebraeorum*. Mainz: Sumptibus Ludovicii Bourgeat, typis Christophori Küchleri.
Stein, Murray. 2019. Psychological Individuation and Spiritual Enlightenment: Some Comparisons and Points of Contact. *Journal of Analytical Psychology* 64 (1): 6–22.
Steiner, Rudolf. 2000. *Aus dem mitteleuropäischen Geistesleben: Fünfzehn öffentliche Vorträge gehalten zwischen dem 2. Dezember und dem 15. April 1916 im Architektenhaus zu Berlin*. Dornach: Rudolf Steiner Verlag.
———. 2001. In *Atlantis: The Fate of a Lost Land and its Secret Knowledge*, ed. Andrew Welburn. Forest Row: Sophia Books.
———. 2017. *Goethe und die Gegenwart: Fünfunddreißig Vorträge in verschiedenen Städten 1889–1912*. Ed. by Monika Philippi. Basel: Rudolf Steiner Verlag.
Stephens, Barbara D. 2001. The Martin Buber-Carl Jung Disputations: Protecting the Sacred in the Battle for the Boundaries of Analytical Psychology. *Journal of Analytical Psychology* 46 (3): 455–491.
Stewart, J.A. 1960. *The Myths of Plato* [1905]. Ed. by G.R. Levy. London: Centaur Press.
Sudhoff, Karl. 1932. Paracelsus und Goethe. *Die medizinische Welt* 6: 1409–1412.
Taylor, A.E. 1928. *A Commentary on Plato's "Timaeus"*. Oxford: Clarendon Press (Reprinted New York: Garland, 1967).
Taylor, Thomas, ed. and trans. 1831. *Ocellus Lucanus, "On the nature of the universe;" Taurus, the Platonic philosopher, "On the eternity of the world"; Julius Firmicus Maternus, "Of the thema mundi; in which the positions of the stars at the commencement of the several mundane periods is given"; "Select theorems on the perpetuity of time"*, by Proclus. London: Printed for the Translator.
———. 2006. *The Theoretic Arithmetic of the Pythagoreans* [TTS, Vol. 30]. Sturminster Newton: Prometheus Trust.
Thiel, Bernward. 2006. Von der Drei zur Vier: Individuationsprozeß und Naturerkenntnis bei Wolfgang Pauli. In *Wegmarken der Individuation*, ed. Thomas Arzt and Axel Holm, 51–82. Würzburg: Königshausen & Neumann.
Tillich, Paul. 1945. Nietzsche and the Bourgeois Spirit. *Journal of the History of Ideas* 6 (3): 307–309.
———. 1959. *Theology of Culture*. Ed. by Robert C. Kimball. New York: Oxford University Press.
Tillich, Hannah. 1973. *From Time to Time*. New York: Stein and Day.
Ulanov, Ann Belford. 2007. The Third in the Shadow of the Fourth. *Journal of Analytical Psychology* 52 (5): 585–605.
Vergely, Bertrand. 2004. *La Foi, ou la nostalgie de l'admirable*. Paris: Albin Michel.
Vidal-Naquet, Pierre. 2007. *The Atlantis Story: A Short History of Plato's Myth* [*L'Atlantide: Petite histoire d'un mythe platonicien*]. Trans. by Janet Lloyd. Exeter. University of Exeter Press.
Wallis, R.T. 1995. *Neoplatonism*. 2nd ed. London: Bristol Classical Press.

Wasserstrom, Steven M. 1999. *Religion after Religion: Gershom Scholem, Mircea Eliade, and Henry Corbin at Eranos*. Princeton, NJ: Princeton University Press.
Weldon, Jane. 2017. *Platonic Jung and the Nature of Self.* Asheville, NC: Chiron.
White, Victor. 1960. *Soul and Psyche: An Enquiry into the Relationship of Psychotherapy and Religion.* New York: Harper.
Whitehead, A.N. 1929. *The Aims of Education.* New York: Macmillan.
Wilberding, James, ed. 2021. *World Soul: A History.* New York: Oxford University Press.
Wilkerson, Stephen Y. 2019. *A Most Mysterious Union: The Role of Alchemy in Goethe's "Faust".* Asheville, NC: Chiron Publications.
Williamson, Rodney. 2007. *The Writing in the Stars: A Jungian Reading of the Poetry of Octavio Paz.* Toronto, Buffalo, and London: University of Toronto Press.
Wilpert, Gero von. 1998. *Goethe-Lexikon.* Stuttgart: Kröner.
Winnicott, Donald W. 2005. *Playing and Reality* [1971]. Abingdon: Routledge.
Wright, M.R., ed. 2000. *Reason and Necessity: Essays on Plato's "Timaeus".* London: Duckworth and The Classical Press of Wales.
Zaehner, R.C. 1992. *Hindu Scriptures* [1938]. New York, London, Toronto: Knopf.
Zeller, Eduard. 1876. *Die Philosophie der Griechen in ihrer geschichtlichen Entwicklung dargestellt,* 4th ed., Part 1, *Allgemeine Einleitung; Vorsokratische Philosophie.* Leipzig: Fues (Reisland).
———. 1881. *A History of Greek Philosophy from the Earliest Period to the Time of Socrates.* Trans. by S.F. Alleyn, 2 vols. London: Longmans, Green.
Zeyl, Donald, and Barbara Sattler. 2019. Plato's *Timaeus.* In *The Stanford Encyclopedia of Philosophy* (Summer 2019 Edition), ed. Edward N. Zalta. https://plato.stanford.edu/archives/sum2019/entries/plato-timaeus/.

Index[1]

A
Abraxas, 97
Adler, Donna M. Altimari, 31
Adler, Gerhard, 7
Aegean Festival, 71, 72
Aegean Sea Festival, 112
Africa, 20, 92, 94, 97, 114
Aion (Jung), 5, 38
Alexander the Great, 114
Allegory of the cave, 18, 129
Altman, William, 40n9
Analogy (*analogia*), 21, 28, 33, 37, 83n7
Analytic third, 3
Andreae, Johann Valentin, 112
Anima, 115
Anthropos, 10, 78, 100, 103, 104
Apelt, Otto, 33, 65
Aphrodite, 37
Apkallu, 19
Apollonius of Rhodes, 85n25
Apuleius, 106
Arab youth, 93, 94, 97

Archetype, 9, 20
Aristotle, 13n5, 20, 30, 54
Assumption of the Virgin Mary, 9
Athanasius of Alexandria, 52
Atlantis, 24, 25, 41n13, 69, 84n19
Axiom of Maria, 56, 114
Axiom of Maria Prophetissa, 60

B
Balduin, Christian Adolf, 99
Basilian Aphorisms (Jung), 10
Baynes, H.G., 6
Becker, Barbara J., 30
Benjamin, Jessica, 3
Bernadete, Seth, 40n12
Bernard of Trevis, 108
Berthelot, Marcelin, 103
Bhagavadgītā, 100
Black Books (Jung), 11, 38, 92, 94
Blumenberg, Hans, 131n3
Brihadāranyaka Upanishad, 35
Brisson, Luc, 31

[1] Note: Page numbers followed by 'n' refer to notes.

© The Author(s), under exclusive license to Springer Nature Switzerland AG 2022
P. Bishop, *Reading Plato through Jung*,
https://doi.org/10.1007/978-3-031-16812-3

152   INDEX

Brown, Norman O., 129
Buber, Martin, 130
Buddhism, 18
Bultmann, Rudolf, 82n3
Burkert, Walter, 85n27
Burnet, John, 26
Bury, R.G., 30, 65

C
Cabiri, 59, 72–74, 105
Cabiri scene, 11, 71, 84n12, 102, 103, 114
Calcidius, 25
Capra, Fritjof, 110
Care of the soul, 26
Chāndogya Upanishad, 100
Chelone, 105
Cherniss, Harold F., 84n15
Christ, 18
Christianos, 103
Cicero, 25, 30, 39n6, 92
Circle, 11, 42n22
Classical Walpurgis Night, 71, 119n25
Clement of Alexandria, 52
Copies of Plotinus's works in Greek, 44n31
Cornford, F.M., 21, 24, 30, 31, 33, 40n12, 58, 67, 69
Creuzer, Friedrich, 72
Critias, 24, 25, 63
Critias (Plato), 24, 42n25, 69

D
Demiurge, 24, 26–28, 32, 35, 64, 68, 81, 94, 96, 97, 107
de Nerval, Gérard, 3
Diogenes the Cynic, 35
Dion of Syracuse, 62
Dionysius II, 62

Dionysius the Elder, 62
Dominey, Charles Kent, 19
Dorn, Gerhard, 11, 54, 56, 77, 82, 108
Drews, Arthur, 11, 36, 37
Driver, Christine, 85n28

E
Edinger, Edward F., 5
Empedocles, 75, 99
Enigma of Bologna, 128, 131n1
Eranos conferences, 22, 38
Euhemerism, 19
Eusebius of Caesaria, 31
Eustratius of Nicaea, 86n31
Ezekiel, 115

F
Faust (Goethe), 8, 11, 84n18, 101, 102, 104, 117n15
Fichte, J.G., 13n3, 20
Fleischer, Heinrich Leberecht, 99
Fludd, Robert, 109
The Fourth, 9–11, 20, 60, 71, 74, 77, 82, 98, 101, 105, 110, 112, 127, 130
Fraccaroli, Giuseppe, 24
Freud, Sigmund, 7, 33, 73, 86n30, 100, 101, 117n13
Friedländer, Paul, 40n12
Fröbe-Kapteyn, Olga, 9, 52
Frobenius, Leo, 41n13

G
Giegerich, Wolfgang, 20, 58, 64, 107, 112
Goethe, Johann Wolfgang, 10, 11, 75, 82, 104, 118n20
Golden Fleece, 105

Gomperz, Theodor, 65, 70
Green, André, 2
Grimes, Pierre, 20
Grube, G.M.A., 21
Guthrie, W.K.C., 21

H
Hamerling, Robert, 102
Happelius, 100
Harding, M. Esther, 7
Heath, Sir Thomas, 58
Hegel, G.W.F., 7, 20, 26
Heidegger, Martin, 93
Henads, 40n11
Hermocrates of Syracuse, 63
Hesiod, 36
Hippolytus, 85n27
The History of Tom Thumb
  (Jung), 74
Holy Spirit, 19
Hypostases, 40n11

I
Iamblichus, 23
Inferior function, 60, 84n13
Inge, William, 6
Isidore of Seville, 55

J
Jeans, Sir James, 128
Joachim of Fiore, 6, 77
John the Lydian, 99

K
Kant, Immanuel, 8
Kepler, Johannes, 109
Kerényi, Karl, 71, 112
Khunrath, Heinrich, 108

Kiefer, Otto, 33, 44n31
Kingsley, Peter, 22, 92
Klein, Melanie, 129

L
Lacan, Jacques, 2, 131n1
Lactantius, 31
Lamborn, Amy, 10
Lang, Bernhard, 130
Latura, George, 31
Laws (Plato), 39n5
Lévy-Bruhl, Lucien, 38n2
Liber Platonis quartorum
  (Plato), 20, 98
Loewald, Hans, 10
Lucanus, Ocellus, 34

M
Macrobius, 30, 55
Maier, Michael, 108, 113
Main, Roderick, 111
Manilius, Marcus, 31
Medtner, Emilii, 92
Metaphysical concepts, 5
Metaphysics, 4, 11
Meyerstein, Walter, 31
Milky Way, 95
Moses, 18
Müller, Hermann Friedrich, 44n31
Mysterium coniunctionis (Jung),
  9, 11, 71, 110, 112, 113
Myth of Er, 30, 42n25

N
Neuhouser, Frederick, 26
Nietzsche, Friedrich, 12n2
  Thus Spoke Zarathustra, 95
  Zarathustra, 18, 120n35
Nowacki, Werner, 33

O

Oannes, 19
Ogden, Thomas, 3
Origen, 52
Ortus, 115
Otto, Rudolf, 52
Ovid, 39n7
Owen, G.E.L., 84n15

P

Parable of the cave, 128
Paracelsus, 7, 104, 118n20, 119n21, 119n22
Paradox, 128
Parapraxes, 73
Parmenides, 13n5, 23, 42n22, 93
Pauli, Wolfgang, 31, 107
Peirce, Charles Sanders, 2
Petrus Bonus of Ferrara, 104
Phaedo (Plato), 42n21
Phanes, 36, 43n30
Philebus (Plato), 42n20
Philo of Alexandria, 17
Philosopher-king, 61
Philosophical midwifery, 44n41
Phoenix, 115
Plato, 10, 17, 18, 21, 22, 36, 39n3, 61, 63, 66, 69, 70, 76, 82, 95, 96, 128
Plato-Jung connection, 22
Platonic myths, 42n25
Platonic riddles, 128
Plotinus, 20, 34, 36, 37, 40n11, 117n14
Plutarch, 81
Pope Julius I, 52
Pope Pius XII, 9
Porphyry, 20, 68
Proclus, 20, 21, 23, 24, 30, 32, 34, 40n11, 40n12, 40n13, 42n23, 68, 83n10

Prophetissa, Maria, 56, 103, 108, 118n19
Pseudo-Aristotle, 115
Pseudo-Dionysius the Areopagite, 18, 52
Psychological Types (Jung), 38
Psychology and Alchemy (Jung), 38, 79, 98
Puer aeternus (Jung), 39n7
   in Roman antiquity, 19
Pythagoras, 54
Pythagoras's theory, 11

Q

Quaternity, 5, 20, 56, 60, 75–80, 82, 115, 127
Quincunx, 67, 82

R

Receptacle, 26, 80, 86n34
Red Book (Jung), 33, 38, 82, 91, 97, 98
The Relations between the Ego and the Unconscious (Jung), 82
Republic (Plato), 25, 26, 30, 62, 83n11, 128
Ripley, George, 115
Robinson, T.M., 21
Rohde, Erwin, 40n12
Rosencreutz, Christian, 72
Ruska, Julius, 99
Russell, Bertrand, 13n5
Ryle, Gilbert, 40n12

S

St Augustine, 38n2, 85n29, 101
St Irenaeus, 17
St Justin Martyr, 31
Schelling, F.W.J., 13n3, 72, 74

Schiller, Friedrich, 84n14, 109
Schopenhauer, Arthur, 36
Septem Sermones ad mortuos (Jung), 97
Shamdasani, Sonu, 37, 72, 92, 128
Siebmacher, Johann Ambrosius, 100, 109
Sigg, Hermann, 92
Silberer, Herbert, 113
Silesius, Angelus, 80
Soul, 27, 35
Stages of psychosexual development, 7
Starkey, George, 118n20
Steeb, Johann Christoph, 99, 100
Steiner, Rudolf, 41n13, 102, 118n20
Stephanos of Alexandria, 103
Suzuki, Daisetz Teitaro, 22
Symposium (Jung), 33, 43n27, 95, 99, 130
Synchronicity, 31, 107

T
Tages, 19, 39n6
Taylor, A.E., 40n12, 54
Taylor, Thomas, 28, 33, 40n12, 41n13, 68, 69
The Third, 1, 10, 11, 20, 56, 60, 98, 101, 110, 112, 127, 130
Thus Spoke Zarathustra (Nietzsche), 12n2
Tillich, Paul, 4
Timaeus (Plato), 11, 22–25, 27, 33, 34, 55, 59, 76, 78, 80, 94, 95, 97, 107, 130
Timaeus of Locri, 24, 63
Tom Thumb, 79, 102
Tractatus aureus (Jung), 38n1
Transcendent function, 7–9

Transformations and Symbols of the Libido (Jung), 34
Trinity, 36, 52, 53, 57, 70, 77, 79, 110
Tzu, Lao, 82n5

U
Ulanov, Ann Belford, 1, 10

V
Valentinus, Basilius, 118n20
van Helmont, Jan Baptist, 118n20
von Franz, Marie-Louise, 39n7, 108
von Harnack, Adolf, 57
von Klettenberg, Susanne, 118n20
von Welling, Georg, 118n20
Vossius, Gerardus, 52

W
Weldon, Jane, 21
White, Victor, 6
Whitehead, Alfred North, 7, 13n5
Wilhelm, Richard, 98, 107
Winnicott, Donald, 2
World Soul, 11, 28, 31, 32, 35–37, 64, 68
Wotan, 93, 94, 97

Y
Yahweh, 70

Z
Zeller, Eduard, 54

The manufacturer's authorised representative in the EU is Springer Nature Customer Service Centre GmbH, Europaplatz 3, 69115 Heidelberg, Germany. If you have any concerns regarding our products, please contact ProductSafety@springernature.com

Printed and bound by CPI Group (UK) Ltd, Croydon, CR0 4YY
23/03/2026
02076447-0012